basketball jones

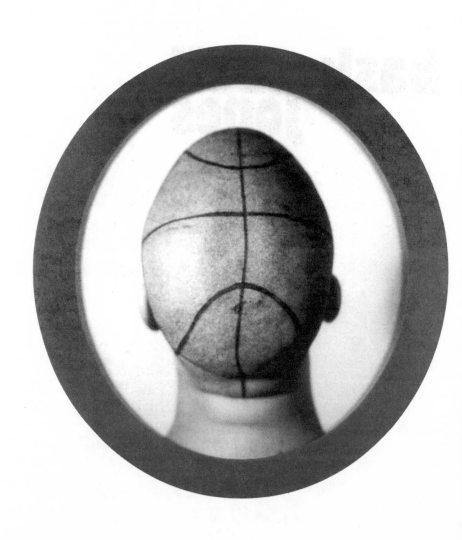

AMERICA
ABOVE
THE
RIM

basketball jones

EDITED BY

Todd Boyd

AND

*Kenneth L.
Shropshire*

new york university press

NEW YORK AND LONDON

new york university press
New York and London

© 2000 by New York University

Library of Congress Cataloging-in-Publication Data
Basketball Jones : America above the rim / edited by Todd Boyd and
Kenneth L. Shropshire.
p.   cm.
ISBN 0-8147-1315-7 (cloth : alk. paper) —
ISBN 0-8147-1316-5 (pbk. : alk paper)
1. Basketball—Social aspects—United States. 2. Basketball—Economic
aspects—United States. 3. Minorities in sports—United States.
4. Discrimination in sports—United States.   I. Boyd, Todd.
II. Shropshire, Kenneth L.
GV889.26 .B28 2000
796.323'0973—dc21   00-008320

New York University Press books are printed on acid-free paper,
and their binding materials are chosen for strength and durability.

Manufactured in the United States of America

10 9 8 7 6 5 4 3 2 1

To all the Ballas and Shotcallas, worldwide.
Stay true to the Game.

contents

preface

the game is to be sold, not to be told

TODD BOYD

The Game. This is the metaphor used by so many Brothas that it ain't even funny. Michael Jordan talks about raising his game to a higher level; Ice Cube incites us to be true to the game; and down in the dirty south, Silk the Shocker encourages us to charge it to the game.

The metaphor has a historical precedent as well. Back in the day, Iceberg Slim pontificated on the game, and Richard Pryor's memorable character from *The Mack* (1973) told us the game was strong. In the present, Snoop Dogg tells us that the game is to be sold, not to be told.

But one must ask, what game are they referring to?

Life in America, for far too many Brothas, has been about playing a concerted game of chance, with the odds definitely stacked against them. These Brothas have attempted to turn a game of chance into a game of skill, and because of this, life itself becomes an ongoing game. This influence pervades Black culture, and because sports has been one of the arenas where there has been a consistent Black presence, even dominance, the notion of the game is that much more a part of everyday life.

The three most commonly referenced games in contemporary Black popular culture are basketball, the rap game, and the dope game. To the extent that rap and basketball are increasingly linked, the dope game becomes the societal model that informs the cultural expression of the other two. These three "games" have certainly been the most visible forms of expression for young Black men since the dawn of the Reagan era, and the dope game often provides a real-life grassroots model that informs these other two areas of culture. One need only observe the evolution of rap mogul Master P from his reputed exploits as a dope dealer, to music impresario, to a tryout with the Charlotte Hornets and Toronto Raptors, to see visible evidence of this connection.

It is also interesting that the common metaphor that links both worlds is the notion of "ballin" or that of a "balla." This has to do not only with the act of playing ball, or even playing ball at the highest level, as the term suggests, but also with *ballin*, a term from the drug culture originally referencing "eight balls," or one-eightieth of an ounce of cocaine. Now the term has come to describe status, money, and power in general—the Big Balla, Shot Caller. In other words, a man in charge of his own destiny.

The idea of "gettin' paid" has come to define a whole generation of people who are most cut off from America's vast wealth. As one would expect, the desire to be represented by dead presidents is far greater when you start off with nothing. Coming up, then, is a victory.

> Let my cash
> invest in stock
> came a long way
> from blastin' techs
> on blocks
> went from Seiko to Rolex
> ownin' acres
> from the projects
> with no chips
> to large cake though.
>   —Nas, "Nas is Like"

Considering that the game of capitalism rewards those with opportunity, Brothas have manufactured an ongoing opportunity in the NBA (National Basketball Association)—"the league," as it were. In this regard, "the league" is not unlike the Black Hand, the Mustache Petes, the Crenshaw Mafia, or the No Limit Soldiers, for that matter, in that disadvantage provided an opportunity, at a grassroots level, for thug life visionaries to organize their peeps. The league here is not to be confused with the NBA, the corporation that allows for the league to exist.

What is important here is that, once again, the formal has provided a place for the expression of the vernacular. The NBA allows for a group of young Black men to make large sums of money, which in turn creates a culture of luxury that few middle-class White people, much less ghetto dwellers, could ever imagine. The pursuit of this exclusive lifestyle, using the racial history of America toward African American males as a direct challenge, makes the game a philosophical quest as well.

This, to me, is what the league is all about: Brothas gettin' paid for their unique contribution to the culture. That's the American Dream, ain't it?

My life has always been about the game, too. The relentless pursuit of some ephemeral sense of successful existence, overcoming the odds, snatching victory from the jaws of defeat. In other words, you play to win, and every potential obstacle becomes an opportunity (similar to breaking a defender down off the dribble and getting your shot off, as Jordan did against Bryon Russell on that historic last shot).

Dealing with the complex maze of life, of being a Brotha in a world where they still drag you behind pickup trucks for sport, where cops stick plungers up your ass just for living, you learn to appreciate the ghetto-fabulous style flaunted by the cats in the league. You live vicariously through their success. You, too, want to get paid. Victory is mine, sayeth the Lord!

In the late 1950s, Miles Davis was residing in a lavish Upper West Side apartment, wearing resplendent bespoke vines, and driving a Ferrari—this, when most Brothas still couldn't get a drink of water. Miles's cheese, his life, his articulation of supreme indifference, his embodiment of cool, was an indication of his skills in the game. He had succeeded, even created art, while all odds were against his very existence.

In the late 1990s, some forty years after Miles invented ghetto fabulous, Michael Jordan can make a commercial in which two attractive and flirtatious white women openly speculate about the contents of his underwear. If this isn't bad enough, Charles Barkley can openly speculate about being a Republican governor of the state whose refusal to come into the twentieth century once put Martin Luther King Jr. on the map.

Then consider the latest generation of hip-hop hoopers like

KG, Kevin Garnett, who can explain the hip-hop definition of the term *dog*—invoking DMX's thesis on man's best friend—to fawning White sportscasters, while "The Answer," Allen Iverson, the man who best symbolizes basketball's new nigga, can do his postgame interview in a designer stocking cap, platinum chain that hangs down to his waist, not to mention the matching quarter-sized diamond studs that he and his baby daughter share in their respective ears.

Damn, it feels good to see people up on it!

Social mobility has always been a common theme in Black life, and basketball provides the modern interpretation of this theme. The world chooses to concentrate on basketball's dark side, no pun intended: the drugs, the life-sized egos, the baby's mamas, and so on. That is real, for sure. But in the game of capitalism, a game that was built on the backs of the free labor of slaves, it seems appropriate that someone other than White people should one day reap some of the benefits.

To succeed is to win. To succeed on your own terms is to win in style, and Brothas have always been about style.

I love this game!

preface

shaka's revenge: not all black men jump

KENNETH L. SHROPSHIRE

The *Hoop Dreams* myth is that an overwhelming majority of Black men single-mindedly and irrationally believe they can make it as players in the National Basketball Association (NBA). The myth has been amplified by various studies in recent years that imply that a disproportionate percentage of Black males believe they can become professional athletes. For example, in 1997, *Sports Illustrated* polled a group of middle and high school students and asked, "Realistically, what could you become when you grow up?" Fifty-seven percent of Black males said yes to pro athlete. Not as well publicized but also unsettling, 41 percent of White males also responded yes to the pro athlete career.[1] I don't fashion social science studies, but there has got to be a way to put one together that says: "Now really, do you think you are good enough to make it to the NBA? I don't care about what you would *like* to do and what you *dream* about doing. Have you been invited to any high school all-star 'you are the greatest' camps? Are you seven feet tall? Do you start on your high school basketball team? Do Sonny Vaccarro and George Raveling have your home number?" Black people are realists, too. We get the message sooner than many commentators seem to believe. What I don't want this book to do is further skew the *Hoop Dreams* misconception; the point is, not all Black men jump.

I grew up in Los Angeles with Elgin Baylor and Jerry West as my basketball idols. LeRoy Ellis and Darryl Imhoff were my models for how to play. Fred Slaughter, then the UCLA center, provided some imagery as well. Ellis, Imhoff, and Slaughter were all relatively obscure big men, but they played the game the way I wanted to play as a kid—the tough, aggressive, scrapping, can-also-take-a-shot-from-the-outside type of big man. Wes Unseld and probably Willis Reed, too, fall into this category. In retrospect, maybe I should have spent more time emulating Baylor.

For whatever reason, I thought I was a big man. I was actually, physically, a big man up through about the eighth grade. I've got pictures of me towering over my classmates. I wasn't Kareem, but I had enough coordination, on occasion, to be dominant. Then it happened. Everyone began to catch up. And then, finally, two guys in particular—Marques Johnson from Louisiana and Tex Walker from, well, his name was Tex—arrived at Audubon Junior High School. They *were* big men. I'm not sure when they grew to be six feet seven inches, but it might as well have been on the day I met them. For a while, Marques and I were on the same "after-school league" team. It was clear that I had to move to the outside. That was my moment. There would be no NBA for me. From their arrival on, I shifted my focus to football.

John Haydel, who coached Dorsey High School to a city championship a few years after my graduation from the school, told me at one point when I was in trouble in the vice principal's office, "I could have made you a good point guard." (I was in the vice principal's office because I had told my Spanish teacher, Miss Aravanis, to "get off my back." This wasn't regular behavior on my part, but the woman *was* on my back that particular day.) At this point I was six feet tall and not growing. Maybe Haydel was right. "Damn, maybe I missed the opportunity," I remember thinking. "Naw, coach, I play like a big man in a guard's body," I told him, thinking this would end my suddenly reemerging fantasy. At least he wasn't giving me a hard time about the Aravanis incident. "I could have taught you," I remember Haydel telling me. "Damn, you can learn to play basketball," I thought. Ball-handling skills did not come naturally to me, so whenever I did play, I continued to play under the basket. That twelfth-grade conversation with Mr. Haydel was my last glimmer of basketball fantasy.

I did not, I can honestly say and my friends will testify, touch a basketball again until my senior year at Stanford University. I wasn't mad at the game; I just wasn't that good at it. I had this thing about not playing sports that I wasn't good at. (I have since overcome that arrogance or whatever it was, as those who have seen me recently on golf courses and tennis courts will attest.) That senior year, a number of the brothers on the football team put together an intramural basketball team. It was my roommate Donny Stevenson

who had the brainstorm. If I was the president of the non–basketball players, he was, at worst, secretary of state. Donny christened
the team "Shaka's Revenge." You students of African history are
rightfully cringing already. We avenged nothing.

When the true gym rats heard that we had put together a team,
they squealed. "Wait, you guys aren't serious?" Mr. Keith—"I *Will*
Skip Class to Get in a Game of Hoops"—Barnes asked me. He
voiced the same impression as others. The team was composed of
Black men who could not and did not play hoops. The team included
future National Football League (NFL) Hall of Famer James Lofton.
We were awful. If there had been videotape back in 1976 and those
games could be shown now, many myths would be destroyed. This
commentary would not be necessary. We were all good athletes—
some track-and-field guys too—but we had put basketball aside.
That game required work, work that the true stars rarely get credit
for. Shaka's Revenge was an all-Black team of future lawyers, doctors, professors, and one future NFL star, without a single false hope
about the NBA. We were all *ballas* to be, as described by my co-editor, but not of the NBA variety.

I still remember that long-ass shot I took from the deep right
corner, at least twenty feet out. Keith Barnes led the hooting and
hollering with a gym-silencing "Oh nooooo!!!!" If I had sunk that
shot, I would have been back. "Nice form," Barnes still reminds me
today. "Need to work on that radar a bit," in reference to the shot
that didn't even draw iron. My comeback shot was an air ball.

My wife and I bought a house in Philadelphia a couple of years
ago. Its former owner had constructed a pole in the driveway that
he intended to put a backboard and hoop on. He left the backboard
in the garage for me, but I have yet to put it up on that pole. We
have young children, so I do plan to install one at some point.

One reason why my game did not go very far, I think, is that we
didn't have the right spot or technology or something to put a hoop
up in our Los Angeles driveway when I was growing up. I wanted
to get good at the game. I remember being on my father's case from
about the fifth grade about putting a backboard up. I recall at some
point there was an elaborate plan to pour concrete in the back-
yard. His brick barbecue grill sits in that spot today. The closest we
came to getting that hoop up was when my father called over his

architect buddy, Cecil McNamee, to see if he had any ideas on how to do it. "Well, to make it ten feet up using your low roof, it's going to look like an oil derrick, there'll be so many steel bars up there." Mr. McNamee puffed on his cigarette and smiled, looking at my father with one of those "You don't really want to try to do this" looks. "Shit," Daddy replied, "that won't look too good." It was McNamee's final response that sealed the case of the hoopless driveway: "Well, Shrop, that's just one of those things. Do you want it or not?" They then retreated to the bar downstairs in the basement. This putting up of basketball backboards is a bigger deal than I had recognized. Others, since I first mentioned this weak-ass excuse for a lack of basketball prowess, have recounted similar backboard construction dilemmas.

So my Jones, such as it is, has never been as a player. Well, maybe for a brief period. But I did have season tickets during "Showtime" in Los Angeles. I, too, caught the end of Dr. J's career and the height of Charles Barkley's in Philly. Occasionally I catch Allen Iverson these days as well. I don't pretend to understand all the nuances of the game. I'm a man's man, but I was the last to understand that the "crossover dribble" is now the thing. Well, it was when I wrote this.

You cannot believe what a social event that "Showtime" era was: take in the game, then to the Forum Club, then to wherever the party was. There didn't have to be a party because the Forum Club was enough. Then there were the half dozen or so times I had my law firm's seats *on the floor. On the floor at the Fabulous Forum.* The Jack Nicholson, Arsenio Hall seats. "You must be somebody," the looks said to me. "Yeah, I lucked up on the seats," I'd think; then some second-tier star like Jermaine Jackson would plop down next to me. I got the seats when the big willies at the law firm I worked for were stuck holding them at the eleventh hour when a client canceled out, or when their wives wanted to spend quality time somewhere other than at a basketball game. The firm partners knew where to find me and that I had no problem hustling up a buddy to go.

I guess when I gave up playing the game, I got one of those benefits like giving up cigarettes and putting the money that you would have used to purchase the cancer sticks in a jar. I put the time in a jar—the time that my closest friends, like Keith Barnes, Reggie

Turner, and Tommy Myers, spent and still spend in the gym, playing and waiting for games, having the Achilles operations, and going to bars after their weekend-warrior events. I lost the camaraderie. I missed out on a lifelong method of exercise. It is tough to find a pickup football game. These days I run, ride on a stationary bike, walk around a golf course, and try tennis here and there. I don't have a sport that I've played all of my life. But I guess I did a few things my buddies didn't get to do. And I don't live in fear of the Achilles' snapping time bomb.

So, when I see statistics that *we* all think *we* can play the game, I know the commentators don't really know *us*. When professors are cited worldwide as making statements like "Consider, for example, the predicament of a young black academic who is tormented by the apparent contradiction between being a professor and being a homeboy and who may also be concerned about the impression he makes on the basketball court,"[2] I wonder who all these people think they are. It's not hard to know when the game is not going to be a career.

Is it just me? No, lots of us are not obsessed, don't regret that we never made it, but still have a Jones for the game. It is a hell of a thing to watch. This is particularly the case when you truly appreciate that you cannot do what those hard-working men and women do. I don't bet on the NCAA (National Collegiate Athletic Association) tournament; I don't fight over who the hometown team should draft; I like that I don't have a full handle on the intricacies of basketball strategy. I just love watching the game.

So, all in all, I guess Mr. McNamee and my father did me a favor. As for the hoop at my house, I *will* put it up eventually. It might not be until a member of Shaka's Revenge stops by, but it will happen. Well, on second thought, maybe it will take a non–Shaka's Revenge member. My Shaka brothers probably never put a hoop up before either.

NOTES

1. S. L. Price, "What Ever Happened to the White Athlete?" *Sports Illustrated*, December 8, 1997, 30, 51.

2. John Hoberman, *Darwin's Athletes: How Sport Has Damaged Black America and Preserved the Myth of Race* (Boston: Houghton Mifflin, 1997), 83.

acknowledgments

Let me begin by giving props to my Peeps, the Fam: Bonnie, Edward, Mozelle, Willis, Kellye, Jason, and Kolbe (the future). Much love. A special thanks to my Mother and Father—two non–sports fans—for remarrying two people who were sports fans.

Big ups to my collaborator, Shrop; handlin' thangs out there in the Illadelph PA. Puttin' our strength together!

Big ups to Christine Acham. Once again, you stepped up in the clutch.

Big ups to my crew, who allow a nigga to pontificate on ball, whenever, wherever, whatever: Rick "the Ruler," Jatty, my homey Robert Hurst, my homeys D. Was and Johnnie, James Scott, my nigga So, MJ, Live Music, and The Queen of the Dirty South, Peace.

Big ups to my man at NYU Press, Eric Zinner.

Big ups to all the cats who have picked up a basketball and transformed it into an art form: Marques Haynes, Bill Russell, Kareem, The Big O, Wes Unseld, Earl "the Pearl," Clyde Frazier, Pistol Pete Maravich, The Doctor, Moses, my homey The Iceman, Magic, Zeke, the 1986–91 Detroit Pistons, MJ, Sir Charles, KG, AI, and Vince Sanity.

Peace.

TODD BOYD
Los Angeles

This one has been a long time coming, and without question, the contributors made it happen. It is their collective vision of the game's impact that brings this all together. For the broader framework in the casting of this book I thank:

the true believers;

my professor colleagues, including Earl Smith, Vivian Gadsden, Peter Vaughan, Elijah Anderson, Tukufu Zuberi, Alfred Mathewson, Richard Shell, Eric Orts, and Timothy Davis, for keeping me true to our game;

Niko Pfund, for believing in round two;

those people in the business of basketball who graciously allow me to be in touch probably more than they would care to hear from me including one or two still running the floor;

my key Philadelphia non-academic foils on these topics, Stan King and Larry Platt—this includes Stan's wife, Sharon, for putting up with our calls when the outrageous in sports occurs;

Vizhier Mooney, for a broad range of insights about the game and the "evil empire" (my words not hers);

members and guests of a few key NCAA committees, for insight I never would have gained in an academic vacuum; that amateur basketball world is largely a cesspool, and the struggle to keep the cess off of the kids must continue;

almost twenty years of students, for keeping me in touch and reeling me back in;

the cast of lifelong influences whom I refuse to light up in print yet again (but do check out the preface);

my collaborator, Dr. Boyd, who remains true to many games, viewing them all through an often more controversial lens than mine but coming up with the same photo album in the end;

Lisa Kmetz, for pulling another manuscript together with superior patience while working with the technological anti-Einstein;

Sharese Bullock, my assistant, for pulling so much together (including the cover). She claims her "J" is still there;

my mother and brother, for again asking about the next book with just that motivating tone of voice;

Theresa and Sam, my young ballers;

and finally, my wife, Diane, who has rearranged her life in part so that I can do more of this. Did I say thanks?

KENNETH L. SHROPSHIRE
Philadelphia

basketball
jones

introduction

basketball jones: a new world order?

TODD BOYD AND KENNETH L. SHROPSHIRE

As he walked through the streets of Barcelona during some off time at the 1992 Olympics, Michael Jordan found himself confronted by an enormous billboard of himself flying through the air in another of his signature balletic basketball moves: the real-life superstar dwarfed by his own larger-than-life image. The fact that this took place in Barcelona, at the Olympics, serves nicely as a metaphor for how Jordan and, by extension, the game of basketball now occupy a prime position on the global stage.

Funny, one could not imagine the same happening to Mark McGwire, or to John Elway, for that matter. Neither baseball nor football has any real significance in the world at large. They are primarily American sports. When most people outside the United States talk about football, they are referring to soccer. At a time when America sought to reassert itself through sport on a global stage, in an increasingly global world, basketball seems in retrospect not only the right choice but the only choice.

The Olympic Games serve as a grand opportunity for the expression of tradition, nostalgia, and nationalism at the highest level. America's political, economic, and cultural prominence in the world is amplified by its massive presence in the Olympics. In many instances, but particularly through the Olympics, sports becomes a direct metaphor for power.

This cultural significance is best evidenced by the first collection of basketball superstars, known as the "Dream Team," assembled to compete in the 1992 summer Olympic Games in Barcelona, Spain. The Dream Team phenomenon is the result of several social and cultural conditions in America in the late 1980s and early 1990s.

After the United States' humiliating loss of the basketball gold medal to the Soviet Union in the 1988 games in Seoul, South Korea, panic set in both overtly, in public media venues, and in

1

everyday conversation among the general populace. Was the United States losing its prowess in yet another area where it had dominated for so long?

In public perception, after World War II, the United States had resurrected West Germany and Japan from the ash heap of war. Yet, throughout the 1980s, Americans were constantly reminded that those same countries had become key players in the world economy, often *beating* the United States, which had been so instrumental in assisting them in regaining their prosperity. Most notable in this regard were repeated news stories, with a not-so-subtle racial subtext, of Japanese corporations purchasing treasured American properties such as Rockefeller Center and media institutions such as Columbia Pictures at an alarming rate. It was suggested often that America was being taken over by a foreign power. Was a similar version of this happening in the sporting world?

In addition to the economic fear generated by Japan and West Germany, the United States, a country which had defined itself against the Soviet Union and communism throughout the cold war, was now running out of acceptable enemies, as Eastern Bloc countries began falling with regularity. War, which involves the same language of dominance and power as sports, had been a defining moment throughout the twentieth century, especially World War II and the Vietnam War. But with communism's seemingly having run its course, America appeared both literally and symbolically, to have no one else to fight.

Though the necessity to exert power was no longer present, the desire to do so remained. This is echoed in President George Bush's declaration of a New World Order in 1988, which further solidified the American preoccupation with power and its need to express this power in direct and indirect ways, as had been initiated in Grenada by President Ronald Reagan and was continued by Bush in Panama and the Persian Gulf. These conflicts provided convenient opportunities for the flexing of the American muscle against much smaller, less-qualified foes.

For the working class, lower class, and otherwise disenfranchised, global political events are often barely noticed. Yet sports, which has always cut across the normally divisive boundaries of race and class, is there for all to see. After teaching the truly American game of basketball to the rest of the world, America had begun to show signs of weakness; everyone else was catching up. The loss in the 1988 Olympics demonstrated this in no uncertain terms.

After this loss, the common excuse offered in the press was that other countries, especially those of the crumbling Eastern Bloc, were using professional players to compete against America's amateurs. Many regarded this as an unfair advantage and suggested that America's professional players be allowed to play. Out of this argument came the idea and actual composition of a Dream Team of the National Basketball Association's (NBA's) most visible stars. This group went on to demolish all competition by an average of forty-four points per game.

Basketball thus became a focal point for what would amount to the undermining of Olympic principles surrounding amateur athletics. Baseball has never played such an important role in the Olympics; nor has football. Because basketball had become omnipresent as an expression of dominance and superiority, it functioned perfectly as a symbol of contemporary Americana, more so than any other sport. The composition, marketing, and symbolic value of the original Dream Team suggests basketball's overall significance as a sport and as a metaphor for our society in the late twentieth century.

Basketball has become a significant preoccupation in American life. With that in mind, this collection of essays focuses on basketball as a sport teeming with issues of race, class, gender, and cultural identity in American society. Using the sport as the model, the essays link the social, cultural, business, legal, and political events of the era with an analysis of the game of basketball.

Basketball is perfectly suited to define American culture because of the ease with which it is represented through the media. By comparison, football seems never to be viewed in this manner. Although football has tremendous television viewership and huge revenues from ticket sales, the game is simply not as intimate as basketball. Unlike baseball and especially football, in basketball the players' faces are easy to see and thus easy to use in advertisements. Because of this intimacy, there is a clearer identification between fans and individual players, or at least with players as we perceive them to be.

The game is also fast paced and easily reducible to the television news format, highlighting dunks and three-point shots. Basketball blends with television like rock with MTV. In 1993 the television ratings for the NBA Finals were, for the first time, higher than baseball's World Series. Unlike baseball and football, basketball is a sport that came into its own in the television age. Baseball grew up in the golden age of radio, and many of those non-visual vestiges remain. Regarded as a sport of minimal national interest in the 1970s, basketball has become mainstream entertainment and popular culture in the 1990s and looks posed to broaden this appeal throughout the twenty-first century.

One can follow this transition by observing the game's escalation in media representation since the late 1970s. The 1979–80 finals between the Los Angeles Lakers and the Philadelphia 76ers were telecast at 11:30 P.M. on tape delay by CBS Sports. The event is now a multinight prime-time event. What was once "filler" on tape delay for CBS's notoriously abysmal late-night programming has become an integral part of prime-time network representation.

Baseball, in the interim, has steadfastly refused to change any rules to speed up the slow-moving game. Though an event such as the Sammy Sosa/Mark McGwire home-run race breathed new life into baseball—this, while basketball suffered labor strife and the retirement of its biggest star, Michael Jordan—basketball remains the media and pop-cultural darling of sports.

In the interest of demonstrating basketball's continued ability to transcend the world of sports, we focus on the late 1970s, when the league began its rise toward mass media popularity, through the present, when the political, social, and cultural changes in America have fundamentally altered the public presentation and reception of the game. This is also a time when America is undergoing a mass identity crisis of its own.

During the Reagan era, America entered a period of transition. The country's overall attempts at redefinition in the aftermath of significant historical events such as the Civil Rights and Black Power movements, feminism, Vietnam, Watergate, the continuing oil crisis, the decline of the cold war, and the necessity of learning to live in a high-tech, postindustrial economy created an environment where many of the commonly held tenets of our cultural identity were simply no longer viable. So much was in turmoil.

As these circumstances helped create an overall anxiety for a new identity, this desire for identity, in turn, opened up possibilities for new forms of culture to emerge to replace those that were suddenly becoming outdated. Over time, the media-friendly nature of basketball, like the sports of baseball and boxing before it, was able to fill a void and provide both a diversion and a realization of these societal circumstances. Basketball became prime time entertainment while simultaneously reflecting society in many ways.

For most of the twentieth century, baseball has been viewed as the sport that defines America. Baseball evokes tradition. Though this traditionalism still exists, especially in terms of baseball's internal politics, it is constantly being challenged, if not completely displaced, by the burgeoning prevalence of basketball.

While baseball remains the key vessel of sports nostalgia and tradition, it is basketball that currently saturates popular culture and permeates our national identity. In this regard, it is not difficult to argue that basketball's Dream Team has become a most glaring sign of American identity in the highly nationalistic discourse that surrounds the Olympic Games. Nor is it be unreasonable to assert that the cult of personality that often defines players as different as Michael Jordan and Dennis Rodman is equivalent to that of the most popular Hollywood celebrities.

This has been a shift from the largely white, working-class, conservative discourse of baseball, focused on icons such as Babe Ruth and Joe DiMaggio. These men were regarded as central to American culture and its representation of itself. The contemporary politics of basketball, as an enactment of popular culture and national identity, offers an opportunity to expose what appears to be a dissolution of the ideals of power and dominance in sports so long associated with white masculinity.

Sports has always been able to produce celebrities who assume larger-than-life proportions and occupy positions as icons of American culture. A closer look at the most significant of these icons over time reveals an interesting pattern. Whereas Babe Ruth's massive appeal as both a baseball player and a cultural symbol defined the early part of the twentieth century, and Muhammad Ali's politics of resistance defined the volatile 1960s and early 1970s, the present ubiquity of Michael Jordan, even in retirement, is perfectly suited for the media saturation of today.

Just as Ruth and baseball aligned perfectly with the white, working-class origins of a large segment of Americans, and Ali represented an evolving American position of racial politics and defiance of authority, Jordan embodies the postintegration moment when race, especially blackness, increasingly informs cultural dialogue, at the same time, paradoxically, rendering race largely invisible within the fabric of sports. Jordan's overall image, while popular, is one devoid of the character substance and specific cultural identity so integral to both Ruth and Ali. In this regard, Jordan's appeal has often been defined as raceless. His seemingly vapid, overmediated image is quite consistent with the void that tends to define much of contemporary American culture.

Consider Jackie Robinson's symbolic "breaking of the color line" in baseball, one of the central events in the public desegregation of American society. Though Robinson's acceptance into the major leagues in 1947 in no way eliminated racism, it certainly suggested to a postwar society that, as Sam Cooke sang, "a change is gonna come."

Serving as a precursor to the Civil Rights movement of the 1960s, Robinson's suggestive entry into one of this country's strongest, most conservative institutions demonstrated that race was inseparable from the progression of American cultural history. But in the same way that Robinson's break offered possibilities, Jordan's dominance and his suggested racelessness are an important prism with which to view contemporary society through basketball.

From the mid-1960s, African American players were increasingly allowed into major college basketball programs. This is highlighted by the all-black Texas Western starting team that defeated all-white Kentucky in the 1966 National Collegiate Athletic Association (NCAA) championship game. Southern universities began recruiting blacks, and soon the college game was dominated by blacks.

In addition, the upstart American Basketball Association (ABA), which merged with the NBA in 1976, featured a large percentage of

African American players and a style of play that closely resembled playground basketball, which is very much in line with the impulses of the black aesthetic. The ABA led in moving the game away from stiff two-handed set shots and bounce passes to behind-the-back alley-oop passes and 360-degree slam dunks. Blackness thus became normalized in discussions about basketball, and the sport was soon to be, in the words of Larry Bird, a "black man's game."

The postintegration era gained momentum at the end of the 1970s and beginning of the 1980s. Following on the heels of the 1960s push for integration and the 1970s attempt at "affirmative action," in the 1980s basketball became increasingly visible in popular culture, and reflective of the nation's racial conscience. The 1979 NCAA championship game featured the Michigan State Spartans and Magic Johnson against Indiana State and Larry Bird. This game signaled the beginning of a rivalry that would spill over into the pros and in some ways marked the dawning of a new era in basketball. As Johnson was drafted by the Los Angeles Lakers and Bird by the Boston Celtics, the tone was set for a narrative of race, history, and evolving social concerns that would play themselves out on the basketball court for much of the next decade.

Johnson's Lakers played in the entertainment metropolis of Los Angeles. With the star of the team appropriately dubbed Magic; the coach, Pat Riley, representing the ultra-hip exterior of Hollywood celebrity; and their style of play referred to as "Showtime," Los Angeles contrasted starkly with the more traditional city of Boston and its working-class idea of substance-over-style basketball. Further, Boston's enthusiasm for a basketball team dominated by white players seemed to echo its racial politics. Boston and thoughts of busing and racial intolerance go in lockstep. Placing a predominantly white team on the parquet floor took a concerted effort, considering the high percentage of African Americans who play the sport.

This battle between Magic and Bird allowed for a displacement debate about race and masculinity present in sports since the days of boxer Jack Johnson and his legendary fights against several "great white hopes." To side with the Lakers or the Celtics was to embrace a racial position and a specific set of cultural politics. As race is in some way endemic to everything in American society, the staging of these racial concerns through basketball allowed for a creative outlet with which to discuss cultural identity in not-so-obvious terms. The battles between Magic and Bird, L.A. and Boston, black and white, could be described as the late twentieth century's version of an acceptable race war.

Yet the representation of the Midwest and the urban identity of postindustrial Detroit through the Detroit Pistons in the late 1980s offered a challenge to the East/West dichotomy. The self-proclaimed "Bad Boys," the Pistons, used a solid defense and what many would consider roughhouse tactics to establish their place among the league's elite. Their style, often dismissed as overly aggressive, if not violent, was quite consistent with the image of the city itself. Detroit, the original murder capital, has long been the epitome of urban blight in the minds of many Americans. The city's large African American population and identity facilitated an image that worked perfectly with the less glamorous style of the Pistons.

By the early 1990s, the Lakers, Celtics, and Pistons were losing their dominance to Michael Jordan and the Chicago Bulls. Jordan and his team ascended to prominence on the premise of transcending race. Jordan's ability to cross traditional boundaries owed a lot to the mass-media popularity of his non-threatening image, and the game's relegation of racial politics to the sidelines, so to speak, demonstrates a new series of concerns for the 1990s.

The shift from a covert discourse about race, which has been fully normalized at this time, to a discussion about class, gender, and even sexuality defines the present agenda in professional basketball. The popularity of the Women's National Basketball Association (WNBA) and women's basketball in general helps expand these possibilities well into the future. These issues are equally instructive in commenting on the American character

Other examples of the racial and class politics that define basketball can be found in the college game, beginning in the mid-1980s with the Georgetown Hoyas and their coach, John Thompson, through the southern elitism associated with the Duke Blue Devils and the street style of the fast-breaking Running Rebels of the University of Nevada Las Vegas (UNLV), to the flamboyant Fab Five from the University of Michigan in the early 1990s. In each case, race and the cultural identity of the represented city has clearly been part of the media representation and popular discourse about the team.

Often the game's racial dilemmas are being played out in different ways in the college game, due to easy associations with concerns of education and intelligence. On the one hand, Duke, a highly regarded elite southern university historically, with few African American players, has been praised for its ability to blend athletics and academics in a successful fashion. This idea was always referenced as part of an older tradition. On the other hand, UNLV, a commuter school in the heart of Las Vegas, a city of glitz, glamour, and no substance, regularly recruited players with checkered backgrounds from junior colleges. The championship games between Duke and UNLV in the early 1990s were pitched as battles between those representing college athletics as it used to be—clean, virginal, and pure—and those who demonstrated what athletics had become—corrupt, immoral, and avaricious. Everything but a direct reference (at least in the media) to white versus black.

Another factor to consider during this time is the NCAA's attempt at reform of college athletics through the passing of Proposition 42 and Proposition 48. Using standardized test scores as the barometer for eligibility to participate, these measures had profound implications for many lower-class black players. Some would argue that these propositions were an indirect way in which to neutralize black dominance in the sport, and that they assisted in restoring the balance of power to the game. They went into effect at the same time that shoe companies (such as Nike and Adidas) were rewarding young athletes for their basketball-playing progress. A world of "street agents" and "uncles" created what has come to be viewed as the "cesspool" of precollegiate basketball. Many caught in this cesspool made it no further.

This "restoration of balance" has allowed schools such as Stanford, with a high percentage of middle-class white players, to compete against some of the schools that have tended to have lower academic standards and recruit a high percentage of black players. In turn, some African American players now opt for the NBA straight out of high school or spend minimal time in college before making the jump to the pros. Even schools like Duke now must face the reality that they will be recruiting players who will stay for only a few years at best.

Further, a generation gap has developed in basketball that continues to exist today. This is articulated largely in class-specific terms. With arguments similar to those made against gangsta rap, the present generation of NBA stars are depicted as synonymous with greed, arrogance, selfish individualism, and an overall disrespect that has often embarrassed the "positive image"–driven league. Consider for a moment the fallout around Allen Iverson's reported comments to Michael Jordan that he doesn't respect anyone. This, for many, was tantamount to blasphemy.

Another example of this generation gap appears when contrasting the first two installments of the Dream Team. The initial team centered on Magic, Jordan, and Bird, who were the beacons of nationalist glory. With the exception of Charles Barkley elbowing a much smaller Angolan player and later joking that the Angolan might have been carrying a spear, the Dream Team rode a crest of popularity that forever enshrined them in the annals of American history. The second incarnation of the team was to play in the 1994 world championships.

This team, which featured young players such as Shawn Kemp, Derrick Coleman (once a *Sports Illustrated* cover subject for a story that decried this new generation of player), and Larry Johnson, turned the games into a playground carnival, often hanging on the rim, grunting, taunting, and displaying an overall disregard for the unspoken rules of basketball social etiquette, particularly in the international realm—behavior for which they were criticized for years after the games were over. Their style of play was such that the older generation's problem child, Barkley, was transformed from a rebel to an elder and became a frequently outspoken critic of their youthful folly.

Basketball has become the preeminent American sport. An analysis of viewership, endorsement power of individual athletes, and the pervasiveness of the game globally all begin to point to basketball as more culturally significant than baseball and football, especially in contemporary society. Baseball has the history and football certainly still plays a prominent role in contemporary America, particularly in terms of the numbers of spectators, both in the stadiums and at home watching. Yet basketball assumes a larger place than either in the lexicon of popular culture throughout the world. This may not be the New World Order that Bush was referring to, but when you consider that a sport once dismissed as a "black man's sport" has come to represent America worldwide, then it is obvious that, if nothing else, the old order has been replaced.

1

privileges and immunities for basketball stars and other sports heroes?

CHARLES J. OGLETREE, JR.

THE UNITED STATES SUPREME COURT has a slogan that represents the underlying principle of our legal system. When ascending the marble steps of the Supreme Court, one can read in bold letters the slogan "Equal Justice under Law." That has long been viewed as the keystone of our legal system. No one is above or below the law.

Debate on the application of this legal principle has been fierce and widespread, especially during the investigation of the president of the United States for "high crimes and misdemeanors." "Is it really true that no one is above or below the law?" "Does our justice system treat people who are differently situated in our society similarly?" Though few people disagree that there *should* be equal justice under the law, the extent to which equal justice truly exists is often contested.

Concerns about disparities of justice arise when people with unusually high levels of status and power repeatedly encounter and too easily escape legal conflicts. When someone is afforded special treatment in the justice system because of his or her status, the notion of equal justice weakens and becomes less credible as a bedrock principle. In particular, equal justice under the law has a tortured meaning when it applies to top basketball players and other successful athletes in America. These sports figures are among the most respected and admired people in society. Unfortunately, a disproportionate number of athletes also commit crimes and engage in immoral acts. Despite their unflattering records, many star athletes continue to receive respect and admiration and are too often protected from the law's just enforcement.

Before exploring the nature and incidence of these crimes and the disproportionate level of justice athletes can receive, we should take note of how athletes are perceived and treated as a privileged class in different contexts. It may well be that these attitudes are fundamental in perpetuating their behavior and even in protecting them from strict enforcement in the justice system.

Our society idolizes successful athletes more than any other figures and provides them with special privileges. Just think about how basketball players have affected our culture. The way we dress, the way we speak, and certainly what we purchase have been heavily influenced by images basketball players project. Arguably more than other sports celebrities, basketball players appear in movies, record their own music, sell products in commercials, and even write books that pass on words of wisdom they have picked up from the game. The impact is undeniable. It is not difficult to find a fan who is willing to stand in line for an entire day to get an autograph from Michael Jordan; in fact, consumer demand for anything related to Michael Jordan created a $10 billion industry.[1] For many of these fans, Jordan was more than just a great basketball player—he was someone to look up to and emulate.

The demand for successful athletes, much less for megastars like Jordan, is unlimited in most popular sports. A strong incentive is

thereby created for various institutions to do whatever they can to
culture new icons. Countless numbers of athletes receive enormous
financial inducements to participate in sports. Many of these athletes are invited to attend colleges or universities despite falling
short of the usual admissions requirements. But these privileges
frequently go beyond simply providing opportunities and rewarding hard work and talent. Instead, athletes may abuse their privileges and develop a fundamental sense of entitlement. Outside
basic scholarships, collegiate athletes can get the privilege of attending special training camps, and they can receive lucrative deals
for their services through inappropriate contact with agents or
would-be agents, obtaining widespread support for family and
friends. In recent years, it was reported that University of Massachusetts basketball player Marcus Camby received illegal funds and
the services of prostitutes from a lawyer hoping to be Camby's
agent. Despite the obvious illegalities of Camby's conduct, he suffered no consequences, signed a lucrative professional basketball
contract, and now plays for the New York Knicks.[2] The problem is
by no means uncommon. In fact, an NCAA (National Collegiate
Athletic Association) committee on amateurism and agents recently estimated that 90 percent of "elite" college athletes have illegal contact with agents.[3]

   Athletes taking advantage of privileges may give us pause: they
are averting institutional rules and obtaining special advantages.
Perhaps we should be concerned about their sense of entitlement
and the leniency with which rules are enforced against them. It is
more disturbing, however, when that sense of entitlement grows
into a feeling of impunity from the justice system, and it is unacceptable when criminal abuse occurs and the legal system responds
with only leniency.

   To begin with, we should recognize the startling incidence of
crimes committed by a wide variety of athletes. The *Los Angeles
Times* reported that 1995 saw 252 nationally reported police incidents where professional and amateur athletes in all sports were
accused of crimes, ranging from shoplifting to murder.[4] In the report, a summary for each offense, along with the charges, is
listed. One needs only to scan the list to realize the severity of
the problem:

OCT. 26: *Latrell Sprewell,* Golden State Warrior basketball player, arrested for various traffic violations in Oakland, including having an outstanding warrant for driving with a suspended license.
RESOLUTION: Judge dismissed charges.

OCT. 26: *Danny Sullivan,* auto racing driver, arrested Sept. 17 on suspicion of grabbing the throat of his girlfriend in Aspen, Colo.
RESOLUTION: Goes to trial on third-degree assault and domestic violence charges March 7.

OCT. 27: *Art Long,* University of Cincinnati basketball player, two incidents in Cincinnati. He was accused of choking his girlfriend in October and faced trial with teammate Danny Fortson [now playing with the Denver Nuggets] after a May 3 confrontation with a mounted police officer.
RESOLUTION: On Oct. 28, a judge ruled the domestic violence charges will be dropped if he completes a 14-week counseling program. On Nov. 3, Long was found not guilty of assaulting a police horse and Fortson was found not guilty of being disorderly while intoxicated.

OCT. 28: *Alvin Robertson,* Toronto Raptor basketball player, two incidents. Arrested after an incident Oct. 28 involving a Toronto woman and faces a common assault charge. Charged June 26 with burglary, assaulting a police officer and resisting arrest in San Antonio after he allegedly kicked open the front door of his girlfriend's home, broke some furniture and allegedly roughed up the woman before taking her wallet. He left, but then returned and is believed to have set fire to some newspaper in the woman's living room.
RESOLUTION: In Toronto case, court date will be set Jan. 4. San Antonio case trial date is April 1.

OCT. 30: *Kevin Johns, Jason Taylor, Richard Schuckman,* University of Dayton football players. After a fight at a campus party: Johns arrested on Oct. 2 on charges of assault on a police officer and disorderly conduct; Taylor and Schuckman charged with disorderly conduct.

RESOLUTION: Johns' charges reduced to misdemeanor attempted assault, probation pre-sentencing Jan. 9. Taylor's case is tentatively scheduled for trial in February. Charges against Schuckman were dismissed Oct. 30.

OCT. 30: *Vernon Maxwell,* Philadelphia 76er basketball player. Two incidents. On Oct. 30, he pleaded no contest in Houston to a misdemeanor marijuana charge after an August arrest. On March 8, he was accused of hitting a patron in a bar in San Antonio with a bottle.

RESOLUTION: Sentence in Houston matter will be handed down upon review of probation reports; charges were dismissed in San Antonio because alleged victim's testimony could not be obtained.

OCT. 31: *Tyrone Williams,* Nebraska football player, accused of firing a gun Jan. 30, 1994, in Lincoln, at a car occupied by New York Jet safety Kevin Porter and a woman. No one was injured.

RESOLUTION: Nebraska Court of Appeals ruled he must face trial on weapons charges.[5]

Even though this represents only five days in October 1995, it is reflective of a trend that shows no signs of slowing down.

Some of the most egregious crimes are committed by the most well known and successful athletes. Even though our society may perceive them as heroes, professional basketball players are frequently perpetrators of criminal acts. In a highly publicized case, Latrell Sprewell assaulted his coach P. J. Carlesimo by choking and punching him during a team practice. This incident served to remind commentators that it was only a single incident out of many reprehensible acts committed by NBA players. A *Wall Street Journal* article cites other, less publicized crimes committed by some of the NBA's best.[6] For example, current New York Knicks forward Larry Johnson was accused by a twenty-eight-year-old woman of pressuring her to abort their unborn child. When she refused, another NBA star and former college roommate of Johnson's threatened her life.[7] A former number-one draft pick and current Sacramento Kings star, Chris Webber, was charged with second-degree assault, marijuana possession, and driving under the influence of drugs.[8] Allen Iverson, offensive specialist of the Philadelphia 76ers, was arrested and charged with possession of marijuana and a handgun.[9] And Isaiah Rider of the Portland Trail Blazers was charged with possession of marijuana and of stolen goods.[10]

Recently, *Sports Illustrated* revealed another disturbing trend: a growing number of paternity suits against professional basketball players.[11] Though they may not be committing felonies, it is startling that so many professional athletes have fathered multiple children, and yet many have allegedly avoided or ignored their paternal responsibilities, despite their incredible wealth. The list of NBA stars who have had out-of-wedlock children reads like a list of the NBA's all-time greatest and most popular players: Larry Bird, Patrick Ewing, Shawn Kemp, Jason Kidd, Hakeem Olajuwon, Gary Payton, Scottie Pippen, and Isiah Thomas.[12] ESPN broadcaster Len Elmore estimated that there is one out-of-wedlock child for every player in the NBA.[13]

The National Football League's players are just as likely to have questionable backgrounds. A study of 509 players in the NFL revealed that 109 had been formally charged with a serious crime, including homicide, rape, kidnapping, and robbery.[14] Some of these players have been charged with multiple crimes. For example, Charles Jordan, wide receiver for the Miami Dolphins, has been charged with murder, robbery, auto theft, and threatening a witness.[15] Damon Jones, tight end for the Jacksonville Jaguars, has been charged with assault, manufacturing and placing a bomb, and vandalism.[16] And Deion Sanders, defensive back for the Dallas Cowboys, has been charged with aggravated assault, disorderly conduct, battery, trespassing, resisting arrest, and leaving an accident scene.[17]

Researchers have identified that some crimes are particularly prevalent with basketball and football players. A 1995 *Sports Illustrated* article exposes the high occurrence of domestic violence cases involving sports stars.[18] The author describes particular cases, including an incident where NFL quarterback Warren Moon struck his wife in the head and proceeded to strangle her before she escaped, as well as multiple incidents where NBA all-star Scottie Pippen choked and hit his wife.[19] Other sports celebrities who have been accused of domestic violence include O. J. Simpson, Dante Bichette, Barry Bonds, Jose Canseco, Michael Cooper, Darryl Strawberry, Duane Causwell, Olden Polynice, and Otis Wilson, just to name a few.[20] A recent research study at Northeastern University and the University of Massachusetts found that this pattern of abuse also exists at the college level. Out of 107 cases of sexual assault at thirty universities over an eighteen-month period, researchers found that male athletes who made up 2.2 percent of the student population were involved in 19 percent of the crimes on campus.[21]

It is difficult to explain why these trends exist. The fact that a large part of our society idolizes athletes and awards them with special attention and privileges may give them a sense of entitlement and freedom from accountability. Alan Klein, co-author of the Northeastern and University of Massachusetts study on athletes and abuse, attributes the high occurrence of sexual assault by athletes to their sense of entitlement, resulting from receiving special privileges and treatment. "Included in that," says Klein "is the view of women as always at one's beck and call. It's a combination of that and never being held accountable for anything."[22] The truth is that the focus on athletes' achievements in sports often overshadows their crimes. For example, Latrell Sprewell attacked and threatened his former coach, but now that he is with the New York Knicks, the focus is on whether or not he can provide the offensive boost to make the Knicks a consistent championship contender. Nobody seems to remember the allegations against Allen Iverson for "maiming-by-mob" now that he has won the NBA scoring title.[23] Who recalls Chris Webber's being charged with second-degree assault when he leads the league in rebounds and scores twenty points a game?[24] But, despite a lack of accountability in society and the media, what about "equal justice under the law"? These perpetrators of crimes and immoral acts should not be treated differently in our justice system, because no one should be above or beneath the law. Yet athletes are getting away with crimes in a way that makes it seem like their elevated social status is translatable to immunity. It's one thing if society decides to admire its best athletes and provide them with special privileges. It is a more serious matter, however, when the law fails to follow its bedrock principle for a privileged class.

Equal justice under law is initially threatened where institutions avoid disciplining their athletes and foster their athletes' feeling of being above the law. While the NCAA rules are strict and detailed, the modern trend is to allow academic institutions to self-report violations, often leading to unbalanced and absurd results.[25] An example of such an infraction includes a case where a recruited athlete received a pair of gloves purchased by a student host while on a recruiting visit. The athlete needed the gloves because of the cold weather. The student host subtracted the cost from the student-host money, and as a result, the recruit lost his eligibility, which could be restored only through an NCAA appeals process.[26] Compare this to cases where more visible athletes receive only token punishments for greater crimes. Boston College freshman basketball star Chris Herren failed a number of drug tests and was never suspended from the team. Without much publicity, he transferred to Fresno State University.[27] Nebraska defensive tackle Christian Peter pleaded guilty to a third-degree sexual assault on a former Miss Nebraska in 1993, had two other women tell the police that Peters had sexually assaulted them as well, and was fined for urinating in public and threatening a police cadet. The only punishment Peters received from his school was to miss a week of spring practice.[28] At Bucknell University, wide receiver Michael Phillip never missed a day of school or a single game, though he was convicted of assaulting another student, fracturing the victim's cheekbone, and causing him nerve damage.[29] Because schools are allowed to set their own disciplinary policies based on NCAA guidelines, rather than punishing their top student athletes, schools actually do very little to hold their best players accountable. In some cases they can even protect their stars from bad publicity. Ironically, the NCAA's desire to give colleges the authority to account for their own student athletes has actually produced the opposite effect.

An athlete's institution may even take measures to help the athlete avoid criminal punishment. These institutions in essence act as accomplices to crimes committed by their athletes. The Northeastern and University of Massachusetts study on athletes and crimes determined that sexual assaults committed by athletes were more likely to be handled by internal college hearings than by the police.[30] Campus officials sometimes encourage victims of sexual assault or rape to leave the punishment up to the college, where the greatest possible sanction is expulsion, rather than to pursue criminal prosecution.[31] In a particularly outrageous case, one alleged victim of a rape stated that instead of any punishment for the athlete, she was paid to get therapy and to transfer to another school.[32] Such immoral behavior demonstrates how academic institutions can act as accomplices that stand in the way of equal justice under the law.

Professional sports organizations also lack internal disciplinary measures that could help the law provide equal justice. Professional basketball player Latrell Sprewell's one-year suspension was the longest in NBA history.[33] Yet, not only was Sprewell not expelled from the NBA, but his marketability within the organization remains healthy. Before the Sprewell incident, the longest suspensions included Kermit Washington's twenty-six-game suspension for punching another player and Vernon Maxwell's ten-game suspension for attacking a fan in the stands.[34]

While the institutions behind the athletes may shield them from the law, it is more troubling when the criminal justice system itself gives special treatment to star athletes. Though the legal system is said to work under the principle of "equal justice under law," justice is not mechanically administered. Human beings make personal judgments during the justice system's stages of enforcement, prosecution, adjudication, and sentencing. And policemen, lawyers, jurors, and judges are just as likely to be sports fans as anyone else.

Examples where basketball players and other popular athletes receive special treatment in the legal system are numerous. After Houston Rocket Charles Barkley threw a man through a bar window, the judge delayed his misdemeanor trial to accommodate his playing schedule.[35] Sun Bonds, wife of all-star baseball player Barry Bonds, discovered what it was like to be in a trial against a sports celebrity. In a legal dispute that followed Sun's allegations that her husband physically and emotionally abused her, the judge not only granted Barry Bonds a 50 percent reduction in family-support payments but also told the baseball star that he was an ardent sports fan and asked for Barry's autograph.[36] And despite the

University of Miami president's insistence that campus police do not give preferential treatment to the school's football players, two women claim that police tried to dissuade them from pursuing battery claims against two of the team's players.[37]

Preferential treatment may even come in the form of affording athletes greater credibility, thus impeding the law's just enforcement. Nancy Saad, former wife of NBA superstar/accused domestic abuser Robert Parish, was directly warned that going against a superstar is futile. Saad stated that Parish taunted her to try exposing him in public: "Who you gonna tell? Who's gonna believe you? They're gonna believe me, and I'll make you look crazy."[38] Unfortunately, Parish may have been right. "The athlete's status in the community often makes it hard for people to believe that these guys are really batterers," says Richard Gelles, for twenty-two years the director of the Family Violence Research Program at the University of Rhode Island.[39] This preferential treatment is more than a series of anecdotes. Researchers in a Northeastern University study of sexual assaults involving athletes claim that athletes arrested for committing sexual assaults were convicted in only 30 percent of the cases, compared to those in the general population, who were convicted in 54 percent of cases.[40]

The impact of athletes receiving preferential treatment is far-reaching. Not only does it negatively affect the victims, but it also weakens the credibility of the bedrock principle of the justice system. In particular, young adults who aspire to be star athletes may believe they can be above the law, just like their heroes. This could not be further from reality, especially for young adults who historically have not been treated with anything approaching leniency in the criminal justice system.

Thirteen percent of the U.S. population is African American, whereas 80 percent of the NBA and 67 percent of the NFL is African American.[41] It should not be surprising that a disproportionate number of young African American boys aspire to be professional basketball or professional football players. A *Sports Illustrated* poll of 1,835 middle school and high school students indicated that 57 percent of black males want to become professional athletes, whereas 41 percent of white males share that aspiration.[42] The danger of young African American boys emulating their sports heroes is that they may erroneously believe they, like their heroes, are above the law. In reality, nearly one out of every three African American men between the ages of twenty and twenty-nine is in some way involved in the criminal justice system. More important, the offenses that professional athletes commit with impunity, such as use of crack cocaine, result in virtual life sentences for many young African American males. The consequences of drug use or other forms of criminality among black males result in stiff sanctions, including not only conviction and incarceration but the loss of such important rights as voting. Thus, though an African American male who is a popular basketball player or football player may commit a crime and walk free, his counterpart, committing the same offense, could spend thirty years to life in prison.

The differential treatment between athletes and non-athletes is not limited to how minorities are treated in the justice system. Anyone who commits a crime may be subject to the law's strict enforcement compared to the lenience that athletes sometimes are afforded. Take, for example, a man in Illinois who knocked out his teeth while he was drunk.[43] He walked to a nearby bank, unarmed and still intoxicated, and said to the teller that he needed a loan. When the teller told him to go to the loan department, he said, "Not that kind of loan," and gave the teller a plastic bag, which she then filled with $6,000.[44] Despite the fact that he had never been in trouble with the law, the judge sentenced him to two years of imprisonment.[45] Though not directly analogous, compare the aforementioned scenario to the case of former Sacramento Kings basketball player Duane Causwell. The NBA player was charged with inflicting corporal injury, battery, false imprisonment, assault, and damaging a telephone in a spousal abuse incident.[46] His charges were suspended to permit him to attend a domestic violence diversion program.[47] Consider also the case of a man in Maryland who was convicted of distributing one gram of LSD. He was sentenced to eighty-four months in prison, pursuant to sentencing-guideline requirements.[48] Compare this to the many cases in which professional athletes are strongly suspected of drug abuse and drug trafficking but are nevertheless not even prosecuted.[49]

In light of the difference between how the justice system treats great athletes and how it treats their non-athlete counterparts, maybe the slogan "Equal Justice under Law" should be changed to "Equal Justice under Law for Some." But rather than give up on our bedrock principle of justice, we should be more adamant about protesting cases where athletes receive undue lenience in the justice system. As previously noted, our attitudes and treatment toward athletes in this society may perpetuate and reinforce unequal justice under law. If this is true, refocusing the strength of our convictions about justice and our attitudes about athletes' position in society should help restore our bedrock principle. We can demonstrate our attitudes by sending a clear message to athletes. Athletes need to be aware that there are privileges with their status, but there are consequences to abusing those privileges. And since being an athlete is a privilege rather than a right, athletes should know that our legal system is based on a principle that does not allow them to commit legal violations and ignore social obligations with impunity.

Any change of attitude will happen over time. Our attitudes are formed through years of believing what we see, hear, and experience. Despite the reality of the matter, it may still be difficult to accept that something is not consistent with what we have always believed. This is why it is so critical to let the youth of America know that not all athletes are heroes and that equal justice under law applies to everyone. While all children need to be taught these important lessons, we need to pay special attention to children who are particularly susceptible to adopting the wrong athletes as role models. We need to make sure that we aren't sending the wrong messages to children about who is a role model and who is not.

Education will be the key to any success in this area. There needs to be further education of young people about the sense of real role models. While we can recognize the incredible talents of professional athletes, it is naive to think that they are role models that young people should aspire to follow. Moreover, if our criminal justice system is to have any credibility in the eyes of those who are subjected to it, there has to be evidence that equal justice under the law, in fact, is more than slogan; indeed, that it is reality. When a young black man, with no other means of self-support, receives twenty years in prison for dealing crack cocaine while a professional athlete receives a slap on the wrist, it is impossible to reconcile the difference in treatment. Credibility requires transparency in the law.

Professional athletes should be encouraged to take the first step to insist on moral obligations among their peers. Rather than requiring the legal system simply to crack down on those who are violating the law, it is far more sensible to require that athletes set their own high standards and to find appropriate sanctions for those who fail to reach that bar.

While it is acceptable to extend privileges and confer respect to those who deserve it, we cannot remove those individuals from responsibility or accountability. The two go hand in hand and are critical parts of our system of jurisprudence.

NOTES

1. See Gregg Krupa, "Losing a '$10 Billion' Icon: Marketing Experts Say Jordan's Absence Would Slow Repair of Lockout Damage," *Boston Globe*, January 13, 1999, at C1.

2. See Mike McIntire, John Springer, Tom Yantz, and Ken Davis, "Lounsbury Investors Bet on Sports Revelation Raises Questions for UConn and the NCAA," *Hartford Courant*, March 7, 1997, at C1.

3. See Steve Wilstein, "Risky Business—All Signs Point to Some Sort of Uprising as College Coaches and Players Alike Scream: 'EXPLOITA-TION.' The NCAA's Survival Could Depend on How Well It's Listening," *San Antonio Express*, December 26, 1996, at 1C.

4. See Julie Cart, "Crime and Sports '95," *Los Angeles Times*, December 27, 1995, at C1.

5. Ibid.

6. See Andrew Peyton Thomas, "NBA: Nasty, Brutish Athletes," *Wall Street Journal*, November 24, 1998, at A22.

7. Ibid.

8. Ibid.

9. Ibid.

10. Ibid.

11. See Grant Wahl and L. Jon Wertheim, "Paternity Ward: Fathering Out-of-Wedlock Kids Has Become Commonplace among Athletes, Many of Whom Seem Oblivious to the Legal, Financial, and Emotional Consequences," *Sports Illustrated*, May 4, 1998, at 62.

12. Ibid.

13. See Thomas, "NBA," at A22.

14. See Jeff Benedict and Don Yaeger, *Pros and Cons* (New York: Warner Books 1998).

15. Ibid., 267.

16. Ibid.

17. Ibid., 270.

18. See William Nack and Lester Munson, "Sports' Dirty Secret," *Sports Illustrated,* July 31, 1995, at 62.

19. Ibid.

20. Ibid.

21. See Maryann Hudson, "From Box Scores to the Police Blotter: 1995 Was a Rough Year for Athletes and the Law," *Los Angeles Times,* December 27, 1995 at C1.

22. Ibid.

23. See Cart, "Crime and Sports '95," at C1.

24. See Thomas, "NBA," at A22.

25. See Greg Hansen, "Most Schools Learn to Fear Mighty NCAA," *Arizona Daily Star,* May 7, 1997, at 1C.

26. Ibid.

27. See Daniel Golden, "When College Athletes Misbehave, Often There's Only Token Punishment," *Boston Globe,* September 11, 1995, at 39.

28. Ibid.

29. Ibid.

30. Ibid.

31. Ibid.

32. Ibid.

33. See Dave Krieger, "Attempts to Free 'Spre' May Be Difficult," *Rocky Mountain News,* March 8, 1998, at 20C.

34. See Jeffrey Rosenthal, "Will the NBA Be Victim of Its Past Leniency?" *New York Law Journal,* January 9, 1998, at 5.

35. See "Judge Delays Barkley Trial," *Washington Post,* January 17, 1998, at H04.

36. See Wahl and Wertheim, "Paternity Ward," at 62.

37. See Darin Klahr, "Two Women Claim That UM Police Gave 'Canes Special Treatment," *Palm Beach Post,* October 26, 1995, at 7C.

38. See Wahl and Wertheim, "Paternity Ward," at 62.

39. Ibid.

40. See Hudson, "Box Scores," at C1.

41. See S. L. Price, "What Ever Happened to the White Athlete?" *Sports Illustrated,* December 8, 1997, at 30.

42. Ibid.

43. See Thomas W. Hillier, "Federal Public Defender," 2 *Federal Sentencing Review* 224 (February/March 1990).

44. Ibid.

45. Ibid.

46. See Cart, "Crime and Sport '95," at C1.

47. Ibid.

48. See Hillier, "Federal Public Defender," at 224.

49. See Jeff Benedict, *Public Heroes, Private Felons* (Boston: Northeastern University Press 1997), 43, 44, 52.

2

why baseball *was* the black national pastime

GERALD EARLY

What is the purpose of a ball game? To win.
—Branch Rickey, Brooklyn
Dodger executive who
signed Jackie Robinson

[Baseball] is a form of Americanization.
—Michael Novak,
The Joy of Sports

People used to ask me at a very young age what I wanted to do when I grew up, and I told them that I wanted to be a ballplayer. I was some black kid from the projects, so they didn't think it was going to happen. But I never lost that dream—I was detoured a couple of times—but I never lost that dream.
—Hall-of-Famer Willie Stargell,
Baseball Weekly interview,
July 22–28, 1998

Prologue

As a black man who is deeply attached to baseball, I find basketball, by comparison, a curiously barbaric sport and am bemused by its popularity. It seems a kind of controlled chaos flowing around two polarities as it aspires, paradoxically, to be a full-contact sport that outlaws contact. I have never enjoyed watching basketball and I loathed playing it. It seems almost in every way inferior to baseball, a game I played in a number of its variants a great deal when I was younger and that I watch almost daily, either at the ballpark or on television, during the season.

What I think I most liked about baseball was what seemed to me to be two contrary ideals: faith and failure. When I was a boy, I believed in the men who played the game more than I believed in myself, and when my favorite players failed, I felt crushed, more disappointed for them than for any failure I ever personally experienced. That was and is baseball for me: a faith in the ability of other people not to let you or themselves down when it really counts the most—but if they do let you down, if they let themselves down, to feel more sorry for them than for yourself. So, for me, baseball was and is about a certain generosity of spirit, a broad and deeply felt empathy in the glory of losing and disappointment. After all, as many commentators have pointed out, losing and failing are bigger parts of the game than success and winning. (Remember that the most famous poem associated with the game, possibly the most famous poem in the English language, "Casey at the Bat," is about losing and defeat. And "Take Me Out to the Ball Game" has the lines "Root, root, root for the home team, if they don't win, it's a shame, 'cause it's one, two, three strikes you're out at the old ball game.")

Maybe that's why African Americans were so attracted to baseball in the 1920s and 1930s, when the Negro Leagues were one of the biggest black businesses in the United States and when baseball was the number-one spectator sport among blacks. Perhaps they liked the idea of having faith in the ability of the black players on the field. It was a way for black folk to believe, if only for a moment, in each other and to pull for one another. But since the game is more about losing and failing than about winning, maybe blacks also felt that baseball was like the blues, an art form that reminds people life is more about losing and failing than about winning. Baseball, therefore, more than anything else, is about the stuff of the black American Dream.

Basketball: The Black Status Quo

It is certainly no news to report that African Americans are closely associated with the game of basketball, both literally and mythically. It might even be said that basketball is their game now, the game that best displays their particular athletic inclinations, their special physical gifts, and their peculiar group genius—if, indeed, one believes in those sorts of highly specified racial or ethnic endowments. Eighty percent of the men who make their living playing in the National Basketball Association are black, which means that although, of course, the odds are very long against anyone of any race becoming an NBA player, it is, as Steve Sailor said in the *National Review*, twenty-five times more likely for a black to reach the NBA than a non-black.[1] Blacks dominate this sport as performers as they do no other glamour profession in mass entertainment, not even popular music, where African Americans have probably exercised their biggest influence on western culture. (The sheer number of metaphorical references by writers comparing basketball to forms of African American music bespeaks both how much blacks dominate basketball and how much music is seen as their most impressive cultural offering.) The most celebrated American athlete in the world is a black basketball player, Michael Jordan. He is, arguably, the most famous—only Muhammad Ali would rival in this regard—and surely the most successful athlete in history. No athlete has ever been such a force in advertising and the promotion of products. Some of the most famous blacks in coaching and sports management are in professional and college basketball, many more so than in any other professional or collegiate team sport, except track and field. In these ways, basketball has become associated with the apogee of black material success and assimilation; for basketball is, after all, an American sport invented by an American on American soil—far more American than baseball, the national pastime, as it were, whose origins are directly traceable to British ball-and-bat games.[2] Is not basketball a perfect example of how African Americans took an American invention and made it their own, of how they defined the meaning of being American in their own terms through this game?

On the one hand, basketball has "uplifted the race," it might be said, in both a Du Boisian and Washingtonian way. From a Du Boisian perspective, basketball has created an elite cadre of narrowly talented, extremely wealthy black men who have visibly and unalterably stamped their style—their racial "elegance," to borrow

a term from Ralph Ellison, Albert Murray, and Stanley Crouch—
on a realm of performance to such a degree that it has changed the
entire nature of how this game is played, changed, indeed, the reality and myth of the game, while elevating African American ethos
and creativity. For basketball now has become a form of *African
American*, not simply *American*, ludic engagement and expression.
Basketball, in the Du Boisian sense, has been an act of the conservation of the race, its sensibility, its Negro-ness, its genius.[3] From a
Washingtonian perspective, basketball is a practical example of
black people exploiting their gifts and seizing an opportunity to
shape the style of a performance art in such a way as to assure their
dominance of it, and thus the relevance and necessity of their continued employment if the sport is to maintain its high level of expression and competitive energy. It is a grand example of the adage
"Cast down your buckets where you are," for seemingly, in dominating basketball, blacks have taken advantage of the ease with
which basketball can be learned under the most harsh social and
economic circumstances, under the most impoverished conditions.
They have also taken advantage of the sports obsession of whites,
who in large numbers make up the audience for professional and
college basketball, and without whom it, like all professional and
amateur sports, would hardly be a lucrative enterprise.

On the other hand, even before the film *Hoop Dreams*, George
Cain's 1970 autobiographical novel, *Blueschild Baby*, about a black
boy who momentarily escapes the ghetto by playing basketball at a
white prep school and who winds up a drug addict, associated basketball with working-class and lower-class black male aspiration
and uneasy, distressing efforts at assimilation and integration
across both racial and class lines. When *U.S. News and World Report* did a cover story (March 24, 1997) titled "Are Pro Sports Bad
for Black America?" Michael Jordan was on the cover and the sub-
head was "A sobering look at the Air Jordan effect." Sports are a
way out of poverty, and poor men, from whites who worked in
mines to Latinos who cut sugarcane, have used sports in just this
way since the heyday of bareknuckle prize-fighting in Regency
England. Unfortunately, sports are not a particularly realistic or
broadly reformative way of helping the poor. Indeed, it can be argued that sports hardly challenge the system of restraints and

degradation under which the poor must function, and in some vital ways, a poor kid's aspiration for a sports career may be interpreted as a particularly tragic or at least dispiriting form of acquiescence to the status quo: that the poor boy as *nouveau riche* sports hero simply reinforces and justifies the values and the power system that made his poverty possible and acceptable in the first place. Some leftists, at least, would argue this. In this way, basketball has become associated with black male "pathology," seen as a symbolic expression of black male frustration, the victim's willing participation in his own exploitation; the black sports obsession as an unlikely, even romantic way out of poverty and as a misbegotten, misdirected ambition.

The black dominance in basketball as the conjunction of both social and material success and sociopathology, of both cultural achievement and cultural perversity, is a point John Hoberman makes in an early chapter of *Darwin's Athletes*.[4] (Whatever one may think about how Hoberman handles this thesis, there seems little question that blacks and basketball have become intricately enmeshed in the popular American mind with achievement, exquisite athleticism, and, paradoxically, black cultural disorder.) This view partly arises from a concern that black dominance in basketball is seen, principally though not exclusively by whites, as the result of something genetic or character related in blacks, a defect, perhaps, or a freakish endowment that has fortuitously found an outlet as a virtue or at least as a socially acceptable skill. This view partly arises as well from a concern about the sociological and political impact of high-performance sports on an oppressed minority population that still has a difficult time finding a full range of opportunities to exhibit its aptitudes or even to find out what its aptitudes are; that, far from being liberating or empowering, an obsession with careers in high-level sports such as basketball further limits and distracts many African American men from more useful, practical, and profitable endeavors. Yet another concern is expressed by this view: African Americans, like everyone else in the United States, are obsessed by the need for group leadership, yet the very people who have most visibility within their own group and with whites, the very people often bestowed with the most charisma because of what they do, such as star basketball players and other

high-performance athletes, are the least equipped or trained or inclined to provide leadership. This, I think, causes a considerable
level of frustration and even contradiction for blacks, who worship
their sports stars as individuals of achievement and figures of conspicuous consumption while expressing disappointment in them
that they are mere sports stars and not people of more serious
substance.[5]

When one couples the fact that blacks dominate both the professional and college basketball ranks with the fact that basketball is
the game of greatest spectator interest for blacks (in part, surely,
because so many black men play it on the highest level, so it becomes a source of racial pride; it is the most commonly played game
that one can see in a casual tour of any black community), one must
ask why this game has become the black national pastime, especially when a sport such as baseball, which has virtually disap-
peared from African American communal life, has a longer, deeper,
and more intricate institutional history in the lives of blacks. Although not nearly as many black men play major-league baseball
(about 17 percent of the players in the majors are blacks; this figure
does not include black Latinos, among whom the game is still very
popular and who would probably swell the ranks of blacks to over
30 percent) as play basketball, there are still enough to interest the
casual black fan.[6] And some of the greatest players ever in the majors were blacks. Moreover, blacks had developed one of the biggest
businesses in their history when they launched the Negro Leagues
in 1920 and again in 1933. And despite the popularity of basketball
today, especially among the young, is not baseball the more deeply
ingrained game, the sport that symbolizes the American national
character, defines us as a people? More casual observers know about
the records in baseball—Roger Maris's (now Mark McGwire's)
home-run record, the number Cal Ripken had to exceed to break
the consecutive-games-played record held by Lou Gehrig, Joe
DiMaggio's fifty-six-game hitting streak—than know virtually
any of the records of basketball or football or, indeed, any other
sport. (What football or basketball player has played in the most
consecutive games? What quarterback holds the record for the
most consecutive games with a touchdown pass, and how many is
that?) It was not simply the popularity of baseball but the power of

baseball as something uniquely and typically American that attracted black people to it at the end of the nineteenth century, when blacks, once banned from playing professionally with whites, tried to form their own leagues, without success, and constantly formed barnstorming teams, with better results.

Baseball, despite the pastoral mythology, is an urban game, invented in New England and New York. Despite all the talk about it being a kids' game, it was invented by adults to be played by adults. After the Civil War, when blacks began to become more urban, they began to form baseball teams along the East Coast, in Baltimore, Philadelphia, and New York in the 1880s and the 1890s.[7] Baseball's attraction was, indeed, the intricacy of its play (these were the days of "inside baseball," where cunning and craft, not home runs, earned teams winning scores) and the necessity of organization. It was proved to black folk, I think, in these post-Reconstruction days, when they were sharply segregated and confined, lynched, and denigrated in academic and scholarly circles as lesser beings, that *organizing* a baseball team, *organizing* a league, would show them to be as good as whites, as capable; it would show them to be Americans, too, since they could *organize* to play this game. Baseball was meant to show the communal strength of blacks. There is no way that black success in basketball compares in magnitude to what blacks accomplished in baseball. So, what happened to baseball in African American life? What did baseball mean to African Americans, and why does it no longer mean what it did?

Baseball: The Black Struggle for an American Dream

Michael Novak's essay on basketball in *The Joy of Sports* lyrically connects blacks to basketball by referring both to jazz and to black literature:

> Basketball players must be improvisers. . . . Basketball is jazz: improvisatory, free, individualistic, corporate, sweaty, fast, exulting, screeching, torrid, explosive, exquisitely designed for letting first

the trumpet, then the sax, then the drummer, then the trombon-
ist soar away in virtuoso excellence.[8]

Novak continues that more and more blacks began to play basketball after the Second World War, as the game came to be thought of
as "the city game" and African Americans, as a result of the major
post–World War II migration, became a more urban people: "The
tempo was now the tempo of the city. . . . The style was the style of
the city: sophisticated, cool, deceptive, swift, spectacular, flashy,
smooth."[9]

Novak then concludes:

> Basketball represents the black experience in yet another way.
> Basketball is, as more than one connoisseur has noted, a game of
> feint, deception: put-on. The very word is a ghetto word. One
> "puts on" the man. . . . Every motion in basketball is disguise for
> yet another. . . . Like the stories and legends of black literature,
> the hero does not let his antagonist guess his intentions; he
> strings him along; he keeps his inner life to himself until the de-
> cisive moment.[10]

Novak's metaphorical comparison of basketball to jazz unfortunately begs the question: What is jazz? It would seem, from
Novak's description, that jazz's major characteristic is that it is improvisational. This is problematic for a couple reasons. First, jazz
players did not introduce improvisation to American music. Improvisation has always existed in music, including European music. It
is only one feature among several that makes jazz a distinctive
art.[11] Also, there is nothing about basketball that makes it more improvisational than other sports, such as boxing (where cuts or hand
injuries may force a fighter to change his approach to his opponent
completely, and in which feints and deceptions are essential to the
sport's execution) or football (with its audibles and broken plays) or
baseball (where, despite its rigidity of structure, in its main confrontation the pitcher is improvising somewhat new patterns to repeatedly get out batters who, through exposure, know his repertoire).[12] Every successful individual athlete or team must rely on
considerable on-the-spot ingenuity, not just mechanical skill, to

win, for sporting competitions nearly always, in a major or a minor way, produce the unexpected.

Second, it is not necessarily the case the blacks are more naturally or culturally inclined toward improvisation than are other groups in America. There has been among blacks as much of a creative urge to write music as to improvise it. (Ragtime, for instance, was a scored music, not an improvised one. Blues, under the pens of W. C. Handy, Clarence Williams, and Perry Bradford, reached its zenith as a professional art form as a written music. One can also mention numerous songwriters and composers from the early days of professional black music, such as the Johnson brothers, Will Marion Cook, Harry T. Burleigh, Andy Razaf.) The African cultures from which black Americans came were as noted for their rigidity of custom and form, practice and tradition, for their prescriptive roles and stunning complexity of proscriptive beliefs, as were most other preindustrial cultures. In other words, nothing from African American cultural products or from their cultural or biological background as Africans argues that blacks are more temperamentally suited to basketball as an exhibition of some innate drive toward improvisation than any other group. (In fairness to Novak, he does mention the contributions of other ethnic groups to basketball, particularly noting that Bob Cousy introduced several of the innovations that black players were to capitalize on and further expand.)

African Americans live in a democratic, capitalist culture that abhors the static and rewards innovation and change. What black people historically saw around them in the United States, despite their own oppression and bondage, were a great deal of fluidity and a huge range of possibilities, quite unlike not only Europe but anyplace else in the world. What struck them was not merely improvisation but adaptability, adjusting and taking advantage of changing conditions that the most successful people in America did well or seemed to do well. As blacks were restricted in circumstance, they took a larger cultural trait, not an inherently racial one, and adapted it as a ritualized style, as a performance, when they created jazz or black basketball or anything else. They also practiced adaptation by using this type of style or flair in the public-performance fields that were open to them in order to distinguish themselves from whites in the same fields, to create a cultural and practical space for themselves. Racism, pride, and a distinct perspective on how to go about problem solving dictated that blacks could not succeed as carbon copies of whites. In other words, Novak, in defining how blacks changed basketball, sees something uniquely black instead of, more correctly, something typically and uniquely American.[13] This sort of thinking leads to misunderstanding precisely what African Americans contributed to the formation of American sports and how they were shaped, in turn, by the sports they played.

In "An Inquiry into the Decline of Baseball in Black America: Some Answers—More Questions," by Don E. Albrecht, the decline of black interest in baseball is structurally linked to the rise of basketball.

During their childhood years, some blacks may choose basketball or football over baseball because the costs for baseball are greater. At a minimum, to play baseball a player must have a relatively expensive baseball glove, which is seldom furnished by the team or league. Such up-front expenses are typically not required for football or basketball. Economics may also play a role because well-financed Little League teams are more common in neighborhoods that are economically well off. The organization and instruction associated with top-quality Little League programs are important because it is more difficult to have pickup baseball games than pickup basketball games. Relevant skills, too, can be more easily developed in basketball, by playing alone or in small groups and generally with less organization than baseball. A related economic factor is that baseball requires a great deal of space, and such space is often simply not available in low-income, inner-city, predominantly black neighborhoods.[14]

Although Albrecht mentions football, his analysis is meant to describe the economic factors that have given rise to basketball as the sport of choice for black kids, particularly inner-city black kids. (Mentioning football, it seems to me, hurts his argument more than aids it.) Nearly all the reasoning here is specious. Surely, a youngster who decides to join his high school football team (and even the poorest inner-city schools have such teams, as those who live near East St. Louis are vividly aware) is given the basic equipment with which to play the game, just as a kid who joins the high school baseball team is given a uniform, bats, balls, and the like. In both instances, the kid is likely to have to buy his own shoes for the sport, but this is no more onerous an expense for baseball than for football, and poor kids manage to scrap together the money to do so to play football. In football, the kid is almost certain to have the expense of getting fitted with a mouthpiece, which he may not have to do in baseball.[15] Moreover, in poor neighborhoods, youngsters can get money to buy what they think is important—expensive sneakers (to play basketball or just to look cool), compact discs, leather jackets, and the like. If a poor kid can buy a pair of Nike sneakers, why he can't he buy an "expensive" baseball glove, which almost certainly is going to be cheaper than the shoes? The argument about expenses simply is not persuasive.

Equally unconvincing is the argument about space in the ghetto. Blacks were taught to play baseball in their own neighborhoods back in the 1930s and 1940s, when these neighborhoods as a rule were far more densely populated than they are now, with just as little green space. These areas now tend to have more vacated space than ever because so many abandoned houses have been torn down and fewer people live there. If the ghetto has anything, it would seem to have space.[16] Moreover, playing football requires a great deal of space, and poor blacks still manage to play it, despite the neighborhoods they live in. They also manage to learn football despite the fact that it is just as difficult to learn the skills of football by oneself as it is to learn baseball skills, and it is just as difficult to organize pickup football games as it is to organize pickup baseball games. This sort of reasoning indicates not only a thorough lack of knowledge of the social and cultural history of African Americans and an at best crude understanding of the intricacies of their consumption habits but also a distorted appreciation of the complexities of their desires and aspirations in sports and, particularly, an ignorance of their relationship with and attempts to create secular institutions. That, it seems to me, is the immense importance of blacks and baseball: that it could be learned, passed on, made a tradition, and professionalized through leagues as a business only through the creation of secular institutions apart from schools.

When Jackie Robinson played his first game as a Brooklyn Dodger in April 1947, a crowd of 26,623 showed up. Fourteen thousand of them were black, more than half.[17] When Robinson played his first game in St. Louis at Sportsman Park, where blacks once had to endure segregated seating but were by that time permitted to sit anywhere, of the sixteen thousand persons who watched the game, six thousand were black, more than a third.[18] Today, African Americans make up only 3.5 percent of major-league baseball attendance. In St. Louis they make up even less, 2.8 percent.[19] This was the cause of some embarrassment in 1997, during the semi-centennial celebration of Robinson's debut with the Dodgers. How can baseball have overcome racism when blacks hardly go to the games?

This I say with some finality: the reason blacks do not go much to baseball games, are not generally as passionate in following the game as whites, and do not pass on the game to their children has little or nothing to do with the expense of attending the game or of learning to play it (even poor blacks have disposable income), or with the fact that black Americans make up only 17 percent of the players (they are still heavily overrepresented in the game), or with the idea that blacks are culturally predisposed to find the game too slow or too rigid (Why do Latin American and Caribbean blacks love the game, in that case? And why did blacks play it so passionately for so many years in the past?), or with the possibility of hearing insults shouted at black players by white fans (as whites make up the majority of the audience for virtually every sporting event, this can happen and has indeed happened at college and professional football and basketball games, yet blacks continue to attend these in greater numbers than they do baseball).[20]

Allen Guttmann perceptively pointed out that baseball is associated with two contradictory myths in American life.[21] ONE IS the myth of pastoralism or a certain type of special, God-ordained, character-defining connection we feel, as Americans, we have with nature, the frontier, the prairie.[22] Baseball begins its season in the spring, following the cycle of rebirth and regeneration; it cannot be played in inclement weather, like football, and thus, sitting under a clear, blue sky in the sunshine has become part of its Edenic myth (even if most baseball games, including the All-Star game and the World Series, are played at night). The other myth associated with baseball is quantification. It is virtually the only game that can be completely replayed in a person's mind if you have a good scorecard in front of you. And more than any other, it is a game where numbers explain its reality. As Michael Novak wrote: "Clean, chaste, nonsubjective, geometric, objective, baseball is of all sports the most suited to the scientific, analytic, empirical temper."[23] Only in baseball are the records so freely and persistently consulted. Baseball, above all other sports, can be contained in its entirety in an encyclopedia of its numbers and records.

If baseball, through nature and numbers, symbolized American exceptionalism, then the moment that blacks organized baseball teams in their community became an extraordinary conjunction in American social and cultural history: American exceptionalism, symbolized by a game, meets America's exceptional people. For black people are America's truly exceptional people, the slaves, the Africans in bondage, the only immigrant group that came to the land of freedom against its will, who helped the country live up to its political creed of freedom because they themselves so believed in it. Certainly, the mythology did not quite work for black folk as it did for whites. Blacks at the end of the nineteenth century were denigrated and degraded by the American pastoral myth, reinvented as the dream of the Southern plantation: in this vision they were loyal, know-your-place darkies; free-playing, watermelon-eating pickaninnies; lazy, shuffling, banjo-picking folk without a care in the world. Whites created this mythological black primitive in response to what they called "the New Negro," the generation of blacks born after slavery ended, who were more assertive than their predecessors and seemed more troublesome. And it was, indeed, this generation of New Negroes who organized baseball teams.

Quantification was never a major attraction for black fans of the Negro Leagues because the Negro Leagues, never kept good player statistics until nearly the time of their demise. This intersection of baseball and black people—where, despite terrible adversity, the African American's belief in the American promise of liberty and self-fulfillment remained true—is where the idea of black urban community emerged in 1920, when Rube Foster formed the first Negro League. For Negro League baseball was always about that for black folk: it symbolized the power of non-protest organizing, of teamwork, of saving yourself through your own effort. Baseball was about black people coming into the modern age as an organized, industrial, urban people. As Sol White wrote, using industrial and technological metaphors:

> [Black ballplayers] should aim to blend the team into a highly polished and magnificent machine. The play itself is a science, if that term may be applied to sport. Compared to town ball or other old-fashioned games, it suggest the present day harvesting engine and its prototype, the scythe.[24]

"Individuality," wrote White later, "is a great hindrance to team work and without team work a team stands a poor chance of beating a bunch of ball players that play the game."[25] Yet, despite the obvious need for teamwork for a baseball nine to succeed, "baseball is an association of individuals."[26] "The game depends . . . on a very high sense of individual dignity and honor. The batter faces the pitcher in utter solitude, depending on no one but himself."[27] Perhaps it was this balance of the individual and the team that made baseball attractive for blacks in an age when they felt they needed both the collectivity of teamwork and the leadership of great individuals. It is no accident that Negro League baseball emerged as black people went to the North and the Middle West, to the cities and to the territory, as Ralph Ellison called it, to form new communities. It is no accident the first Negro League succeeded after blacks had experienced World War I and had fought for the ideal of democracy in Europe under the presidency of Woodrow Wilson, one of the most racist presidents this country ever had. It is no accident that the first Negro League succeeded after many black men had experienced life overseas as a result of the war, had experienced the hard knowledge that they had not fought for anyone to enjoy democracy, least of all themselves. It is no accident that the Negro Leagues succeeded after blacks had experienced some of the worse violence ever committed against by whites, in horrible race riots that occurred in many places after the war.

African Americans organizing themselves to play this game has both a tragic and a lyrical quality. Baseball for African Americans was about demanding their place as Americans while defying the practice of a racist America. It has cost blacks a great deal to play this game. This is why, despite the misplaced efforts of some cultural nationalists and Afrocentrists, Negro League baseball does not represent a golden age for blacks or some sort of communal ideal when, as some foolish young people think, living under segregation was an idyllic of enclosed self-determination because blacks were, supposedly, unified. That baseball is no longer the black national pastime is not because of integration or the end of the Negro Leagues. The Negro Leagues were precarious, undercapitalized businesses that could not compete with white major-league baseball once the market was opened. Moreover, it must not be forgotten that the Negro Leagues were started, in large measure, to show whites that blacks were capable of playing big-league baseball and should be permitted to compete with everyone else and not solely or even principally as a nationalistic venture. I think baseball is no longer the black pastime because blacks never were attracted to baseball as whites were—black newspapers and black writers did not build up the personalities of the players in the Negro Leagues in the same way that white newspapers glorified white players. Thus, I think, black interest in the game was broad but not especially intense; blacks were not permitted to extract from the game what whites got from it: the myth of the pastoral and of quantification. What the end of the Negro Leagues meant was the end of the ability of blacks to pass down the tradition of "their" game in the defective way that they did. But I do not think blacks were ever particularly interested in what whites got from the game or in how the baseball myth worked for them.[28] African Americans experienced the game through their flawed Americanism, imposed on them by whites, and this is why they are somewhat alienated or distanced from the game today.

Epilogue

About five or six years ago, around the time when I was first able to afford to buy season tickets, I took my youngest daughter, Rosalind, to a St. Louis Cardinals baseball game. She was not, by any means, a baseball fan, or any sort of sports fan that I could discern. She generally finds sports boring. But this was during the year when we played catch on the front lawn. I bought a glove and a ball and at first played catch by myself, just tossing the ball in the air or against the side of the house. But she became curious about it all. Why did I play catch by myself? Isn't it better to play with someone else? I told her I didn't think she would be interested, being a girl and all. She took a bit of umbrage at that and told me that her gym teacher thought she threw a ball pretty well, "not like a girl at all," she said proudly. So, Rosalind joined me. I bought her a glove, and we started a brief ritual. She liked playing catch a lot. She could never catch the ball well, but her gym teacher was right: she could throw like anything! Rosalind thought playing catch was a lot better than baseball or that baseball should only be this, catching and throwing back. "Why does it have to be a game where somebody's got to win?" she asked. But at least she seemed in a frame of mind to think about baseball a bit during those days. I thought she might find going to a game to be something of an experience worth having. It was the first time she had ever been to a game or had ever been in a sports stadium.

It was a warm spring night. The opposing team was the Atlanta Braves, with John Smoltz pitching. Rosalind had seen the Atlanta Braves play on television, so she knew something about the team. Indeed, she insisted on seeing them if she were to go to a ball game at all, because she wanted to see David Justice, who was something of a celebrity ballplayer in African American circles at the time. She was at first, not surprisingly, impressed by the size of the ball park, not having realized how big it is from watching games on television. The playing field was very green (Busch Stadium then had an artificial playing surface), very hard-looking, very even, and very flat.

"It looks like a pool table," she said. "The bases could be pockets."

She naturally had a hot dog or two, some cotton candy, ice cream, and the like. What else would a child who doesn't like baseball go to a ball game for? I was amazed she could be so skinny and eat so much! I tried to show her how to keep score, but she wasn't very much interested, although she was more than willing to help me. She corrected a couple of mistakes I made. She found it perplexing that people wanted to keep score.

"What do you do with that when the game's over? Keep it like a memento or something? Who wants to remember old ball games? Why do you want to write that stuff down, anyway? Aren't you watching the game? Isn't that enough?" she asked. She could rattle off questions like that when she got started on something.

I thought she wanted to leave after about the fourth inning. The Braves were clobbering the Cardinals at that point, 9-0.

"I know you must be bored. I think you have eaten everything the park has to offer. So, let's go," I said, starting to get up from my seat.

"I don't want to go," Rosalind responded, looking intensely at the game.

"Why not?" I protested, mildly disappointed since the Cardinals were, as the saying goes, "getting their clock cleaned." It wasn't a very pleasant game for St. Louis fans to watch. "You don't like baseball and I don't want you to stay to make me happy. We can go."

"But I told you, Daddy," she said somewhat impatiently, "I don't want to go. I like this game. Besides, the Cardinals are going to win."

I smiled, feeling superior as the all-knowing baseball expert.

"That'll be some comeback for the Cardinals, nine runs down, against the best team in baseball and one of that team's best pitchers," I said.

"Just sit down, Daddy, the Cardinals are going to win," she said, her hands folded under her chin as she watched the action.

Amazingly, the Cardinals came back, two runs here, three there. By the seventh inning, the boys with the birds on the bat had tied the game, 9-9. During these innings we wandered around the stadium, watching the game from various perspectives—behind the bleachers, at the topmost level of the stadium, and the like. Rosalind gets restless, and it is good to walk with her when she finds sitting impossible; otherwise, instead of being good company, she becomes something of a brat. But her attention never wandered from the game. She followed the action closely.

At one point between innings, though, very much out of the blue, she asked me what an earned run is. I told her, and she simply shook her head.

"Why aren't all runs earned" she asked, bewildered, "since the team batting has done something to get the run, even if the fielding team makes an error? Or why aren't all runs unearned, since scoring runs is all luck and chance and getting a break anyway? You know, Daddy, baseball is doing something that you can't do in life: it's trying to distinguish between what you deserve and what you don't deserve."

"Yes," I said, "baseball does distinguish between what you deserve and what you don't deserve. But it makes no judgment on the matter. A run's a run, for all that. Life does not make a judgment, either. If baseball made judgments about whether you deserved what you got, then it would be a sport about justice. But baseball is not a sport about justice at all. It is about power of caprice and whim upsetting the beauty of a design, the beauty of order."

I don't think she quite understood what I was saying as she was only eleven or twelve at the time and I sometimes spoke to her as if she were an adult. That was a bad habit of mine that I sometimes regretted.

"Do you think the Cardinals deserve to win this game?" she asked me.

"I don't know," I honestly answered. "Do you?"

"What kind of an answer is that?" she asked. "I thought you were the one who told me how you rooted for your favorite team when you were a boy, no matter what. How you had faith in the guys on the field and all that stuff."

"I was a little boy, then. I had a lot of hero worship and—"

"But you said it was life. You didn't say anything about hero worship. You said it was life." She looked at me a bit disbelievingly, as if she were disappointed by what she felt was my blatant hypocrisy. Did I believe in this game or not?

"A game can't be life," I answered lamely.

"Why not?" she retorted. "Anything else can be. You don't believe in this stuff anymore, do you?"

"It's a game," I said. "And I'm not a boy anymore. It's not very important who wins."

"If you believe, it's important," she said.

"You didn't answer my question," I said, shifting ground on her, "Do you think the Cardinals deserve to win?"

"Well, I don't know if they deserve to win, but I think the Braves deserve to lose. If you can't keep a nine-run lead, why should you win?"

And so we stayed for the entire game, and the Cardinals did indeed win, 12-10. As we walked to the car (I parked a bit away from the stadium in a free space, as I could not, at that time, afford the $5 parking fee in the lots that were closer to the park) through the warm spring night air, the brilliant stars against the nearly black-blue sky; the crowd of people walking in our direction slowly thinning out, excited by the thrilling victory; the crickets throbbing and singing in the sweet darkness, I congratulated Rosalind on her prognosticating skills. It was a good night all the way 'round.

"It was nothing," she said with true modesty. "I just felt the Cardinals were going to win. I believed they were going to win. I truly believed it and believed in them, well, just for tonight, and they won."

She was silent for a moment. "It must have been what you felt like when you were a boy and you were rooting for your team. Now I know what that feels like. It's a good feeling. To have the faith."

"So," I said, with a bit of pride, "baseball has taught you to believe, has taught you to have faith in others."

"Naw," she said, a bit surprised at what I had said. "Baseball didn't teach me anything like that. The Cardinals didn't win because I believed they would. What do you think? That's a silly thing to think. The Cardinals would have won no matter what I believed. I believed in them because you gotta believe in somebody if you're gonna watch a baseball game. The Cardinals were whim tonight, you know. Every night, two teams play. One is whim and the other is design. Tonight the Cardinals were whim. Tomorrow night they won't be. What I learned about baseball is just what you said about earned runs. If you got a game between whim and design, take whim as the winner most of the time. Whim rules."

"On the doorpost," I said, grinning, but she did not get the Emersonian joke, of course. But we now had reached the car. And with that, she climbed into the back seat of the car, stretched out, and even before I found the highway home was fast asleep.

NOTES

1. Steve Sailor, "Great Black Hopes," *National Review*, August 12, 1996, p. 37.

2. The fact that basketball is, far and away, internationally the most popular of all American sports, played in virtually every country on earth, has made the African American athlete in this realm something of a global figure, a cosmopolite in his far-ranging influence, unlike his more "provincial" brethren who play football or baseball, both with a smaller (in football's instance, much smaller) international reach.

3. One need only read such classic W. E. B. Du Bois works as "The Conservation of the Races," *The Souls of Black Folk*, his pieces on the preservation of the Negro college, his pieces on Negro art and literature, to understand how it could easily be interpreted that Du Bois would see blacks in basketball as a watershed in the history of the preservation of the race. Du Bois would see black basketball as, properly interpreted, hugely effective race propaganda.

4. John Hoberman, *Darwin's Athletes: How Sport Has Damaged Black America and Preserved the Myth of Race* (Boston: Houghton Mifflin, 1997), pp. xiv–xxvi, chaps. 1 and 2, *passim*. For a history of blacks in basketball, see Nelson George, *Elevating the Game: The History and Aesthetics of Black Men in Basketball* (New York: Fireside Books, 1992).

5. Gunnar Myrdal provides an instructive discussion of leadership and race in America in *An American Dilemma: The Negro Problem and Modern Democracy*, vol. 2, (New York: Pantheon Books, 1972), pp. 709–719.

6. I had a conversation with sportscaster Bob Costas in which he told me he hoped that blacks were not attracted to any team sport simply to see black players or that a majority of the players had to be black to hold black interest. He said that whites went to see basketball and football in great numbers—were, in fact, the majority of the audience—and that most of the players are not white. I thought it was a good point. One would hope that sports partisanship and allure transcend the color or ethnicity of the athletes and that spectators judge them simply on the nature of performance. Indeed, as Michael Novak brilliantly pointed out, as athletes are representative of a location, place, work site, a geography of some sort, it is a sign of considerable advance in our society that whites can have a black team or a team with a number of black players be representative for them. Whites, however, are the majority group in the United States and the most powerful by far, and they can afford to have more liberal attitudes about the color of the players. African Americans, as an embattled minority, are in a far more precarious position. They must often attend sporting events

surrounded by a sea of beer-swilling whites. This can be a little unnerving. Moreover, historically, it is hard for blacks to have whites stand as representatives for them, as the country for a very long time prevented blacks from having such an identification. Blacks were constantly reminded that the United States was "a white man's country" and that, indeed, most sporting events were for the competitive pleasure of white men. Finally, as athletics are a form of entertainment, whites are used to having blacks entertain them. To see blacks playing basketball is no more threatening to them than seeing blacks sing spirituals. It is, of course, an advance in our society that whites no longer wish to see black athletes as comic, noncompetitive, almost like minstrels, as they once did. But athletes, despite their fame and fortune, are not held in the same regard as high-level businessmen or scientists.

7. For a firsthand account of the early days of black baseball, see Sol White, *Sol White's History of Colored Base Ball, with Other Documents on the Early Black Game, 1886–1936* (1907; reprint, Lincoln: University of Nebraska Press, 1995).

8. Michael Novak, *The Joy of Sports: End Zones, Bases, Baskets, Balls, and the Consecration of the American Spirit* (Lanham, Md.: Hamilton Press, 1988), p. 101.

9. Ibid., p. 105.

10. Ibid., pp. 106–107.

11. Jazz might be said to be a series of stylistic innovations that became orthodoxies that had to be overthrown by new generations of musicians. First came New Orleans style, which led to the revolt of swing. Swing was overthrown by bebop. Cool, Third Stream, and finally avant-garde were all movements against bebop. Jazz rock was opposed to the avant-garde and nearly all the styles and schools that preceded it. In short, jazz is not so much about improvisation (indeed, aspects of various styles such as swing, Third Stream, and jazz rock had little distinctive improvisation associated with them) as about the establishment of stylistic ideologies, which take on the characteristics of arbitrary taste tyrannies in relation to those who oppose them.

12. Black baseball was particularly noted for its aggressive, tough, cunning methods:

> Despite the presence of undisputed power hitters, like Josh Gibson, black teams also emphasized speed, baserunning, and what they called "tricky baseball." "You know in boxing there's two rules, Queensbury and the one they called 'coonsbury,'" explained second baseman Newt Allen. "We played the coonsbury rules. That's just

any way you think you can win, any kind of play you think you can get by with."

Jules Tygiel, *Baseball's Great Experiment: Jackie Robinson and His Legacy*, (New York: Oxford University Press, 1993), p. 21.

13. In his article "Great Black Hopes," Steve Sailor also suggests that improvisation is a racial trait of some sort. Indeed, he posits it as a form of intelligence:

> White coaches long resisted their black players' ability to make it up as they went along. . . . Yet, "playground jungle ball" eventually routed predictable white-style basketball. Obviously the occasional Larry Bird or John Stockton shows that some whites can master the black game. Still, whites seem less often able to meet modern basketball's demands for creative improvisation and on-the-fly interpersonal decision-making. As Thomas Sowell notes, "To be an outstanding basketball player means to out-think opponents consistently in these split-second decisions under stress." These black cerebral superiorities in "real time" responsiveness also contribute to black dominance in jazz, running with the football, rap, dance, trash talking, preaching, and oratory. (p. 39)

All of these are, of course, skills that whites find entertaining but do not take seriously or see as particularly important. And that, it seems to me, is precisely why Mr. Sailor and other whites for many decades have conceded them to blacks.

14. Don E. Albrecht, "An Inquiry into the Decline of Baseball in Black America: Some Answers—More Questions," *Nine: A Journal of Baseball History and Social Policy Perspectives*, vol. 1, no. 1 (Fall 1992): 34.

15. The crucial question is what has happened to the tradition of black high school baseball. In St. Louis, for instance, the games between the two black high schools—Vashon and Sumner, the latter the first black high school west of the Mississippi—constitute one of the major sporting events of the 1920s and 1930s. Even players from the St. Louis Stars, the black professional team in the area, came out to watch. This is how Quincy Troupe was discovered by the professionals when he played in high school. See Quincy T. Troupe, *Twenty Years Too Soon: Prelude to Major-League Integrated Baseball* (St. Louis: Missouri Historical Society, 1995), pp. 19–21; and Donn Rogosin, *Invisible Men: Life in Baseball's Negro Leagues* (New York: Atheneum, 1983), p. 50. Did the tradition of black high school baseball slowly come to end when the Negro Leagues died? And, in response to Albrecht's economic argument, if money is the huge obstacle for

blacks to play baseball now, how can it be that blacks, adult and youngster, managed to scrap together the money to form teams back at the turn of the century and through the 1920s and 1930s and 1940s, when they were, as a whole, a poorer population—with virtually no government aid during most of those years—than they are now?

16. This assertion about the lack of space as a reason for the inability of inner-city blacks to play baseball was posited in article in the *St. Louis Business Journal* titled "Cardinals Market to Blacks with Wash. U Students' Help," by Josh Gotthelf, March 3, 1997. I was quoted in this article as disagreeing with this assumption, but my reasons were not given. For more about the ghetto as an empty space, see William Julius Wilson, *When Work Disappears: The World of the New Urban Poor* (New York: Vintage Books, 1996).

17. See Tygiel, *Baseball's Great Experiment*, p. 178; and David Falkner, *Great Time Coming: The Life of Jackie Robinson, from Baseball to Birmingham* (New York: Simon and Schuster, 1995), p. 163.

18. Vahe Gregorian, "Summer of '47: Breaking the Barriers," *St. Louis Post-Dispatch*, May 18, 1997, sec. B, p. 5. It is interesting to note that had blacks not made up such a large percentage of the crowds that were coming to see Robinson, these games would have been rather sparsely attended. Even when one factors in the possibility that some whites stayed away in protest that Robinson was playing, especially in a town as conservative as St. Louis, the presence of blacks still was clearly an economic boon for the game.

19. The St. Louis Cardinals have been making some modest efforts to get more blacks to come to Busch Stadium. One of the major reasons blacks do not go, despite the fact that the stadium is located in downtown St. Louis and that blacks make up over 37 percent of St. Louis city's population, is that they feel they are not wanted there. See Paul Hampel, "Ballclub's Marketing Campaign Aims to Attract African-Americans," *St. Louis Post-Dispatch*, June 5, 1998, p. 1. Despite efforts to increase black attendance, it is surely not the desire of any major-league baseball owner to have blacks make up the kind of attendance percentage they did when Robinson debuted in 1947. It would, indeed, be a cause of unease, if not downright unrest, if blacks made up over a third or a half of the audience for a major-league game.

20. Ralph Wiley suggested this as a reason that blacks may not go to ball games (not entirely without his tongue in his cheek) in "Why Black People Don't Often Go to Baseball Games," in *What Black People Should Do Now: Dispatches from Near the Vanguard* (New York: Ballantine Books, 1993), p. 42.

21. Allen Guttmann, *From Ritual to Record: The Nature of Modern Sports* (New York: Columbia University Press, 1978), pp. 91–116, esp. pp. 100–116.

22. The American intellectual's preoccupation with nature and American space as a symbol of American exceptionalism has been long-standing, from Ralph Waldo Emerson's *Nature* (1836), to Herman Melville's *Moby-Dick* (1852), to Frederick Jackson Turner's theory of the frontier, to Leo Marx, Perry Miller, Bernard De Voto, and Van Wyck Brooks.

23. Novak, *Joy of Sports*, p. 66.

24. White, *Sol White's History*, p. 71.

25. Ibid., p. 81.

26. Novak, *Joy of Sports*, p. 59.

27. Ibid., p. 58.

28. It must be remembered that baseball has not only the longest history of any team sport in the United States but the longest history as the most popular team sport. Americans were crazy about baseball before the Civil War. As a result, the game brings with it much more *remembered* historical baggage than either football or basketball. And it is remembered in very different ways by blacks and whites. As Jules Tygiel wrote in *Baseball's Great Experiment*, "The formative years of baseball as a professional sport coincided with the emergence of segregation as an American institution" (p. 12). The emergence of professional football and basketball as true national pastimes came after World War II, during the age of integration, and blacks played pivotal roles in the broad acceptance of these sports. This, which I learned in part in a conversation with Bob Costas, is crucial in understanding why blacks may feel one way about baseball and another about football and basketball.

3

gladiators, gazelles, and groupies

basketball love and loathing

JULIANNE MALVEAUX

Game on West 4th Street

There really ought to be music
More like ballet
Than a game you play
Long, lean warriors
Sleek gazelles
In syncopated rhythm
Or poised and still
Heads up, running
Like giraffes
An anxious motion
Choreographed
Vultures circling
Round the ball
Bouncing, rebounding
Toss, swish, fall
Muscles taut
There really ought
To be music.

—Julianne Malveaux,
July 1976

THE WOMAN IN ME LOVES THE SHEER physical impact of a basketball game. I don't dwell on the fine points, the three-point shot or the overtime, and can't even tell you which teams make me sweat (though I could have told you twenty years ago). I can tell you, though, how much I enjoy watching mostly black men engage in an elegantly (and sometimes inelegantly) skilled game, and how engrossing the pace and physicality can be. In my younger days, I spent hours absorbed by street basketball games, taking the subway to watch the Rucker Pros in upper Manhattan, hanging on a bench near the basketball courts on West Fourth Street in the Village. I didn't consider myself a basketball groupie—I was a nerd who liked the game.

Still, there is something about muscled, scantily clad men (the shorts have gotten longer in the 1990s) that spoke to me. Once I even joked that watching basketball games was like safe sex in the age of AIDS. Yes, the woman in me, even in my maturity, loves the physical impact of a basketball game, a game where muscles strain, sweat flies, and intensity demands attention.

The feminist in me abhors professional basketball and the way it reinforces gender stereotypes. Men play, women watch. Men at the center, women at the periphery, and eagerly so. Men making millions, women scheming to get to some of the millions through their sex and sexuality. The existence of the Women's National Basketball Association hardly ameliorates my loathing for the patriarchal underbelly of the basketball sport, since women players are paid a scant fraction of men's pay and attract a fraction of the live and television audience. To be sure, women's basketball will grow and develop and perhaps even provide men with role models of what sportsmanship should be. I am also emphatically clear that basketball isn't the only patriarchy in town. Despite women's participation in politics it, too, is a patriarchy, with too many women plying sex and sexuality as their stock in trade, as the impeachment imbroglio of 1998–99 reminds us.

The race person in me has mixed feelings about basketball. On one hand, I enjoy seeing black men out there making big bank, the kind of bank they can't make in business, science, or more traditional forms of work. On the other hand, I'm aware of the minuscule odds that any high school hoopster will become a Michael Jordan. If some young brothers spent less time on the hoops and more in the labs, perhaps the investment of time in chemistry would yield the same mega-millions that professional basketball does. This is hardly the sole fault of the youngsters with NBA aspirations. It is also the responsibility of coaches to introduce a reality check to those young people whose future focus is exclusively on basketball. And it is society's responsibility to make sure there are opportunities for young men, especially young African American men, outside basketball. The athletic scholarship should not be the sole passport to college for low-income young men. Broader access to quality education must be a societal mandate; encouraging young African American men to focus on higher education is critical to our nation's fullest development.

Professional basketball bears an unfortunate similarity to an antebellum plantation, with some coaches accustomed to barking orders and uttering racial expletives to get maximum performance from their players. While few condone the fact that Latrell Sprewell, then of the Golden State Warriors, choked his coach P. J. Carlesimo in 1997, many understand that rude, perhaps racist, but certainly dismissive treatment motivated his violent action. The race of coaches, writers, and commentators, in contrast to that of the players, often has broader racial implications. White players whose grammar needs a boost often get it from sportswriters, who make them sound far more erudite than they are. The same writers quote black players with exaggerated, cringe-producing broken English— "dis," "dat," "dese," and "dose"—almost a parody of language. White commentators frequently remark on the "natural talent" of black players, compared to the skill of white ones. Retired white players are more likely to get invitations to coach and manage than are their black counterparts.

Despite this plantation tension, there are those who tout the integration in basketball as something lofty and desirable and the sport itself as one that teaches discipline, teamwork, and structure. In *Values of the Game*, former New Jersey senator and 2000 presidential candidate Bill Bradley describes the game as one of passion, discipline, selflessness, respect, perspective, courage, and other virtues. Though Bradley took a singular position as a senator in lifting up the issue of police brutality around the Rodney King beating, his record on race matters is otherwise relatively unremarkable. But Bradley gets credit for being far more racially progressive than he actually is because he, a white man, played for the New York Knicks for a decade, living at close quarters with African American men.

As onerous as I find the basketball plantation, the race person in me wonders why I am so concerned about the gladiators. Few if any of them exhibit anything that vaguely resembles social consciousness. Michael Jordan, for example, passed on the opportunity to make a real difference in the 1990 North Carolina Senate race between the former Charlotte mayor and Democratic candidate, the

African American architect Harvey Gantt, and the ultraconserva-
tive and racially manipulative Republican senator Jesse Helms, pre-
ferring to save his endorsements for Nike. Charles Barkley once ar-
rogantly crowed that he was not a role model, ignoring the biblical
adage that much is expected of those to whom much is given. Few
of the players, despite their millions, invest in the black community
and in black economic development. Magic Johnson is a notable
exception, with part ownership in a Los Angeles–based black bank
and development of a theater chain that has the potential for re-
vitalizing otherwise abandoned inner-city communities. Johnson's
example notwithstanding, basketball players are more likely to
make headlines for their shenanigans than for giving back to the
community.

With my mixed feelings, love and loathing, why pay attention to
basketball at all? Why not tune it out as forcefully as I tune out
anything else I'm disinterested in? The fact is that it is nearly impossible to tune out, turn off, or ignore basketball. It is a cultural
delimiter, a national export, a medium through which messages
about race, gender, and power are transmitted not only nationally
but also internationally. As Walter LaFeber observes in his book,
Michael Jordan and the New Global Capitalism, Mr. Jordan's imagery has been used not only to sell the basketball game and Nike
shoes but to make hundreds of millions of dollars for both Mr. Jordan and the companies he represents. Jordan is not to be faulted for
brokering his skill into millions of dollars. Still, the mode and
methods of his enrichment make the game of basketball a matter of
intellectual curiosity as one explores the way in which capitalism
and popular culture intersect. Jordan's millions, interesting as they
may be, are less interesting than the way in which media have created his iconic status in both domestic and world markets and offered him up as a role model of the reasonable, affable African
American man, the antithesis of "bad boy" trash talkers who so frequently garner headlines.

From a gender perspective, too, there is another set of questions.
What would a woman have to do to achieve the same influence,
iconic status, and bankability as Jordan? Is it even conceivable, in a
patriarchal world, that a woman could earn, gain, or be invented in
as iconic a status as a Michael Jordan? A woman might sing—but

songbirds come and go and aren't often connected with international marketing of consumer products. She might dance—but that, too, would not turn into international marketability. She might possess the dynamic athleticism of the tennis-playing Williams sisters, Venus and Serena, or she might have the ethereal beauty of a Halle Berry. In either case, her product identification would solely be connected with "women's" products—hair, beauty, and women's sports items. The commercial heavy lifting has been left to the big boys, or to one big boy in particular, Michael Jordan.

To be sure, the public acceptance of women's sports has changed. Thanks to Title IX, women's sports get better funding and more attention at the college level than they did only decades ago. After several fits and starts, the professional women's basketball league seems to be doing well, although not as well as the NBA. In time this may change, but my informal survey of male basketball fans suggests that some find women's basketball simply less entertaining than the NBA. "When women start dunking and trash talking, more people will start watching," said a man active in establishing Midnight Basketball teams in urban centers. If this is the case, then it raises questions both about women's basketball and about the tension between male players and officials about on-court buffoonery. Do officials kill the goose that laid the golden egg when they ask a Dennis Rodman to "behave himself"?

My ire is not about gender envy; it is about imagery and the replication of gender-oppressive patterns by using basketball, especially, to connect an image of sportsmanship, masculinity, with product identification. In a commercial context that promotes this connection, there is both a subtle and a not-so-subtle message about the status of women.

There is also a set of subtle messages about race and race relations that emerges when African American men are used in the same way that African American women were used in the "trade cards" of the early twentieth century. In the patriarchal context, hoopsters become hucksters while the invisible (white) male role as power broker is reinforced. In too many ways the rules and profit of the game reinforce the rules, profit, and history of American life, with iconic gladiators serving as symbols and servants of multinational interests. Black men who entertain serve as stalkers for white men who measure profits. Neutered black men can join their white colleagues in cha-chinging cash registers but can never unlock the golden handcuffs and the platinum muzzles that limit their ability to generate independent opinions. Women? Always seen, never heard. Ornamental or invisible assets. Pawns in an unspoken game.

A subtext of the basketball culture relegates women, especially African American women, to a peripheral, dependent, and soap-operatic role. These women are sometimes seen as sources of trouble (as in the imbroglio with the Washington then Bullets, now Wizards, where apparently false rape charges spotlighted the lives of two players and perhaps changed the long-term composition of the team). Or they are depicted (for example, in a 1998 *Sports Illustrated* feature) as predatory sperm collectors, whose pregnancies are part of a "plot" to collect child support from high-earning hoopsters.

There are aspects to some women's behavior in relationship with basketball stars that are hardly laudable. (Some of this is detailed in the fictional *Homecourt Advantage*, written by two basketball significant others.) At the same time, it is clear that this behavior is more a symptom than a cause of predatory patriarchy. After all, no one forces a player into bed or into a relationship with an unscrupulous woman. But conditions often make a player irresistible to women whose search for legitimacy comes through attachment to a man.

The disproportionate attention and influence that the basketball lifestyle gives some men makes them thoroughly irresistible to some women. This begs the question: In a patriarchy, just what can women do to attain the same influence and irresistibility? In a patriarchy, male games are far more intriguing than female games. Women, spectators, can watch and attach themselves to high-achieving gladiators. There is little that they can do, in the realm of sport, capitalism, and imagery, to gain the same access that men have. Again, this is not restricted to basketball but is a reflection of gender roles in our society. One might describe this as the "Hillary Rodham Clinton dilemma." Does a woman gain more power and influence by developing her own career or by attaching herself to a powerful man?

This dilemma may be a short-term one, given changes in the status of women in our society. Still, a range of scholars have noted that while women have come a long way, with higher incomes, higher levels of labor-force participation, and increased representation in executive ranks, at the current pace, income equality (which may not be the equivalent of the breakdown of patriarchy) will occur in the middle of the twenty-first century.

Those who depict the basketball culture have been myopic in their focus on the men who shoot hoops, because their coverage has ignored the humanity of the women who hover around hoopsters like moths drawn to a flame. Those writers who are eager to write about the "paternity ward" or about "Darwin's athletes" might also ask how the gender relations in basketball replicate or differ from gender relations in our society. Unfortunately, gender relations in basketball are too often the norm in society. Men play, women watch. To the extent that the basketball culture is elevated, women's roles are denigrated. Why are we willing to endow male hoopsters with a status that no woman can attain in our society? Sedentary men sing the praises of male hoopsters, sit enthralled and engrossed by their games, thus elevating a certain form of achievement in our society. This behavior is seen as normal, even laudable. Yet it takes women, often the daughters or sisters of these enthralled men, out of the iconic, high-achievement mix and pushes them to the periphery of a culture that reveres the athletic achievement derived from the combination of basketball prowess and patriarchy.

The combination of prowess and patriarchy denigrates the groupie who is attracted by the bright lights, but it also dehumanizes the swift gazelle, the gladiator, and the hoopster, whose humanity is negated by his basketball identity. Media coverage depicts young men out of control, trash-talking, wild-walking, attention-grabbing icons. Men play, women watch. Were there other center stages, this would be of limited interest. But the fact is that this stage is one from which other stages reverberate. Men play, women watch, in politics, economics, technology, and sports. And it is "blown up" into international cultural supremacy in basketball.

This woman watches, with love and loathing, the way basketball norms reinforce those that exist in our society. It is a triumph of patriarchy, this exuberance of masculine physicality. It is a reminder to women that feminism notwithstanding, we have yet to gain economic and cultural equivalency with Michael Jordan's capitalist dominance. While we should not, perhaps, ask men to walk away from arenas in which they can dominate, we must ask ourselves why there is no equivalent space for us; why the basketball tenet that men play, women watch, reverberates in so many other sectors of our society.

SOURCES

Bradley, Bill. *Values of the Game*. New York: Artisan Press, 1998.

Ewing, Rita, and Crystal McCrary. *Homecourt Advantage*. New York: Avon Books, 1998.

Frey, Darcy. *The Last Shot: City Street, Basketball Dreams*. Boston: Houghton Mifflin, 1994.

Hoberman, John. *Darwin's Athletes: How Sport Has Damaged Black America and Preserved the Myth of Race*. New York: Mariner Books, 1997.

LaFeber, Walter. *Michael Jordan and the New Global Capitalism*. New York: W. W. Norton & Co., 1999.

Wahl, Grant, and L. Jon Wertheim. "Paternity Ward." *Sports Illustrated*, May 4, 1998, at 62.

4

mo' money, mo' problems

keepin' it real in the post-jordan era

TODD BOYD

> No matter what I do ... I just
> can't win at this game of
> basketball.
> —Dennis Rodman

> The future for us
> young shooters and old killers
> Who become rich as dope
>   dealers
> Nothin' left for us
> but hoop dreams and 'hood
>   tournaments
> thug coaches
> with subs sittin' on the bench
> either that or rap
> we want the fast way outta this
>   trap
> whether it be nine to five or
>   slingin' crack.
> —Nas, "We Will Survive"

"What's the Matter Boss, We Sick?"

It was Oscar Wilde who once said that "living well is the best revenge." This sense of what Manthia Diawara once called the "Black good life" is no more evident than in the *über*-spectacle of our time, the modern NBA.

As I have noted elsewhere, because of the predominance of Black bodies in the league, the issue of race is normalized. To the extent that race is always present, the league has, more and more, become a theater for class warfare on the scale of Berthold Brecht. As the end of the cold war in the early 1990s exposed a new world order, the end of the Jordan era promises to expose new rifts. Who's gonna take the weight?

The 1999 champion San Antonio Spurs are a good nigga's nocturnal emission. The three most important members of this squad, Tim Duncan, David Robinson, and Avery Johnson, all fulfill the requirements of the non-threatening Black man at the highest level.

The sports media's seemingly unanimous embrace of Duncan and constant discussion of his gentlemanly nature and good work ethic cannot be separated from his West Indian heritage and the continued perception that this ethnic group has been easier to assimilate than African Americans.

Mr. Robinson, also known as the Admiral, is the true embodiment of the team's middle-class aspirations. He is a graduate of the Naval Academy who delayed his entry into the NBA while fulfilling his service commitment. Robinson, like so many others, is also quick to announce his religious beliefs whenever being interviewed. A naval officer and a Christian—what better credentials for all-American citizenship?

The cartoonish Avery Johnson rounds out the trio. Johnson, who sounds something like a southern Daffy Duck, also a devout fundamentalist, echoes Robinson's religious sentiments. The fact that these Spurs are the first team to win a championship in the post-Jordan era is especially significant in that they had to overcome thug life personified, otherwise known as Latrell Sprewell, in the process.

White Man's Burden

It seems as though sports, especially basketball, remains one of the few places in American society where there is a consistent racial discourse. This is not to say there are not other areas of society where race is a significant part of the conversation, but in basketball, race, directly or indirectly, *is* the conversation, at all times.

During the 1999 Eastern Conference finals, *New York Times* writer Ira Berkow was producing another celebratory column about Indiana Pacers coach Larry Bird. In describing Bird's character, Berkow states that "unlike others in basketball, who have never had to work at anything else in their lives, Bird worked on a garbage truck one year at home." Berkow goes on to extol Bird's blue-collar ethic and attributes to this Bird's overall success, both as a coach and as a legendary player.

Those of us who have watched basketball for some time know that Bird is undoubtedly the last true great White hope of the twentieth century, first as a player for the Boston Celtics and now as a coach. When Bird was a player, the game of basketball was in its final stages of transition from the primarily White game that it had been to the predominantly Black game that it has become. So, during the 1980s, Bird and his Celtics were routinely considered by many commentators to be a shining example of White dominance in sports. This in spite of the fact that Magic Johnson's Lakers won five championships to Bird's three and that, in head-to-head competition, the Lakers beat Boston two series to one. This is not unlike the boxing rivalry between Jake LaMotta and Sugar Ray Robinson during the 1950s. Though Robinson defeated LaMotta five out of six times, it is LaMotta who has been immortalized in the classic film *Raging Bull*.

Sometime during Bird's first year as a coach, it became known that former basketball great Kareem Abdul-Jabbar was also interested in being a coach. Yet it was said that Abdul-Jabbar needed some experience before he could be considered for a head coaching position. Now, Bird had never coached a day in his life, but he was handed over a veteran Indiana team that had been to the conference finals twice already in the 1990s. But Kareem, who won six Most Valuable Player awards to go along with six championship rings during his career, retiring as the leading scorer in league history, needed some experience? Kareem, who at one point could only find a coaching position with a team on a Native American reservation, was finally hired to serve as an assistant for the lowly Los Angeles Clippers during the 1999–2000 season. I guess Al Campanis was right when he said that Blacks do not have the "necessities" to be coaches in professional sports.

Bird's work on a garbage truck is considered a character-building moment in his life, but having to navigate the ghetto, as so many others have done, is insignificant. This is not considered work. For a young man with a basketball in his hands to carry the hopes and aspirations of an entire family, and by extension an entire community, on his shoulders is not work, and certainly not as important as driving a garbage truck after having been unable to cut it with one of the top basketball programs of your time. It is always interesting how mainstream society can turn failure into virtue when it concerns White people but seems unable to find virtue when its concerns others.

Larry Bird was a great player and has, in his short tenure as coach, been quite impressive. In both cases, the overwhelming support of the masses aided in his success. Even Black players go out of their way to let the world know how significant Bird has been to the league. In other words, they are saying that in spite of the perceived limitations of his race, he got game!

Thus, Bird, as player and coach, remains significant to the overall mythology of sport in America. He is the hard-working White lower-class individual who pulled himself up to prominence and national adoration, the Babe Ruth of the latter half of the twentieth century. He is undoubtedly the great White hope, and maybe the last White hope as well.

I say this because the game has changed, a change in full swing when Bird played that has now fully taken over. The contemporary discourse of the NBA is undoubtedly a Black discourse, and this is one where Whiteness is the other. This shift also brings about a redefinition of the racial politics surrounding the game. Set against the backdrop of that other dominant Black entity of the late twentieth century, hip-hop, basketball has become a place where we can guarantee a recurring series of racial incidents that demand public attention. In this regard, the case of Latrell Sprewell stands out.

"Everybody Wants to Be Bougie, Bougie . . ."

Prior to the 1999 finals, Utah Jazz forward Karl Malone went home with his second undeserved Most Valuable Player Award in a three-year period. The first he collected in 1997, at the expense of Michael Jordan, so it was really no surprise when he walked away with the 1999 trophy in a Jordanless league. In spite of the fact that Karl has consistently failed to deliver when it has truly mattered—against Seattle in the conference finals in 1996 and twice against the

Chicago Bulls—the sportswriting establishment and the league still choose to embrace him.

They ignore his petulance, his cheap shots, and even the eighteen-wheeler he drives through the streets for no apparent reason; in turn, they embrace the fact that Karl is a self-described "Black redneck." The rap group Outkast has a line that says, "Some say we're country, but we're only southern." Karl Malone is definitely country. In other words, he is a non-threatening Black male figure in a sport where race is always lurking beneath the surface of any potential situation. The fact that he plays in Utah, a citadel of conservatism, adds to his acceptance.

So it stands to reason that the people who embrace Karl Malone could never understand, much less embrace, Latrell Sprewell. The original 1999 Sprewell And 1 commercial demonstrates this to the fullest. In the commercial, Spree is getting his hair braided into his signature cornrows while he makes several statements about his place in the NBA world. Jimi Hendrix's version of "The Star-Spangled Banner" plays in the background. In his final statement Spree says, "Some say I'm what's wrong with sports today. I say, I'm the American Dream."

This is not the first time that a company has used a controversial basketball player to sell their product. First we had Charles Barkley's famous "I am not a role model" Nike commercial, and later a plethora of commercials that tried to capitalize on Dennis Rodman's eccentricities. Nothing, though, has been like this.

Barkley presented a position that people could and did argue with, but there was no real cloud hanging over his head. Dennis Rodman, the Jar Jar Binks of basketball, manufactured his own see-through image, and thus he was never really controversial as much as he was a clown. Spree, though, has, for some, looked a gift horse in the grill, and that, for those same people, is another example of what they see as wrong in professional sports.

First of all, Spree's actions from the 1998 season were blown completely out of proportion. I cringed every time I heard someone say that "anyone who chokes their boss should be fired." Though that was the idea NBA commissioner David Stern had in mind, Spree had not done anything deserving of banishment from the game, as was recognized by the judge who decided that the league had resorted to cruel and unusual punishment when suspending him.

If you have spent any time around college and pro sports, you know that this is not a normal workplace, so the rules of the typical workplace do not apply. The environment of a basketball practice is filled with expletives, dehumanization, and an overall level of disrespect directed toward the players. All this comes from the coach and is considered motivation, much like in a military environment. In any other workplace this would be harassment, but in basketball it is par for the course. Add to this the high testosterone levels, the egos, and the money involved, and you have a very volatile mix. It surprises me that this type of incident doesn't happen more often.

The sentiment that underlies public assumption is that because these athletes make so much money, they should accept whatever treatment they get. Well, for whatever reason, on that day, Spree was not going for it, and Golden State Warriors coach P. J. Carlesimo had to bear the weight of this, around his neck. Besides, how can you call a coach a boss in a real sense, when most of his players make more money than he does?

This, too, is something many people find problematic, and it is for this reason that in the late 1990s coaches have been receiving unprecedented deals, even coaches like the deposed Nets coach John Calipari and Larry Bird, neither of whom had any prior NBA coaching experience before getting their respective jobs.

Interestingly enough, the Sprewell incident is not the first time this type of thing has happened in the NBA. In the early 1990s, Alvin Robertson, a journeyman who was then playing for the Detroit Pistons, got into a physical altercation with Pistons executive Billy McKinney. This story was never made into the national drama that the Sprewell incident became. The reason: both Robertson and McKinney are Black.

Even though McKinney's position was actually higher in rank than that of coach, it is assumed that Black people are constantly at odds among themselves anyway; so what significance is there when two Black men have beef? *They all kill each other anyway, don't they?* Yet, when a Black player—with cornrows, mind you—chokes a White coach, this is deemed reason for public lamentation over what's wrong with sport.

Don't Nothin' Move but the Money

It is important to understand that Black men, especially young Black men, are held in the highest contempt by a large segment of society. This has always been the case, and this contempt has always been exposed through sport. Yet, in modern society, these same Black men are often entertainment for the masses. Though it is acceptable for these men to entertain, they are held in contempt for the money they make because of their entertainment.

This was never more evident than during the most recent NBA lockout. Though the owners "locked" the players out, though they would not allow the players to work, the players were still perceived as being on strike. The assumption was that the greedy players wanted even more undeserved money, and thus we get stories like the one that lampoons Kenny Anderson, who says he has to sell one of his eight cars to make ends meet. Instead of greedy players who wanted more money, it was the greedy owners who felt that the players were making too much, though the players were the ones who paid the bills.

Not one fan in the history of basketball has gone to a game to see David Stern—or any of the owners, for that matter—yet Stern makes $8 million a year, and no one complains. In the end, the players were forced to accept a deal that was the equivalent of communism, with an absolute cap on the maximum amount they could make as demonstration of this. This defies every fair-market convention there is.

America loves their Black entertainers when they behave "properly" and stay in their place. These entertainers are socialized at an early age, live under a microscope, and are constantly held to the expectations of a mainstream society that has no understanding for the fact that not everyone shares the same worldview. When the players realize their value, their significance to the game, and try to capitalize on this, they are held in the highest contempt. These circumstances, both in basketball and in society as a whole, produce a particular response, and this response is what informs the And 1 Sprewell commercial.

Throughout their presence in America, Black men have used a calculated indifference as a strategic weapon against the constraining demands of an unsympathetic society. This philosophy, in modern parlance, is known as "I don't give a fuck!" In other words, the individuals in question have decided not to buy into the propaganda of America, which has always been articulated by those in power and is seldom applicable to those who live on society's margins. So, when you reject the system and all that goes along with it, when you say, "I don't give a fuck," you then become empowered, liberated, the controller of your own destiny. This is certainly the case in basketball, because the players make enough money to be able not to give a fuck, as money is the ultimate source of liberation in capitalist America.

This is why you hear so many rappers talk about things like "gettin' theirs," "stacking chips," "makin' cheddar." These are all metaphors for making the most money you can, so as to further distance yourself from the "playa haters" of the world. This is their critique of the dictates of capitalism. They exploit the concept to its fullest, thus making a mockery of it. As the character Eddie says in the film *Superfly*, "I know it's a rotten game, but it's the only one the man left us to play, and that's the stone-cold truth."

Spree knows this, and thus he can use this attitude to sell shoes and, ultimately, sell himself. He realizes, at the end of the day, his skills on the basketball court translate into cheese off the court. The cornrows suggest a distinctly Black, even ghetto style. Hendrix suggests a deconstruction of the national anthem, a rejection of tradition at the highest level. Spree's words in the commercial flip the script on mainstream sentiment. In other words, "I don't give a fuck."

Sprewell's rereading of the American Dream is not unlike the forward movement of Francis Ford Coppola's operatic *Godfather* saga. From the marginalized position of Italian immigrant to the throne of American capitalism, we watch first Vito, then Michael Corleone make the arduous journey through the social fabric of America. Once outlaws, the family moves, with much difficulty, from Italian to Italian American to American. This is fully realized in *The Godfather, Part II*, when Michael sits down at the table in Cuba with all the leaders of industry, a legitimate businessman; this is, of course, after his father, in a similar scene in *The Godfather*, sat down with the heads of the five families to conduct business, mafia style.

Just as *The Godfather* exposed the underside of the American Dream, so does Sprewell's success in the NBA. For any of today's troubled young Black men to make it to the league is evidence of people taking advantage of a bad situation, making the best of what they have been given. With his success, Sprewell can now say that he truly went from "ashy to classy."

The rapper Nas proclaims to his detractors, "You can hate me now"; now that I'm paid, is what he means. Spree is saying the same thing. Though he had committed an act many deemed unpardonable the year before, after the lockout broke, teams clamored for his services—including NBA legend Larry Bird. This gnashing of the teeth suggested Spree's value as a player. If he was so reprehensible, why were so many people going after him? Not because they were benevolent, but because they knew Spree could help their team win. This was affirmed as the Cinderfella Knicks made their way to the finals, with Spree as one of the main reasons they had come so far.

Near the end of the 1999 regular season, *New York Times* beat writer Mike Wise wrote an extensive piece about Spree's being the reason for the Knicks' dismal year up to that point. The Knicks are a consistently overrated organization who have not raised a championship banner since Superman was a boy, but suddenly it was Sprewell, a player who has been on the team for only a few months, who posed the problem. Wise had to eat his words.

Latrell Sprewell knows he will be second-guessed the rest of his career. Whatever he does will be contrasted against the Carlesimo incident. So why should he give a fuck? With these circumstances, it's important to do what you do best: play ball. Let the playa haters hate. That's what it's all about, and you can laugh all the way to the bank.

I, for one, was pulling for the Knicks to win it all. Not that I'm a Knicks fan—Spike Lee's sycophantic presence at courtside assures this will never be the case—but if they did win, the public would have to further digest the latest Amerikkka's most hated and reconcile this hatred with Spree's championship ring. Damn; maybe next time.

As the late Biggie Smalls once said, "Stereotypes of a Black male, misunderstood . . . but it's still all good."

5

the white shadow

LARRY PLATT

ONE NIGHT, LATE IN THE SECOND SEA-
son of Matt Maloney's excellent NBA adventure,
the most improbable of NBA starters sat in a
Houston bar that played U2, his favorite band, over
the loudspeakers—as opposed to the rap music that
usually serves as the NBA's soundtrack—and he
was talking about what he has spent his life doing:
shooting a basketball.

Shooters like Maloney, it turns out, live in fear
of the same thing: the almost imperceptible foul
on the all-important follow-through, after the
ball's been released. It's rarely called, because most
refs consider the shooter fair game once the ball's
out of his hands. That's what Maloney, then sec-
ond-year point guard for the Houston Rockets,

claimed happened earlier that night on his first four attempts in a game against the Boston Celtics. Defensive players running at him nicked his hands—maybe even his fingertips—on his extension after he'd launched the shots. Refs discount the shooters who complain of such seemingly incidental contact; indeed, most chalk it up to the softness of shooters, assuming that those content to stand outside and drain jump shots have an aversion to physical contact.

But that doesn't hold true in Maloney's case. He's a big point guard—six feet, three inches, but more important, a solidly built two hundred pounds—who actually likes to guard his man down low. He doesn't mind being banged around while being run through picks. No, Maloney can bear that. What he can't stomach are the fouls that the refs consider ticky-tack but that he knows mean the difference between a made and a missed shot. Against the Celtics, the refs cost him maybe six or nine more points. It's not fair, he argued: There is a box score after games that reviews how players have performed, but nothing that indicates what kind of game the refs have had.

So, after getting whacked following his fourth straight miss, he spoke his mind.

"I haven't gotten a call since I've been in this league," he called to the ref, who just shrugged.

When Maloney told this tale that night at the Houston taproom, his brother, Paul, offered his own analysis. "Well, last year, you were a rookie," said Paul, pointing out that everyone knows rookies get no breaks. Like any other night, the brothers were dissecting that night's on-court action. And, as on those other nights, the issue of race was never far beneath the surface.

"But it's no different this year, and it happens to other guys I talk to," Matt responded, rebutting Paul. "The truth is that white guys get porked in the NBA. I'm telling you, it's prejudice. Brent Barry and Mark Price have experienced the same thing. We don't get the calls."

Maloney, not a big drinker, sipped at the beer he'd been nursing all night and looked at his watch. Practice would be at ten the next morning. It was time to get home and put the night behind him.

Matt Maloney is the living embodiment of every white suburban kid's fantasy, as those of us who spent our youth in the driveway with a hoop, a ball, and the sound of our own play-by-play in our heads can attest. He has, at various times, been the rarest of minorities in the NBA: a white starter. In a league that is close to 80 percent black—and the percentage of black starters is even higher—Maloney has long battled racial stereotyping to get where he is.

There is, for instance, the preconception of white ball players' slow-footedness that, in Maloney's view, leads to refs' looking the other way when fouls should be called. Calling fouls on whites' "quicker" defenders, after all, concedes that the defender was out of position, something most refs—not to mention coaches and broadcasters—are loath to recognize, given the preconception.

It's only one example of how race plays a major role in Maloney's life. In fact, in a culture that finds the majority—whites—complaining about how often blacks think and talk about race, it should come as no surprise that, in turn, Maloney and other white basketball players—the league's minority—see racial implications where others don't. Maloney has had to overcome prejudice just to get where he is.

"Granted, only a small percentage of guys from the inner city make it, but the chances are greater that someone from there will make it than someone from Haddonfield, New Jersey," he says. "So my situation is almost the reverse of what you would think. It's like a black guy from the inner city becoming CEO of a Fortune 500 company."

Of course, Maloney is not alone in the NBA. Throughout the league, many white guys hold down roster spots, but not without the stigma of special privilege, akin to recipients of affirmative action in the real world. "It's the reverse in our industry," New York Knick Buck Williams told the *Washington Post* on May 11, 1997. "If you come in as a white ballplayer it's taken that you're a token, whereas in corporate America we're looked at as tokens."

But, as Maloney is quick to point out, at least in that real world he and his white counterparts still come from a relative place of privilege—an advantage that still accrues in the NBA, despite their minority status. Case in point: mediocre center Jon Koncak's stunning six-year, $13 million contract a few years back. Throughout the league, countless black players expressed the view that, were

Koncak black, he never would have been so rewarded for scoring all of six points and grabbing all of six rebounds per game.

Call it affirmative action, NBA style. "I think diversity is a good thing," Williams told the *Post*. "I think we should have more diversity in corporate America."

Maloney agrees. "I had to work twice as hard to get the opportunity to make the NBA," he says. "But here I am."

Haddonfield, New Jersey, is an upper-middle-class suburb in the shadow of Philadelphia. It was there, in the driveway, that Maloney honed the skills—the dead-eye shooting, the sure-handed dribble—that he'd later, quite improbably, display in the NBA.

Once in the NBA, the labeling continued. He was "heady"; he made up in "work ethic" what he lacked in "athletic ability." In college it was the same story. He starred at the University of Pennsylvania, an Ivy League school not known as a basketball powerhouse. His backcourt mate Jerome Allen and he were widely regarded as one of college basketball's premier guard tandems. Allen, who is black, hailed from North Philadelphia.

Though Maloney was named the Ivy League player of the year their senior year, it was Allen who was drafted into the NBA. Not only didn't Maloney get drafted; he wasn't even invited to the major postseason tournaments that offer graduating seniors a chance to show off for the NBA scouts. Maloney was thought to be too slow, unlike Allen.

The stark contrast in how the two players were perceived was a constant source of amusement between Allen and Maloney. They understood the racial coding going on when Allen was called the "athlete" and Maloney the "cerebral" player. The truth was that both players had incorporated urban *and* suburban style into their games.

Though Allen had grown up in North Philly, he starred at Episcopal Academy, a tony prep school on the ostentatious Main Line in the suburbs. And though Matt was raised in Haddonfield, he was the son of Jim Maloney, an inner-city Irish Catholic kid who became an assistant coach and brother in all but blood to John Chaney, the legendary head coach at Temple University. Every morning during high school, Matt would accompany his father to Temple's 6 A.M. practices, and he wouldn't just watch. He'd suit up, often guarding Temple's all-American guard Mark Macon, before showering and barely making it in time to homeroom at his suburban high school.

"Matt's dad grew up in the city, so Matt's got some of that in him, and my game only started to gel when I went to Episcopal in ninth grade," points out Allen, now playing professionally in France. Yet the two were constantly reminded of their labels and went so far as to compile a list of adjectives that they felt were informed more by their pigmentation than by what they showed on the court.

"It's funny, because I knew what I was doing against those guys at Temple, how I was breaking ankles against players like Macon," Maloney says. "It's frustrating, because it's like you are what the media wants you to be."

As a white man in a black man's world, Matt Maloney says his eyes are opened every day. "This is a great education," says the history major who posted a 3.0 grade point average at Penn. In the Continental Basketball Association, where he toiled for a year before signing as a free agent with Houston, he roomed with Cuonzo Martin, a six-foot six-inch black man from East St. Louis. "Basketball made it possible for a kid from the ghetto in St. Louis and a kid from Haddonfield to become best friends," he says. "I don't know where else that happens. I guess the army. And what was cool was that neither of us are sensitive about our differences. So we'd bust on each other all the time. I'd get on him about rap music."

Indeed, it is one of the great paradoxes of sports' place in popular culture. Those who chronicle sport may lag behind the cultural zeitgeist—witness the *New York Times's* insistence on calling Muhammad Ali "Cassius Clay" for years after his name change— but sport itself has long served as an egalitarian model. The civil rights movement, after all, didn't start with *Brown vs. Board of Education;* it started with Jackie Robinson.

And, as Maloney knows, with the possible exception of the military, professional sports in America is a shining example of meritocracy in action. "The best thing about sports is that it's color-blind," Maloney's Houston teammate Charles Barkley often observes. "In the locker room, we're all the same. Sports brings us together. I mean, if you can play, you gonna play, no matter what color you are."

As Barkley suggests, unlike most of the American workplace, discrimination isn't an impediment to opportunity in sports. Partly that's because performance in sports can be so easily measured: If you can score twenty points and make half your shots, there's a good chance you'll find yourself on an NBA roster. Whites like Maloney still have to counter misperceptions, but they nonetheless get the opportunity—if they perform, they're in. And if they don't perform, it will have little to do with pigmentation. Yet subtle racial preferences do exist—off the court, especially when it comes to the game's hierarchy and its marketing. How else to explain New Jersey's Keith Van Horn, the league's latest "Great White Hope"—a good player whose hype his rookie year overshadowed fellow rookie Tim Duncan, a *great* player who happens to be black?

In fact, it is in the economic realm that Maloney has, quite ironically, countered stereotypes. It's become fashionable, after all, to lambaste today's black athletes for pursuing a "show me the money" agenda at the expense of time-worn values. But they at least realize they're the assets in a multibillion-dollar business. One would expect that Maloney, an Ivy League product, to follow suit and make smart bottom-line decisions. Instead, after his Cinderella rookie year with Houston, he turned down more lucrative offers to sign for the league minimum with the Rockets, out of a sense of loyalty to the team that had discovered him and given him his shot. At the same time, guys like Jerry Stackhouse and Derrick Coleman, good players who had come from less and were dead set on striking lucrative deals for themselves, actually exhibited superior business acumen. Maloney did sign a new, more lucrative contract prior to his third NBA season.

Now in his third NBA season, Maloney still gets frustrated at the repeated labeling that has racial roots, but at least he's in the NBA, countering the stereotypes, night after night. And he's open to alternative views: It doesn't always have to be about race. On the night that found him bemoaning the refs' racial predispositions with regard to shooters, he conceded that factors besides race could have accounted for the silent whistles. "The only other thing I can think of is that I'm stronger than a lot of point guards, so that when I get fouled, if I don't flop around, it may look like incidental contact," he offered with a shrug.

But then, the next morning, he heard a sound bite in which a talking head called him a "smart player" who is "quick enough." He laughed to himself while he searched his memory for the last black point guard who was referred to as "quick enough."

6

deconstructing the nba

KENNETH L. SHROPSHIRE

Introduction

"Some of that Ian Ayres stuff might be going on here," a law professor friend said to me two days before the 1998–99 National Basketball Association (NBA) lockout of the players by management ended. He was referring broadly to the series of studies by Professor Ayres that examine car dealers' treatment of car buyers according to race and gender.[1] In that venue, Ayres found price discrimination against Blacks. His analysis points out that Blacks are likely to pay more than Whites for the same vehicle.[2] Ayres concludes that it is difficult to pinpoint whether racial animus or something else causes this pricing discrimination to occur.[3] The something else is the statistical belief in the minds of auto dealers that Blacks will, on average, pay more than Whites; that, in fact, they will accept an inferior deal.[4] If one wants to reach a non-abrasive conclusion, these car dealers are simply being good businesspeople and bargaining for the best deal possible from their viewpoint. In relation to the lockout, my law professor friend's view was that the negotiations dragged on and the White owners made few concessions because of similar views the owners may possess about Blacks who happen to be talented athletes: They should be willing to accept an inferior deal.

The lockout's end was an exclamation point on a unique moment in basketball. A moment that allows us to deconstruct this presumably racially pristine venue. Much of the Latrell Sprewell saga unfolded simultaneously. Sprewell is a basketball player who was found to have choked his coach during a practice session while he was a member of the NBA's Golden State Warriors. Sprewell explained that the attack on his coach was provoked by the in-your-face coaching techniques Coach P. J. Carlesimo employed. In the end, Sprewell was suspended from the league for sixty-eight games, at a cost to him of $6.4 million.[5] It is important to note that both the lockout and the Sprewell matter had varying undertones of the dominant form of racism that permeates American society: aversive or unconscious racism. According to John Dovidio:

> In contrast to "old-fashioned" racism, which is expressed directly and openly, aversive racism represents a subtle, often unintentional, form of bias that characterizes many white Americans who possess strong egalitarian values and who believe that they are nonprejudiced.[6]

Both basketball events, in their own way, signaled enough being enough with regard to largely financially successful or soon-to-be-successful Black males. Dovidio points to this as a need for power and control: "In a world of limited resources, one of the ways that people maintain their control or power is by resisting the progress of competing groups."[7] But if you mentioned an aversive- or unconscious-racism theory in either case, some would maintain that you were overreacting, particularly with regard to the basketball business.[8] The informed view, some argue, is that the owners, like car dealers, were merely being good businesspeople, and the sanctions against Latrell Sprewell were merely punishment for inappropriate behavior.

Sprewell and the players, in the two different contexts and to varying degrees, represented a stand against power. Violence steps over the line of civility, but much may be gained by discussing Sprewell in conjunction with the players in the lockout in the context of this response to a traditional power base.

It is rare today that racism is blatantly displayed. We no longer see Bull Connor ordering that powerful fire hoses be aimed to assault innocent Black women and children. On lesser levels, we rarely hear (unless secretly recorded) comments such as that commentator and former basketball player Rod Hundley made in 1966 in reference to the first all-Black starting team to win the NCAA tournament: "They can do everything with a basketball but autograph it."[9] Occasionally we are made aware of outrageous events, such as the dismemberment of a Black man in Texas[10] or the assault by New York police officer Justin Volpe on Abner Louima, where Volpe shoved a wooden stick into Louima's rectum in the stationhouse bathroom.[11] We also have heard in recent years about the Texaco tapes[12] and the discrimination by Denny's restaurants against, among others, African American Secret Service agents in Annapolis, Maryland.[13] But these events are the exception.

What occurs in basketball is probably a clearer vision of today's dominant version of racism. "How much do *you* want, and how far do *you* think you are going to be allowed to go" is the difficult-to-detect theme. The Denny's scenario may be closest to the basketball frame of mind. There have been numerous allegations of discrimination against Denny's restaurants, but probably the most publicized instance involved six African American Secret Service officers. These gentlemen received extremely slow and rude service while in a Denny's restaurant, at the same time that fifteen White colleagues received rapid and pleasant service. The African American customers complained to the manager to no avail; as one of the agents reported, "His [the manager's] attitude was so nonchalant, you knew where he was coming from."[14] After suits filed by these agents and others, Flagstar Companies, the holding company for

Denny's, entered into a settlement agreement.[15] Imagine the
Denny's waitress having the power to state, without literally saying it, "Be happy we're letting you eat in here, but don't expect good
service."

For some, it is hard to perceive the NBA as relevant to this conversation. There is no higher concentration of Black millionaires
anywhere. The NBA evolved to this predominantly Black state
nearly two decades after Rod Hundley's negative pronouncement
on the intelligence of Black basketball players—a statement that,
incidentally, turned out to be wrong at the time. More West Texas
players received their degrees sooner and went on to traditional
jobs than did the entirely White Kentucky players they defeated in
that championship game, where Kentucky was coached by the legendary Adolph Rupp (who said in reference to the speed of black
athletes, "[In Africa] the lions and tigers caught all the slow
ones").[16] According to Frank Fitzpatrick in his book on that 1966
Texas Western–Kentucky matchup:

> Nine of the twelve Miners, four of the seven blacks, eventually
> got their degrees. The remaining three left within a semester of
> theirs and did not suffer because of it. . . . What no one mentioned
> at the time was that until the mid 1970s, four of Kentucky's five
> starters, including All Americans [Pat] Riley and Louie Dampier,
> had not yet earned their college diplomas.[17]

Today there is largely equal opportunity on the court, and even the
representation in the front-office and ownership positions (although there are still no African Americans with a controlling
ownership interest) has changed to include the greatest percentage
of African Americans in management in professional team sports.

Studies conducted during the 1990s have brought to light various inequality issues in the NBA. To some extent, with the declining presence of White ballplayers in the NBA, the statistics lose
their value; the sample of White players is just too small, representing over this period of time just 20 percent of the league. Even
with that in mind, some of the results are troubling.

One study finds a wage gap between White and Black players in
the NBA, favoring Whites by anywhere from 11 to 25 percent.[18] A

more staggering study, published in 1999, concludes that there is
"exit discrimination" in the NBA: "White players have a 36 percent
lower risk of being cut than black players, *ceteris paribus*, translat-
ing into an expected career length of 7.5 seasons for an apparently
similar player who is white and 5.5 seasons for the same player who
is black."[19] As the authors of that study amplify, exit discrimination
is easier to identify in a sport than in other businesses. Athletes are
most often fired from the NBA (or any other sport, for that matter)
before they quit. In other businesses, employees may move from
one firm to another voluntarily, with no visible pressure from the
firm to do so.[20]

Latrell Sprewell

In 1998, Latrell Sprewell brought a lawsuit against the NBA, alleg-
ing that the actions the NBA took against him were racially motivated.[21] He offered no evidence in the complaint. The lawsuit
specifically alleged that the Golden State Warriors and the NBA
"conspired to violate Mr. Sprewell's civil rights and violated his
freedom of contract, because of his race, which is Black and African
American."[22] A judge threw the case out. When Sprewell filed the
action a second time, it was thrown out again.[23]

The *New York Times* reported that former Chicago Bull Craig
Hodges brought a similar lawsuit in the early 1990s. He maintained
that "the owners and operators of the 29 N.B.A. member franchises
have participated as co-conspirators" in "blackballing" him from
the league "because of his outspoken political nature as an African-
American man."[24]

The facts in the case of Craig Hodges pose an interesting segue
into and amplification of the mysteries of modern-day racism.
After ten seasons in the NBA, the last four as a three-point specialist for the Bulls, the Bulls chose not to re-sign Hodges, and no other
team in the league even offered him a tryout. Hodges's suit maintained that the blackballing occurred because, among other things,
he wore a dashiki to the traditional championship team meeting
with President George Bush; he delivered a letter to Bush asking

him to do more to "end injustice toward the African American Community"; and he worked with Nation of Islam minister Louis Farrakhan.[25] The arguments to the contrary were that "he couldn't guard a post" and that the Bulls had simply signed a better player.[26] In the end, it is all so subjective; who knows what the truth is?

How do you prove it? How do you really know when racism is occurring, often so subtly? This difficulty in uncovering the subtleties of racism is imbedded in American law. As we see the burdens of proof shift in American jurisprudence, much of that shifting is based in presumptions of the decline of racism.

I remember many late college nights in the 1970s at the Denny's restaurant on El Camino Real in Palo Alto, when my Black friends and I found the service to be unbelievably slow and rude. Similarly, I recall one Las Vegas afternoon when my father shouted for a waitress, embarrassing the family but detecting a racism that he had known throughout his life. That occurred at a Denny's as well. The treatment of the Secret Service agents and other related actions validated a problem I never had evidence to prove. When the Denny's settlement was announced, I heard from many of my late-night dining brothers, and this was twenty years later.

The disbelief or doubting of what others *know* to be true is one of the oldest stories in the world. The biblical epigraph "Blessed are they that have not seen, and yet have believed" is from the story of "Doubting Thomas," who would not believe that Jesus Christ had risen from the crucifixion until he personally felt the holes in the hands and sides of Christ. These 1990s basketball issues amplify the illusory status of discrimination. This is counter to the trend in the most prominent criminal cases, where science now thoroughly convinces us of the guilt or innocence of a party. The press is now filled with cases where DNA evidence *proves* the innocence or guilt of the respective parties. There is no DNA to uncover the most sophisticated versions of discrimination, those where the reasons for the action are retained in the mind of the perpetrator, undetected by any fact finder.

That the arbitrator in the Sprewell case reduced the penalty the ballplayer initially received infuriated many. The rancor over the penalties assessed against racial minorities for violent acts— Latrell Sprewell, Roberto Alomar, and, in a sports-removed setting, O. J. Simpson—has not been mirrored by any expressions of concern at sanctions against Whites, such as Carolina Panthers football player Kevin Greene. Kevin Greene endured only a *one-game* suspension for attacking his linebacker coach Kevin Steele *on national television*. The cost to him was $117,647 the equivalent of a one-game check of his $2 million salary.[27] Latrell Sprewell, in contrast, suffered a sixty-eight-game suspension for attacking his then head coach, P. J. Carlesimo, at a cost to Sprewell of $6.4 million of an $8.3 million annual salary. This occurred at a *non-televised practice session*. But racism cannot be proven in these cases. Speaking to the Greene incident, Sprewell contemplated, "My case was behind closed doors. His happened on national TV and no one can really deny it. And still, ESPN's Sports Center buried the whole thing in the middle of their segment. It wasn't on World News Tonight or those types of things like I was." The irony of the treatment of a Black man with corn-rows and a goatee contrasted with that of a White man, with a ponytail and Fu Manchu mustache did not escape Sprewell. "If a white guy has long hair pulled back in a ponytail, what does that mean? It's not like he's a thug or anything. I know prejudice is out there. I know it's just the way things are. But so much was made about my braids, about my deal with P. J. Then Greene's thing was on national TV. And nobody really cared."[28]

Interestingly, there had been numerous instances of player violence in the NBA prior to the Sprewell incident, but none of the penalties applied begin to approach the severity of the one imposed on him. The broad allegation was that Sprewell, "without provocation, attacked him [Coach P. J. Carlesimo], choked him and screamed death threats." That he "returned to the practice floor about 15 minutes later, fought his way through several players and coaches and engaged in a premeditated attack on the Head Coach." Finally, he "again threatened to kill him."[29] The greatest variation in the telling is the level of provocation and the degree to which Sprewell "cooled down" before the second attack. Sprewell and the National Basketball Players Association asserted in this regard, "There was no premeditated second attack. . . . [Sprewell] never calmed down to an emotional state where he could premeditate anything. . . . The incident was an instantaneous reaction resulting from a month of tension and confrontations between [Sprewell and] the Head Coach [P. J. Carlesimo]."[30]

Was there really choking? Sprewell testified that "He grabbed Carlesimo around the neck with his arms fully extended . . . he applied some pressure but he did not consider it to be choking."[31] Sprewell further asserted that "his intent was to just have the Head Coach leave him alone . . . he was slightly squeezing Carlesimo's neck but he was not trying to choke him, and that [Carlesimo] was not gasping for air, changing color, or resisting."[32] In Carlesimo's testimony, the coach asserted, "It was difficult to breathe and getting more difficult."[33]

Ronald Klempner, general counsel of the National Basketball Players Association (NBPA), testified about other instances of violence, emphasizing how severe Sprewell's penalty was relative to others. These incidents included the following: Two players were fined $25,000 each by their team for fighting; one player had a swollen lip and also needed stitches. Los Angeles Laker Shaquille O'Neal slapped an opposing player, Greg Ostertag, in the face for remarks that upset him; O'Neal was fined $10,000 and suspended for one game. And the longest previous suspension in NBA history was for twenty-six games over sixty days; this was for a punch thrown by Laker Kermit Washington that hit opposing player Rudy Tomjanovich and shattered his jaw.[34]

Even more revealing was that Klempner, as well as all others who testified, "could not recall an instance of violence between a player and a head coach, noting that often things are kept behind closed doors."[35] Relatedly, the NBA commissioner David Stern testified that "up until the [Sprewell] incident . . . off court incidents were generally kept behind closed doors." Stern also said that there was "no other event that he recalled where a team and the NBA both imposed discipline for the same physical altercation."[36]

The instances Klempner recalled that did not involve player-on-player violence were the following: NBA player Alvin Robertson grabbed his team's director of player personnel around the throat and fell with him over a banister into a row of seats. Robertson was suspended indefinitely, but he was traded before any commissioner-imposed discipline. Player Vernon Maxwell was suspended for ten games and fined $20,000 for attacking a fan in the stands.

Player Dennis Rodman was fined $20,000 and suspended for six games for head-butting a referee; Rodman also kicked a photographer in the groin and was suspended for approximately one month. No team discipline was imposed.[37]

Even across sports the Sprewell sanction seems uniquely severe. Eugene Orza of the Major League Baseball Players Association testified that the longest suspension he was aware of in baseball was for thirty days. In that incident, Lenny Randle "punched his manager in the jaw and knocked him down, and when he was on the ground, punched him several more times. The manager ended up in the hospital."[38]

Much was unique about the Sprewell incident. It occurred on the heels of Shaquille O'Neal's slapping Greg Ostertag, Dennis Rodman's kicking a cameraman in the groin, Nick Van Exel's going after a referee, and Charles Barkley's throwing a man through a plate-glass window. There was a pervading sense that something had to be done to get the players back in control. Sprewell's act was characterized by some as the last straw, where severe punishment was mandated.[39] As Sprewell himself stated, "I never said I shouldn't be punished for what I did. We just said that the punishment was excessive."[40] In response to this view, Stern responded, "Yes, I was trying to send a message. You cannot choke your coach in the NBA. That's the one and only message I was trying to send."[41] Sprewell had become the whipping post for all that was wrong with the game. The reality is that the Sprewell imagery is precisely what broader American society has pushed against. Sprewell is not the role model desired for Black America. In short, those Black performers who have been widely accepted project images that are raceless, colorless, and apolitical. The best examples are, of course, Michael Jordan and the reconstructed Muhammad Ali.

The Lockout

The NBA's lockout of its players and the dominant public reaction epitomized the "you should be grateful for what you have" sentiment. The race issues that emerged sporadically in 1998–99 were evident in the most recent NBA collective-bargaining scenario as well. Again, however, no one could say for certain that racism was present. The labor, the stars, are predominantly Black, at around 80 percent of the league. The owners, at least those with controlling interests, are White—that's 100 percent on the ownership side. This necessitates that any collective-bargaining process is (if only in the simplest manner) Black against White.

The book *Money Players* highlights even more acrimony in the 1995 NBA collective-bargaining negotiations than appeared in those of 1998–99. Charles Grantham, an African American, was the executive director of the NBPA at the time. Just before the negotiations got underway, he left the position; a variety of unsubstantiated reasons have been given for his departure.[42] Grantham's replacement was Simon Gourdine, another African American, who at one point in his career had been the deputy commissioner of the NBA, the party on the opposite side of the bargaining table. The union president at the time was Buck Williams.[43] Williams and Gourdine received much criticism during the course of those negotiations. In response, Williams stated:

> You see it all the time: blacks don't believe that another black man can do for them what a white man can. I'm not a racist person, but here you have all these white, Jewish attorneys on both sides, and in the middle you have black players questioning the intelligence of their black union leaders.[44]

Money Players chronicled the public view of the negotiation's conclusion best:

> The worst thing, said veteran forward John Salley, was the underlying racial tensions and the specter of failed black leadership. Gourdine's intelligence and intentions were publicly challenged time and again. Buck Williams's dedicated service was forgotten. Charles Grantham's reputation was smeared. Even black agents such as [Len] Elmore and Fred Slaughter resented how [Eric] Fleisher and [David] Falk [both White agents] were held up as the brains behind the rebellion.

As for the players, Salley said they had let the NBA and the agents divide them into warring factions the public perceived as the haves against the have-nots. They came off looking, he said, like "house Negroes and the field Negroes."

Salley knew enough American history to understand this wasn't the first time something like this had occurred. "Blacks in this country have always been divided and it never did us any good," he said. "The NBA is a very black league, so we must be careful of the message we send." In effect, Salley's message was that no matter how successful it became, how big it got, 1970s racial perceptions would never go away for a predominantly black league selling to a white corporate crowd.[45]

It is difficult, if not impossible, to measure whether the public's reaction to this predominantly Black league is any different from that to predominantly White baseball or hockey when those players are demanding more. The animus toward Black basketball players seemed to be stronger during the 1998 lockout. The usual images provided were of Black players huddled around Black NBPA executive director Billy Hunter and of the White leadership around the White commissioner David Stern. As much as the desire has been expressed, we are not a color-blind society, and those stark black-versus-white competitive images were real.

Conclusion

For Sprewell to want more respect and for players in the lockout to want more money are both broadly acceptable goals—unless someone perceives that you have enough already. Absent an uncharacteristic public revelation (à la Jimmy "the Greek" Snyder or Al Campanis), we'll never know the motivations of the opposing parties for sure. But with this in mind, we should follow the game beyond the court with open eyes. The potential for racism and other forms of discrimination is still with us, regardless of what anti–affirmative action legislative successes in California and the state of Washington and elsewhere may tell us.

The most memorable moment in the whole Sprewell incident came when San Francisco mayor Willie Brown was asked his view of the incident. "His boss may have needed choking," the politician responded.[46] He went on to say, "I'm not justifying what [Sprewell] did as right. But nobody is asking why he did it or what might have prompted him."[47] I'm not sure what was truly behind Brown's later retracted statement. But what he probably perceived, in the language of Johnnie Cochran, was a "rush to judgment." The instant condemnation and severe sanction against Sprewell probably reminded Brown of the innumerable instances of rushed judgments he had witnessed over the years as a practicing attorney and an African American.[48] Sprewell had feuded with his previous coach, Don Nelson; his driver's license had been revoked or suspended six times; and he had been under house arrest for three months for a reckless-driving incident.[49] These incidents, coupled with past allegations of violence against fellow players, including an alleged two-by-four assault, made him no one's ideal client.[50]

An examination beyond the game tells us much about our society. In the past, I've written that sports is a microcosm of society.[51] That is an overstatement, just as it would be to hold up the game of basketball to that status. Among other differences, the absence of societally related gender issues reduces the value of sports as the ideal model. Further, the basketball model is Black and White, quite different from the real America.[52] But the reality behind a business perceived to be a bastion of equal footing does provide some insight as to where we are in broader American society. In order for greater progress in legislatures, courts, and other sectors of society to occur, more of those who have not directly felt or seen racism need to *believe* it still exists even in the most meritorious of settings.

NOTES

1. See Ian Ayres, "Further Evidence of Discrimination in New Car Negotiations and Estimates of Its Cause," 94 *Michigan Law Review* 109 (1995); Ian Ayres, "Fair Driving: Gender and Race Discrimination in Retail Car Negotiations," 104 *Harvard Law Review* 817 (1991).

2. Ayres's study observes the negotiations with Black males, relative to other groups.

3. Ayres, "Fair Driving."

4. Ibid. Relevant text from Ayres that summarizes this view maintains:

Airlines, for example, do not charge businesspeople higher fares because of animus or higher costs; the difference in fares is an attempt to charge higher-valuing customers a higher price. In the retail car market, the dealer's ultimate goal is to maximize profits by charging each consumer his or her reservation price—the maximum amount the consumer is willing to pay. Under this theory, race and gender serve as proxies to inform sellers about how much individual consumers would be willing to pay for the car.

"Fair Driving," 843–844.

5. Ira Berkow, "Sprewell Has Golden Opportunity," *New York Times*, February 3, 1999, D1.

6. John F. Dovidio and Samuel L. Gaertner, "On the Nature of Contemporary Prejudice: The Causes, Consequences and Challenges of Aversive Racism," in Jennifer L. Eberhardt and Susan T. Fiske, eds., *Confronting Racism: The Problem and the Response* (Thousand Oaks, CA: Sage, 1998), 5.

7. Ibid., 6.

8. Unconscious racism has probably best been defined by Professor Charles Lawrence:

Americans share a common historical and cultural heritage in which racism has played and still plays a dominant role. Because of this shared experience, we also inevitably share many ideas, attitudes, and beliefs that attach significance to an individual's race and induce negative feelings and opinions about nonwhites. To the extent that this cultural belief system has influenced all of us, we are all racists. At the same time, most of us are unaware of our racism. We do not recognize the ways in which our cultural experience has influenced our beliefs about race or the occasions on which those beliefs affect our actions. In other words, a large part of the behavior that produces racial discrimination is influenced by unconscious racial motivation.

Charles R. Lawrence III, "The Id, the Ego and Equal Protection: Reckoning with Unconscious Racism," 39 *Stanford Law Review* 317, 322 (1987).

9. Frank Fitzpatrick, *And the Walls Came Tumbling Down: Kentucky,*

Texas Western and the Game that Changed American Sports (New York: Simon and Schuster, 1994), 34.

10. Claudia Kolker, "Trial Opens in Black Man's Savage Dragging Death," *Los Angeles Times*, February 17, 1999, A1.

11. Helen Peterson, "Louima Jury Reviews Cop Testimony; No Verdict," *New York Daily News*, June 8, 1999, 8.

12. See Bari-Ellen Roberts, *Roberts v. Texaco: A True Story of Race and Corporate America* (New York: Avon Books, 1998).

13. See Howard Kohn, "Service with a Sneer," *New York Times Magazine*, November 6, 1994, 42, 47.

14. Ibid.

15. Ibid.

16. Fitzpatrick, *And the Walls Came Tumbling Down*, 58.

17. Ibid., 34.

18. Ha Hoang and Dan Rascher, "The NBA, Exit Discrimination and Career Earnings," *Industrial Relations*, vol. 38, no. 1, (January 1999): 69.

19. Ibid.

20. One can move from this hard-to-explain-away statistic to the final-stance argument for affirmative action. At various points along the path of progress are gatekeepers. Absent the lever of the law, one of these sophisticated gatekeepers may be a racist and, without any disclosure, disproportionately bar the group toward which he or she has ill, without a hint of intent or animus. If queried, the gatekeeper's response could be "I made the determination based on the merits." Is there some aversion in the minds of NBA gatekeepers that causes this disproportion in cutting players to occur? Is there such aversion in the mind of the auto salesman? in the mind of the Denny's waiter or waitress? in the mind of an employer? in the mind of a college admissions officer?

21. He also sued his agent, Arn Tellem, because Tellem did not negotiate the disciplinary clause out of Sprewell's contract with the Warriors. That case was unsuccessful as well.

22. Complaint, *Latrell F. Sprewell v. Golden State Warriors and National Basketball Association*, U.S. District Court, Northern District of California, www.courttv.com/legaldocs/newmakers/latrell.htm.

23. "Judge Dismisses Sprewell Lawsuit," UPI, March 29, 1999.

24. Ira Berkow, "The Case of Hodges vs. the NBA," *New York Times*, December 25, 1996, B11.

25. Ibid.

26. Ibid.

27. "Scorecard," *Sports Illustrated*, December 28, 1998, 31. "Raiders Add Another Heisman," *St. Petersburg Times*, June 3, 1999, 8C.

28. Johnette Howard, "Sprewell Runs Hard to Leave Thug's Image Behind," *Newsday*, February 7, 1999, C4.

29. Dean John Feerick, "Arbitration Opinion and Award in the Matter of National Basketball Players Association on Behalf of Player Latrell Sprewell and Warriors Basketball Club and National Basketball Association," March 4, 1998, at 12.

30. Ibid., 13.

31. Ibid., 18.

32. Ibid., 19.

33. Ibid., 39.

34. Ibid., 35.

35. Ibid., 35.

36. Ibid., 72.

37. Ibid., 36.

38. Ibid., 33.

39. Johnette Howard, "Sprewell Runs Hard to Leave Thug's Image Behind," *Newsday*, February 7, 1999, C4.

40. Ibid.

41. Ibid.

42. The stories ranged from "philosophical differences" to financial discrepancies. Regarding the latter, Grantham maintained, "The allegations were not substantial. I'm not going to tell you if you looked at my expense accounts, I didn't have a dinner here, a car there. I didn't steal money." See Armen Keteyian, Harvey Araton, and Martin F. Dardis, *Money Players: Inside the New NBA* (New York: Pocket Books, 1997), 84.

43. Ibid., 85.

45. Ibid., 91.

46. "San Francisco Mayor Says Choking Might Be Deserved," *Chicago Tribune*, December 5, 1997, 2C.

47. Ibid.

48. See James Richardson, *Willie Brown: A Biography* (Berkeley: University of California Press, 1996).

49. Howard, "Sprewell Runs Hard," C4.

50. Ibid.

51. See Kenneth L. Shropshire, *In Black and White: Race and Sports in America* (New York: New York University Press, 1995).

52. For an analysis of the changing demographics of America, see Dale Maharidge, *The Coming White Minority: California, Multiculturalism, and America's Future* (New York: Vintage Books, 1999).

7

blue-collar law and basketball

MARK CONRAD

THE JUNE 1998 DECISION OF THE NBA owners to impose a lockout of the players and jeopardize the basketball season brought the issue of labor relations and basketball into public view—with all its accompanying distrust and divisions. Giving the basketball fan a taste of the often acrimonious and high-stakes posturing also demonstrated how a sixty-year-old series of laws has applied, rightly or wrongly, to a professional sport comprised of wealthy (even superwealthy) employers and, at times, almost equally wealthy players.

Of course, basketball is not the first sport to be affected by labor–management disputes. Baseball, football, and hockey have seen their share of

strikes and lockouts. But the NBA lockout and its results gave basketball fans a strong education in American labor laws, notably the
National Labor Relations Act of 1935.[1]

These days, the basketball news forms an adjunct to the labor
and financial pages of the local newspaper. In the "good old days"
when sports was sports and news was news, the two rarely met.
Now they engage in a tango of conflicting goals, resulting in frequent arguments.

The Labor Law Model

American labor law concepts—conceived to protect blue-collar
workers in their quest to improve working conditions—have been
injected into the world of professional basketball as well as other
sports, over the last quarter of the twentieth century. Although
basketball fans may hate to admit it, labor law in sports is here to
stay.

In one sense, it is incongruous. Professional basketball employs personnel to represent elite, skilled practitioners of a sport
barely a century old. Their working conditions (about six or
seven months per year, arguably less than thirty-five hours per
week) and their compensation scales are beyond the hopes and
aspirations of the ordinary or even not-so-ordinary American
worker. With an average salary of $1.5 million per season in
1998, players in the National Basketball Association surpassed
the averages for partners in the nation's largest law firms and all
but the very top surgeons; some salaries even exceeded those of
many CEOs of Fortune 500 corporations.

Also, unlike the automobile and steel industries, professional
basketball is a relatively new business, which came to fruition
well after New York Senator Robert Wagner drafted the National
Labor Relations Act in 1935. At the time of the law, Senator Wagner most likely did not consider it applicable to the weak professional basketball leagues of his day, which could not compete
with the successful college basketball game of the 1930s. At Wagner's death in 1951, the modern NBA—conceived from the

merger of the Basketball Association of America and the National Basketball League—was just two years old.

The passage of the National Labor Relations Act (NLRA) in 1935 marked a milestone in American labor. Called the "Magna Carta of Labor," the NLRA was intended to protect auto workers, printers, and clerical employees in their quest to unionize and bargain collectively with management without the fear of retaliation. The enactment of this law changed the nature of labor-management relations.

Before 1935, "workplace democracy" often collided with the mantra of laissez-faire capitalism. Unionization, a difficult process confronted with subtle and not-so-subtle threats of employee harassment or dismissal, was a legally unprotected act. Legal attempts to give workers greater rights previously had been incremental. But the New Deal period marked the emancipation of American labor. Senator Wagner, an ally of President Franklin Roosevelt, shepherded the NLRA through the Congress. Wagner firmly believed in the government's duty to take an active role in promoting the public good.

The NLRA guarantees workers the right to be represented by a union and provides for specific methods to attain union representation and employer recognition of a particular "collective bargaining unit" to negotiate on behalf of a group of workers.[2] Elections are held, and if the National Labor Relations Board certifies the results, the union is recognized. Usually, if union recognition is granted, individual employees lose their right to negotiate on such subjects as "wages, hours or working conditions."

The NRLA also gives employees the right to strike.[3] Most strikes occur when a satisfactory collective-bargaining agreement, usually an attempt to secure better wages, hours, or working conditions, cannot be reached. This pits the collective economic power of the unionized workers against the employer's attempts to go on without the aid of their labor. Employers may replace striking workers with temporary or permanent replacements or get by with managerial employees who are not part of the collective-bargaining unit.[4] (This was done in the 1987 National Football League strike.)

The flip side of the strike is the lockout, a tactical measure taken by employers to prevent the union members from working. Just as the strike is an economic pressure tactic taken by the union, the lockout is a similar strategy for management. With the expiration of a collective-bargaining agreement, management may prefer to "call the shots" in determining the shutdown of an operation, rather than wait for the union to seize the opportunity. This tactic was employed by the National Hockey League (NHL) in 1994, resulting in a disruption of almost half the season. In 1998 the NBA owners, possibly taking their cue from the NHL outcome, declared a lockout in basketball.

One of the central components to the NLRA involves a series of actions known as "unfair labor practices."[5] Both employers and employees may be liable for these violations, which include interference with the unionization process, discriminatory treatment against employees for union-related activities, and most important, the refusal by either side to bargain in good faith. The last condition requires both sides to negotiate on the "mandatory" subjects—wages, hours, and working conditions. The law also established the National Labor Relations Board as the administrative agency to enforce the mandates of the NLRA.

Senator Wagner's goals for industrial justice centered on the steelworker, auto assembly-line employee, and sandhog, not the professional basketball player. Probably the farthest thing from his mind was the idea of the likes of Michael Jordan, Patrick Ewing, and Shaquille O'Neal as unionized workers.

Although Wagner's labor ideals did not center on labor in relation to sports, his one connection with sports was a case involving the suspension of baseball player Carl Mays, who had been traded to the New York Yankees. The Yankees wanted the suspension lifted, but American League president and baseball's de facto leader Bancroft "Ban" Johnson refused to reconsider. The case went to court and was heard by then New York Supreme Court justice Wagner. Wagner ruled in favor of the Yankees, enjoining Johnson from interfering with the player's performing for the Yankees. A quotation from the decision is quite prophetic:

The commercialization of baseball is a highly-profitable undertaking, rendering lucrative returns to the member clubs, to their stockholders and to their players. . . . The suspension of a player not only interferes with his individual contract; it may also interfere with the reputation and collective ability of the club.[6]

In limiting Johnson's power, this decision served to weaken his authority over the game and was one factor in his fall from grace. Just a few years later, baseball reorganized and created a commissioner's office to govern the sport. The commissioner system came to be used in every other professional sport, including basketball. The quotation is timeless in its applicability and could describe the sports environment today. This language could have been included in the recent arbitration involving Latrell Sprewell, where arbitrator John Feerick ruled that the NBA was unjustified in terminating Sprewell's contract after the player assaulted his coach.[7]

After the passage of the NLRA (which the Supreme Court subsequently upheld as a legitimate exercise of congressional power,[8] the blue-collar workers of the nation's central industries took advantage of the act and unionized. The resulting improvements in wages, hours, and general working conditions are a testament to the success of the law. In fact, many felt that the law was too pro-union, and in 1947, the so-called Taft-Hartley Amendments were passed to ensure that unions themselves do not engage in unfair labor practices.[9]

Application to Basketball

To keep operating costs down, the NBA originally copied the system employed in professional baseball and football to restrain player salaries. That device, the use of a "reserve" system to hitch players to their respective teams, severely restricted players' right to test their talents on the open market. This de facto monopolization achieved its effect and resulted in considerably lower player salaries, due to the lack of a free market for the players. The use of a contractual limitation on the right to secure employment remains a unique element of sports law and one of the most hotly contested issues in labor–management relations to this very day.

Yet trade unionism in the NBA came slowly. The National Basketball Players Association (NBPA) was formed in 1954, with Boston Celtics great Bob Cousy as its leader. Taking a cue from the nineteenth-century captains of industry, the NBA at first refused to recognize the association. In 1957, Commissioner Maurice Podoloff reluctantly conceded its validity, in part because he feared the NBPA would affiliate itself with a larger and stronger union, such as the steelworkers or teamsters. But the union's mettle was not seriously tested until 1964, when the NBPA threatened a strike at the 1964 All-Star Game.

In the 1950s, most professional sports "unions" were more like medieval guilds than modern labor organizations. The idea of collective bargaining between the union representatives and basketball owners did not begin in earnest until the 1960s, at just about the time that the percentage of unionized American workers began to shrink. Union membership in the United States peaked in 1953 to 37 percent of non-agricultural workers and has dropped steadily since. By 1991, the figure was 16 percent.[10] Though sports unions, including the NBPA, were late bloomers, in recent years they have crafted a singular position among American labor.

It was during the regime of union executive director Larry Fleisher that the NBPA began to think of itself in the same mold as other trade unions. Fleisher, called "the most successful labor leader of the 20th century" by former New Jersey senator Bill Bradley,[11] served as the head of the union until 1988 and negotiated the groundbreaking 1983 and 1988 collective bargaining agreements (CBAs), which created the salary-cap structure but also guaranteed the players a percentage of league revenues in either salary or benefits. In 1967, the average salary of an NBA player was $9,400; when Fleisher retired, it was $600,000. Not as well known as his compatriots Marvin Miller in baseball and Ed Garvey in football, Fleisher ably guided his players gradually, without protracted litigation and strikes.

In those days, the NBPA's representation dovetailed some of their experiences with those of other unions. Some thought their labor battles were a central component to trade unionism, as was stated by the late sports commentator Howard Cosell, in the epigraph to this chapter.[12] In the 1960s, Cosell's assessment accurately reflected the kinship between sports unions and unions at large. Today it serves as cant, glossing over major differences between the American labor experience on the one hand and the NBA and its players on the other. The differences far outweigh the similarities, legally, economically, and practically.

The Peculiarities of Basketball Labor Law

As *New York Times* sportswriter Murray Chass has noted, collective bargaining in professional sports has been described less as negotiating over working conditions than as "two mega-corporations talking to each other about mergers or splits or sales."[13] In the recently expired 1995 NBA collective bargaining agreement are sections that would be unheard of in a typical CBA.

First, much space was devoted to revenue sharing between the employer teams and the players. Players shared 59 percent of "gross defined revenues" and were guaranteed 48 percent of all NBA revenues—a staggering $700 million in 1994–95. Such revenues included fees from arena signage, sponsorships, parking, concessions, and luxury boxes. Players were entitled to share in the moneys generated from licensing and merchandising. True, some indications of a traditional labor contract exist, such as the minimum salary. But that amount, which began at $225,000 per season and rose to $272,500, towers over the $500-per-week minimum one frequently finds in the general labor force. And we are not even considering the complicated salary-cap structure.

The very nature of this agreement is more akin to a European Social Democratic partnership between labor and management than to the typical American model. It is both an irony and a success story that such sharing of the wealth has the potential to make both the employers and the employees very rich.

This brings us to the nature of the services and the public loyalty to the services provided. Brand loyalty occupies a sacred place in the dreams of a marketer. If a company's brand name exudes stature and quality, it will retain a following among consumers of that type of product. And that will be the case even if the actual quality of the brand suffers. To paraphrase that often-stated theme from the 1992 presidential campaign: "It's the perception, stupid."

Most buyers do not care who makes the cars they drive, as long as the vehicles run dependably, are well designed, and have reasonable comfort and performance. Even in a service industry, one doesn't care about who the individual employees are but rather about the service itself. So, while the employee is a cog in the overall scheme, the replacement of that person with another will not necessarily cause consumer discomfort (unless the service declines in quality).

Contrast this with professional basketball players. The fan loyalty to a star player may be of incalculable value. Only a very small number of athletes play professional basketball in the United States; they make up an elite group by definition, especially considering the millions who play the game. Only a select few make the cut through high school, college, and the draft to get in and stay in the NBA and to occupy an exalted place there. And unlike other industries, where a choice of products abounds, the NBA has one—basketball. Without any rival, the NBA is the ultimate brand, and its employees are the ultimate makers of that brand.

The athletes' clout is a function not only of their unique skills but also of the unique relationship consumers have with the service they deliver. The players' agents and their union leaders know this all too well. With the value of the individual players far from being equal, basketball stars such as Michael Jordan, Patrick Ewing, Kevin Garnett, and Shaquille O'Neal can command huge salaries, bonuses, and other contractual perks negotiated through a position of tremendous strength. They and the other elites who dominate their franchise get the top marquee billing. The less-talented players, good enough to play but not to star in the NBA, do the job but are not irreplaceable. The wide disparity in value of the talent makes the NBA players a widely diverse union, a group of employees with great differences of wages. Consequently, it is a union that is very hard to hold together. Fleisher could do so; things have become more difficult since.

In the 1980s, the union and the NBA negotiated novel CBAs that dramatically changed the landscape of professional sports. In 1981, sixteen of the then twenty-three teams lost money. Rumors of rampant drug use and escalating salaries resulted in declines in game attendance, television ratings, and league revenues.[14] Sensing the desperate situation, both the NBA and NBPA concluded the 1983 CBA, the first to include revenue sharing (53 percent of gross revenues, including the national TV contract, local gate profits, playoff profits) in return for a team cap on salaries. This CBA was further refined in 1988.

The league and the union became victims of their success. As professional basketball attained new heights of popularity both in the United States and worldwide, the marquee value of teams and players increased. Today, a great disparity in salaries exists. In 1998, 40 players made over $5 million per season and 120 made the league minimum. Free-agency rights apply only to certain veteran players. The salary-cap structure is porous, permitting the elites to command whatever the market will bear as long as they stay with their teams. While the union negotiates many working conditions on behalf of all the players, it does not mandate the actual money individual players make. The resulting disparity adversely affects union solidarity—difficult in many situations but far more challenging for the leader of the NBPA.

Union Rules?

Tensions exist in many unions. But the kinds of tension that now exist at the NBPA reflect the huge differences between castes of players. For the best and the brightest, the union may be a hindrance and can put them in a weaker position than if they were "on their own." As the CBA does not involve individual salary negotiation, the impact that player agents have on the process is not insignificant. The major agents representing the big-time players do not have any built-in loyalty to the NBPA or to its continued existence. Indeed, attempts at decertification of the NBPA were seriously considered in 1995, during a period of contentious negotiations, Michael Jordan, Patrick Ewing, and Reggie Miller signed decertification notices because they were dissatisfied with the leadership of the union. They feared that the union would capitulate into accepting a "harder" salary cap. A tentative agreement exacerbated the issue. Ultimately, the union prevailed by a 226–134 vote, or 63 percent against decertification. The union accepted a final collective bargaining agreement the next year. Yet the issue of player "haves" versus player "have-nots" will not go away, and decertification may be revisited. The following statement by Tom Heinsohn, a former NBPA president who retired from playing in 1965, illustrates the dilemma:

> The players today take everything for granted. . . . Players all travel first-class, have plenty of meal money and they stay in separate rooms. The players have a very cavalier attitude about the union itself. Now, I'm fearful that if they decertify the union, all of the players are going to have to fight for those things individually in their contract.[15]

These problems represent an inner weakness in a union of such disparate members and a systematic weakness of individual (both in the performance sense and in the negotiating sense) employees attempting to band together. The greater the salary disparities, the more untenable the NBPA is. The structure of these labor–management relations also has led to use of a legal tactic that has probably done as much or more to accomplish union goals than collective bargaining: invocation of antitrust laws.

The Antitrust Tango

As every law student knows, antitrust law ranks as one of those subjects full of theorists, long on explanation, and brimming with complex judicial determinations. Most unions do not partake of antitrust theory in their dealings with employers. The NBPA (along with the National Football League Players Association) has made antitrust application a virtual art form.

The basic antitrust laws—the Sherman Antitrust Act[16] and the Clayton Act[17]—date from 1890 and 1914 respectively and apply to concerted activities that restrain trade in interstate commerce. The

intentions of these laws were to stop monopolistic activities that
often resulted in large "trusts" in such industries as oil, sugar, and
tobacco. To avoid the argument that union activity may constitute
restraint of trade, section 6 of the Clayton Act states that "the labor
or commerce of a human being is not subject to antitrust laws."[18]
The scope of that provision has been a matter of considerable academic debate and practical application in the field of sports law.

Ostensibly, section 6 protects unions and employers from engaging in concerted activities such as strikes and lockouts. But what
if there are sections in a collective bargaining agreement that may
have antitrust implications? For example, does a salary cap or a limitation of free agency become a restraint of trade under antitrust
laws? Because of the history of free-agency limitations and salary
restrictions in all professional sports, including basketball, this
issue has occupied the time of a number of courts over the last two
decades of the twentieth century.

In the NBA, the issue has been the continuing validity of the exemption during and after the expiration of a collective bargaining
agreement. In the case of *Wood v. NBA*,[19] Leon Wood, a point guard
on the 1984 gold-medal U.S. Olympic team, was picked by the
Philadelphia 76ers in the first round. Because of salary-cap con-
straints, Wood was offered a $75,000 one-year contract, well below
his true market value. Ultimately, when cap room became available,
his contract was amended to a four-year $1 million deal. Neverthe-
less, he sued the NBA, claiming that the cap violated antitrust laws.
Wood was still in college at the ratification of the 1983 CBA that
created the system and alleged that he should be a party to its pro-
visions. The court rejected his claims, as the agreement was subject
to the labor exemption. Otherwise, the court noted, federal labor
policy would be subverted.

Also in 1987, a lower federal court, ruling in *Bridgeman v.
NBA*,[20] concluded that the labor exemption continues to apply after
the conclusion of a CBA during an impasse stage, if the employer
"reasonably believes that the practice or a close variant of it will be
incorporated in the next collective bargaining agreement." Junior
Bridgeman challenged the cap rules but also lost. Shortly afterward, the 1988 CBA was concluded. In 1995, a similar ruling occurred in *National Basketball Association v. Williams*.[21]

The results of the *Bridgeman* case demonstrate how the NBPA turned a defeat into a victory. Even though the NBA won, the union, in a daring and ingenious move, threatened to decertify itself—meaning that no collective bargaining process would be in place and the owners would be wide open to antitrust suits. The plan worked; the NBA capitulated, not wanting anything to do with negotiating individual contracts with players in a free market, subject to antitrust laws. Shortly afterward, the parties concluded the 1988 agreement.

The ingenious tête-à-tête between labor and antitrust has benefited the NBPA. It is difficult to conceive of a non-sports union working the legal realm in such a way. Given the recent vintage of the NBPA, the disparity of talents and of payments made to its members, and the power of the player agents, it is ironic that the basketball players union could utilize the labor laws—especially the decertification threat—as a negotiating tactic to get its way. Or maybe, because of these attributes, the decertification sword had to be utilized to make the union's point.

In fact, a strong possibility for decertification exists in the not-too-distant future. The elite twenty-five players who help establish the worldwide recognition of the NBA don't need a union. They could thrive in a non-union market because their services are in demand. But the lesser stars and journeymen would suffer in an environment where the gulf among the players may be as wide as the disparities between the players and the owners.

A Few Last Words

Despite the fissures in the union, the disparate interests, the pressures from the agents, and the difficulties of bargaining with a league composed of twenty-nine separate entities, the NBA players have done exceedingly well. And for most of the 1980s and 1990s, management has also done well in this fascinating industrial partnership. But the events of 1998 could turn out to be a watershed, signaling a rocky road for both sides.

For any basketball fan, the 1998 owners' lockout represented a

sad state of affairs; a situation of prior union–management cooperation had become a victim of its own success. The grand scheme
turned the NBA into a marquee product worldwide, with multibillion-dollar television contracts and a cadre of $100 million
ballplayers who could do just as well without a union as with
one. And even if a prolonged lockout occurred in 1998 or sometime in the future, a setup including matches between teams
composed of the likes of Scottie Pippen, Kevin Garnett, Shaquille
O'Neal, Juwan Howard, Allen Iverson, and Patrick Ewing would
attract fan and television coverage. A group of striking coal min-
ers cannot do the same.

The worst-case scenario for the NBA and the NBPA would have
been a season-long shutdown of operations. As hard as that would
have been for the players and the owners, they could rest assured
that the league would not easily go out of business. Major-league
Baseball is testament to a sport that has come back, attendance-
wise, after the 1994 strike. Boosted by the home-run exploits of
Mark McGwire and Sammy Sosa, baseball in 1998 and 1999 experienced a wave of popular goodwill not seen in many years. Attendance at games increased by 12 percent.[22]

But when all is said and done, the fact remains that in a splintered union of six-figure employees, millionaires, and multimillionaires using the labor and antitrust laws to win concessions from
multiparty employers who are multimillionaires or billionaires
themselves, something is askew. Is this what Robert Wagner had in
mind when he drafted the landmark National Labor Relations Act?
That's hard to believe.

NOTES

1. 29 U.S.C. sec. 151 *et seq.*
2. Ibid.
3. 29 U.S.C. secs. 157, 163 (1982).
4. See *NLRB v. MacKay Radio and Telephone Co.*, 304 U.S. 333 (1938).
5. 29 U.S.C. secs. 157, 158(a)(1)–(a)(5); 158(b)(1)–(b)(7) (1982).
6. See Harold Seymour, *Baseball—The Golden Age* (New York: Oxford University Press, 1971), 268.

7. See Dean John Feerick, "Arbitration Opinion and Award in the Matter of National Basketball Players Association on Behalf of Player Latrell Sprewell and Warriors Basketball Club and National Basketball Association," March 4, 1998.

8. See *NLRB v. Jones and Laughlin Steel Corp.*, 301 U.S. 1 (1937).

9. 61 *Statutes at Large* 136 (1947)

10. See also Melvyn Dubofsky, *The State and Labor in Modern America* (Chapel Hill, University of North Carolina Press, 1994), 130, cited in Deborah A. Ballam, "The Law as a Constitutive Force for Change, Part II: The Impact of the National Labor Relations Act on the U.S. Labor Movement," *American Business Law Journal* 123, 126 (1995).

11. "Fleisher Is Eulogized," *New York Times*, May 9, 1989, D30, col. 1.

12. Howard Cosell, *What's Wrong with Sports* (New York: Pocketbooks, 1991).

13. See Murray Chass, "As Trade Unions Struggle, Their Sports Cousins Thrive," *New York Times*, September 5, 1994, 1; Kenneth A. Kovach, Patrizia Ricci, and Aladino Robles, "Is Nothing Sacred? Labor Strife in Professional Sports," *Business Horizons* (January 11, 1998): 34.

14. Martin Greenberg, *Sports Law Practice* (Charlottesville, Va.: Michie, 1993), vol. 1, 210.

15. See *Akron Beacon Journal*, August 23, 1998, cited in *Sports Business Daily*, vol. 4, no. 220 (August 24, 1998).

16. 26 *Statutes at Large* 209 (1890), as amended; 15 U.S.C. secs 1 *et seq.*

17. 38 *Statutes at Large* 730 (1914), as amended; 15 U.S.C. sec. 12 *et seq.*

18. 15 U.S.C. at sec. 17.

19. 809 F. 2d 954 (2d Cir. 1987).

20. 675 F. Supp. 960 (D.N.J. 1987).

21. 45 F. 3d 684, 689 (2d Cir. 1995).

22. Major League Baseball's total attendance of 70,589,505 in 1998 is a 12 percent increase over 1997's 63,016,136. See *Sports Business Daily*, vol. 5, no. 18 (October 15, 1998).

8

african american ownership

bob douglas and the rens

SUSAN J. RAYL

THERE IS A DEARTH OF AFRICAN AMERICAN
team ownership in professional basketball today.
Such has not always been the case, however. A
dominant owner in early professional basketball
in the United States was Robert L. "Bob" Douglas
of the New York Renaissance Five. Bob Douglas
organized the New York Renaissance Five professional basketball team in 1923. Over the next
twenty-six years, the "Rens" accomplished many
remarkable feats, including an eighty-eight-game
winning streak in 1933, winning the first national
professional title in 1939, and serving as the first
all-black team in a league—the National Basketball League—in the 1948–49 season. Without the
marketing ability and business acumen of owner-

manager Bob Douglas, however, the Rens would never have survived the depression of the 1930s.

Bob Douglas was an immigrant of African descent from the British West Indies. At a time when black ownership comprised just 10 percent of all businesses in Harlem, Douglas and men like him were the exception to the rule. Such people served a vital role in the African American community, both in Harlem, New York, and across the country. In Jim Crow America, Douglas and his Rens survived with all odds against them. This chapter discusses Bob Douglas and the networking and marketing tactics he employed that enabled his business, the Rens, to thrive over a twenty-six-year period. It also presents an ironic contrast to the present state of minority ownership in professional sports.

Born in 1882 in St. Kitts, British West Indies, Bob Douglas arrived in New York in 1902. For the next several years he worked as a messenger and porter for The Musical Courier in New York City.[1] The son of a commercial ship purser, Douglas followed his father and many other immigrants from the Caribbean into the New York business world. In his 1930 book *Black Manhattan*, James Weldon Johnson noted that many black immigrants from the British West Indies went into business.[2] This was reaffirmed over thirty years later by Gilbert Osofsky in his study of Harlem in the 1920s and 1930s, where many of the blacks who owned businesses during this period had their roots in the Caribbean. According to Osofsky, black immigrants from the British West Indies such as Douglas possessed attitudes that differed from the American perspective. These immigrants (1) placed importance on class distinctions rather than on color; (2) did not understand the racial discrimination prevalent in the United States and would not accept it; (3) saw menial labor as degrading and motivated themselves to improve economically, thereby becoming the top businessmen and leaders of the community; and (4) believed in strong family ties with traditional attitudes and values concerning male and female roles.[3] These sorts of Caribbean attitudes affected the way in which Bob Douglas ran his life and his business.

By 1923, when he organized the Renaissance Five, Douglas was a respected member of the Harlem community who had come to know the game of basketball well. After observing his first game in

1905, he became an instant convert. Three years later he helped organize the Spartan Field Club, an organization that provided amateur sports competition in cricket, track, soccer, and basketball for the black youth of Harlem. Until 1918, when he became the manager and coach, Douglas played on the Spartan Braves basketball team.[4]

With tremendous knowledge of the game and strong business sense, Douglas organized the Renaissance team. He approached the owners of the newly built Renaissance Ballroom with a proposal: trade practice and playing space for use of the name Renaissance. Advertising the ballroom with a basketball team that played every Sunday night drew patrons in for both dancing and entertainment. Unlike other dance clubs in Harlem, the Renaissance Ballroom was owned and managed by blacks, which brought pride to the people of Harlem and served as an example of black achievement in the business world.[5]

Though the Rens were a basketball team, they were also a business. Douglas knew he had to employ tactics that would keep the Rens financially solvent. During their twenty-six-year existence, Douglas kept the Rens in business through such strategies as networking, benefit games, capitalizing on traditional rivalries, contracts with his players, barnstorming, playing many games against white teams, establishing ties between his team and music and dance venues, requiring guarantees and percentages of the profits, creating farm teams, and consistently demonstrating honesty.

By the time Douglas organized the Rens, he had come to know several prominent members of the Harlem community. Two of those people were the Reverend John Johnson of St. Martin's Episcopal Church and Romeo Dougherty, entertainment and sports editor of the *New York Amsterdam News*. West Indian immigrants gravitated toward the Episcopal Church because of the relationship of the West Indies to the Church of England. Douglas looked up to Father Johnson, even though the priest was twenty years younger than the entrepreneur, and the two had a common interest in athletics. Before going into the ministry, Johnson had played basketball at Columbia University. In addition, before and after World War I and during the 1920s, many churches sponsored youth athletic teams, and Father Johnson coached a basketball team, the St.

Cyprian Keypies. Considered a religious man, Douglas stopped by St. Martin's frequently, and the church's dances were always held at the Renaissance Ballroom. In the 1940s, Johnson became the Negro National League president.[6]

Romeo Dougherty was a great supporter of Bob Douglas and his Rens, as is evidenced by headlines and commentary in the *Amsterdam News* leading up to big games and results reported the week after the games. Dougherty noted in February 1925, "No colored team in the country today stands a chance with the crack players under the guidance of the astute Bob Douglas."[7] Christmas and New Year's night games against rival teams, such as the Original Celtics, the SPHA (South Philadelphia Hebrew Association), and the Visitations, attracted capacity crowds at the Renaissance Ballroom and drew tremendous interest in the black community. These games were covered extensively in the *Amsterdam News* and other black newspapers.[8] In March 1930, at the onset of the depression, Dougherty credited Douglas as being a top owner-manager, saying, "By many personal sacrifices Bob has made it possible to keep the game alive with his professional team."[9] Douglas's networking with Dougherty created a basis for free advertising, and the *Amsterdam News* covered the Rens games. Douglas used Dougherty's newspaper to announce his lineup for each season.[10]

According to Dougherty, the Rens had "become an institution in Harlem. The colored fans find in it a vent for their emotions and an outlet for their pride in race."[11] The Rens were a team that Harlem could rally behind. They served as ambassadors for Harlem and for fellow black citizens. Regardless of broader society's edict, if the Rens achieved equality on the court, then there was hope for blacks to achieve equality in other aspects of life. In this way the team made dents in the color line, as it drew both black and white fans at home and on the road. The Rens' first defeat of the Original Celtics was in their fifth matchup, in December 1925. A capacity crowd witnessed the game, while one thousand fans who were turned away at the door waited in a chilly December night for the results. Called the "battle of the gods," the Rens' victory was a symbolic one for blacks. Reflecting on the game, Dougherty stated, "All Negroes have asked is a fair chance, and when given that chance, they have more than made good."[12]

Regardless of whom the Rens played, however, Douglas refused
to allow discriminatory behavior, such as an occasional biased referee, to determine the success of his team. For example, in a game
against the Celtics in Cleveland in 1933, twenty-seven fouls were
called against the Rens while only seven were called against the
Celtics. The Rens won in overtime, 36-35.[13] In addition, white players such as John Wooden, Nat Holman, and Joe Lapchick appreciated the teamwork and play of the Rens.[14]

Today, critics and the general public believe that professional
athletes have an obligation to serve as role models both on and off
the court, which they do not always do. This expectation also held
true for the Rens early in their tenure. Renaissance Five fans were
disappointed when players did not play well or when they misbe-
haved off the court. Bob Douglas cared about his players as if they
were his sons. He stood up for them but disciplined them and even
removed players from the team for not following rules, regardless
of their athletic ability. The *Amsterdam News* endorsed this type of
action. Romeo Dougherty attributed a string of losses in December
1925 to player behavior off the court; evidently, the players spent
late nights in the cabarets after the game. Dougherty warned the
Ren players, via the newspaper, to take their job seriously, because
through basketball they had a rare opportunity to help blacks
achieve in a white world. Dougherty suggested that the Rens follow the example set by their owner-manager.[15] In December 1926,
the Rens lost a close game to the Bronx Professionals. Douglas had
benched Fats Jenkins for not following team rules.[16] George Fiall
was removed from the lineup in February 1928 because he broke
training rules. He returned the next season but lasted only a couple
of weeks because he could not maintain the training rules that
Douglas established.[17] At the end of the 1927–28 season, the *Amsterdam News* reported that the Rens lost fifteen of their games due
to carelessness, lack of conditioning, breaking training rules, or discipline problems. The newspaper reiterated the belief the Rens had
a responsibility to represent the black community and reminded
Douglas to keep this in mind when selecting the team for the
1928–29 season.[18]

In the 1920s, before the Rens began to barnstorm extensively,
and later during World War II, Bob Douglas allowed his Rens to

play for, or "revolve" to, other teams on nights when the Rens were not playing. For example, Rens Hilton Slocum and Harold Mayers played for the Manhattan Elks in March 1924,[19] and George Fiall, Frank Forbes, and Leon Monde represented the Grand Central Red Caps in January 1925.[20] In early 1941 and during the war, Rens players revolved to various teams during the week, including the Washington Bruins/Bears, Harlem Yankees, Philadelphia Toppers, Passaic Crescents, Grumman Long Island Flyers, and Hammerlund All-Stars.[21] Douglas did not require his players to sign contracts during the war because of the uncertainty of who could play, due to job conflicts. The Rens owner appeared to put the players first, but he expected loyalty and allegiance in return, especially when a conflict of interest occurred. When Rens players decided to play for the Washington Bears in the 1943 professional tournament, Douglas was forced to withdraw his Rens team from the competition. After winning the tournament as Washington Bears, several players wanted to return to the Rens for the Worcester Tournament. Douglas turned them down. He felt these players had shown ingratitude, especially since they "learned how to play" under him, and he was embarrassed by the incident.[22] Eight months later, Douglas released Dolly King and Pop Gates from the Rens for refusing to play in the game against the SPHA unless they were paid more. The *People's Voice*, a local Harlem newspaper, backed Douglas's actions, noting that he always had paid King and Gates when crowds were small. Douglas also felt Gates and King had encouraged other players to put the Bears ahead of the Rens when there was a conflict.[23]

Bob Douglas was a respected citizen of Harlem. His experience as an honest owner-manager and promoter kept him in good standing, as did his desire to give back to the community. The Rens played dozens of benefit games during their tenure, both at home and on the road. The first may have been in December 1925, for the New York American Christmas Fund.[24] The Rens played a benefit game against the Celtics in April 1932 for the Boy Scouts of Harlem, to help support the purchase of a thirty-piece brass band. Musician Cab Calloway, a former basketball player and a fan of the game, entertained on that occasion.[25] In March 1934, the Rens helped raise money for the Welfare Fund of the Philadelphia Sporting Writers Association by participating in a six-team basketball

carnival. A week later they played a group of college and profes-
sional all-stars in a effort to boost the Scottsboro Defense Fund.[26]
The Rens played a benefit game in December 1935 against the Jew-
els, with proceeds going toward the American Jewish Congress
Fund. Many Jewish sports stars attended the game, including Jack
Dempsey, Hank Greenberg, and Nat Holman.[27]

In March 1940, Bob Douglas donated the use of the Renaissance Ballroom for a doubleheader benefit for Eddie "Bricktop"
Wright. Wright, a member of the amateur Original Collegians
basketball team, had been convicted of assault in connection with
a fight at the 1939 Penn Relays. Though a white Temple University student received a thirty-day workhouse sentence for his
part in the fight, Wright was sentenced to one to three years in
prison. The doubleheader featured four amateur teams, Alpha Phi
Alpha, Phi Beta Sigma, the Harlem YMCA Seniors, and the Original Collegians, and it gave Douglas an opportunity to scout talented players for the Rens. Wright himself joined the Rens in the
1942–43 season.[28]

After World War II, late March 1947, the Rens defeated the
SPHA in Madison Square Garden in a Basketball Association of
America preliminary game. Douglas had canceled two previous
dates in order to boost attendance for this benefit game for the
African Academy of Arts and Research.[29] All in all, benefit games
drew crowds and also endeared the Rens to Harlem and the African
American community.

Amateur and professional "B" teams provided opportunities for
talented players in the community and also served as a farm system for Douglas and his Rens. Douglas organized the amateur Eastern Colored League in December 1925. Teams such as the Scholas-
tics, Metro Diamonds, Buffaloes, and Majestics played preliminary
games to the Rens games every Sunday night at the ballroom, and
the top team at the end of the season won a "loving cup." This
league lasted for over five years, into the early 1930s.[30] In January
1927, Douglas formed the Harlem Big Five. This team, made up of
former Spartan Braves and Renaissance team members, served as a
B team to the Rens and played home games every Wednesday
night.[31] At the height of the depression in the mid-1930s, Douglas
formed two new amateur teams and a coed club at the Renaissance

Ballroom, in order to bring black youth off the street and redirect their energies. Douglas coached both the Rens Cubs, boys weighing up to 135 pounds, and the Rens Juniors, boys of unlimited weight, in amateur basketball. The Cubs and Juniors played one game each month at the ballroom. Future Ren John Isaacs started playing for the Rens Juniors. The Renaissance Co-Eds club drew over one thousand members.[32]

Organized in fall 1937 by Frank Richardson, an assistant to Bob Douglas, the Harlem Yankees replaced the Harlem Big Five as the B team to the Rens. The Yankees played weekly Sunday-night games at the ballroom while the Rens were on the road and also barnstormed in the northeast. Players such as Hank DeZonie, Sonny Woods, Puggy Bell, Pop Gates, Lou Badger, Benny Garrett, Bricktop Wright, Charlie Isles, Dolly King, and Ed Younger all played for the Yankees and then moved to the Rens. Though the Harlem Yankees disbanded in 1943, they reorganized in the fall of 1946 and were coached by former Ren Eyre Saitch. Again, the Yankees played games at the ballroom while the Rens were on tour.[33]

What caused the Rens to stand out from other teams was their strategy and style of play, a style they may have obtained from the Original Celtics and embellished.[34] Unlike the individualism favored today, the Rens key was teamwork, with no single player dominating. Fast breaks made up of passes from player to player highlighted their play. They established themselves as a serious basketball team with consistent wins over white teams. Rens player Fats Jenkins noted that the success of the team was due to the camaraderie among the players.[35] Because team personnel changed little from year to year, the players came to know one another's styles and moves quite well. Fans were attracted by the endurance of the players on the court, as well as by their overall playing and shooting ability. In the 4 December 1929 *Amsterdam News*, Pappy Ricks, Eyre Saitch, and Fats Jenkins were referred to as the "Triple Threat" for their offense.[36] Other teams attempted to imitate the passing style of the Rens, as in the case of the Rankin Spartans of Pennsylvania in the mid-1930s.[37]

The Rens used a strategy of gaining a large lead in the first half and then either using reserves or displaying their passing ability in a bit of showmanship in the second half, giving up opportunities to score.[38] The game then appeared to be a close contest. Such strategy was good for business. When barnstorming in the midwest and the south, close scores guaranteed future contests with the same team. It was important for the Rens to win, but not by a high score. When playing black college teams in the south and professional teams in the midwest, the Rens usually won their games by exactly ten points.[39]

During an era of legalized segregation, the Rens played both black and white teams, with most of their games against white teams. Douglas realized the value of a black-versus-white game, both for profit and for race relations. Games between a black team and a white team usually drew a much larger and more diverse crowd than games between teams of the same color. Decades-long rivalries developed with white teams such as the Original Celtics, SPHA, and Visitations. Douglas was not afraid to take on the top white teams. Though the SPHAs and Visitations served as major rivals of the Rens, the Rens biggest rival was the Original Celtics. When the Rens defeated the Celtics in 1927, Douglas reportedly received notes of congratulations from all over the country.[40] Games between the Celtics and the Rens were rough, but they drew large crowds through their displays of passing, shooting, and teamwork.[41]

Douglas rarely scheduled games against top black teams, such as Cumberland Posey's Loendi Five of Pittsburgh in the early years or Abe Saperstein's Harlem Globetrotters of Chicago during the 1930s and 1940s. Several attempts were made, usually by sportswriters, to arrange a Rens-Globetrotters game, but the two teams didn't play until the Chicago Professional Tournament in 1939, and they never played a game during the regular season. Organized three years after the Rens in 1927, the Globetrotters were originally a serious team but turned to clowning and showboating in the 1930s. Douglas disliked Saperstein's portrayal of the players as clowns, believing this perpetuated the white stereotype of blacks as subservient and lacking in intelligence. Douglas believed basketball should be played seriously, and he viewed the game as a vehicle for gaining equality with whites.[42]

When serious discussion did take place in 1939 concerning a Rens-Globetrotters match, it came down to financial arrangements, and Douglas and Saperstein could not agree on terms. Saperstein would not agree to give the Rens a $150 guarantee and 40 percent of profits, even though the Rens commanded 50 to 60 percent of profits in many areas.[43] As the two black teams invited to the first world professional tournament in 1939, the Rens and the Globetrotters were placed in the same bracket. This ensured a black-white matchup in the championship round. In the second round, the Rens defeated the Globetrotters, 27-23, and went on to win the tournament.[44] The next year, the Globetrotters defeated the Rens and went on to win the professional tournament.[45] In all, the Rens and the Globetrotters faced each other three times, all at the professional tournament, with the Globetrotters winning two games and the Rens one.

John Isaacs noted that "it was every kid's dream in Harlem to be a Ren."[46] While not every kid became a Ren—John was one of the fortunate few—many made the attempt each year. Bob Douglas ran intensive preseason workouts and tryout exhibition games for prospective players every October. Even during World War II, sixty young men attended tryouts for the team. Douglas kept the lineup to himself a while before announcing it to any newspapers.[47] Though his word and his handshake would have been good enough for most people, he followed the pattern of the Original Celtics in protecting his business through contracts with his players. He also carried an option on his players from year to year; this prevented other teams from raiding his team. Ironically, it was the Celtics that attempted to sign four of the Rens in the fall of 1929.[48] Renaissance players earned $150 to $250 per month during the season, with bonuses of $25 to $50 for defeating the Celtics. At a time when an average laborer earned $100 per month and a teacher $165 per month, this could be equated to a middle-class income. Top players such as Clarence "Fats" Jenkins may have earned up to $2,000 per season. During World War II, however, Douglas could not compete with the Washington Bears financially. The Bears paid $500 for a twenty-three-game series, while the Rens paid $500 for over one hundred games. Though Douglas had written agreements with most of his players, the Bears required no contracts.[49] This, along with wartime job conflicts, forced Douglas to be flexible with his players during the war.

Like any good businessman, Bob Douglas used several strategies to draw fans to games at the Renaissance Ballroom. During
the Rens' first season in 1923–24, admission to the game was
fifty cents and included music and dancing provided by Vernon
Andrades and his orchestra before and after the basketball
game.[50] According to the *Amsterdam News*, by limiting his own
salary and catering to the public, Douglas was able to maintain
the Rens in the mid-1920s while many other professional teams
went out of business.[51] Traditionally, the Rens opened each season with an election-night game against a top white team such as
the SPHA or the Visitations. Douglas recruited known personalities to throw out the ball or speak to the crowd, among them
Tiger Flowers, a light heavyweight boxing champion in 1927; Nat
Holman, a former Original Celtic and the City College of New
York basketball coach in 1943; former Ren Eyre Saitch in 1944
and 1945; and UCLA football star Kenny Washington in 1945.[52]
Radio broadcasts of Rens games began in the fall of 1928, over
New York City station WPCH. Imitating Negro League baseball,
Douglas initiated "Ladies Night" at the Renaissance Ballroom in
February 1932, allowing women to attend for free. He also intro-
duced new bands at the ballroom from time to time to increase
business. Jimmy Lunceford and his orchestra played on opening
night in 1933.[53]

When the depression hit, the Rens did not entirely escape hard
times as a business entity. Crowds at Rens games decreased by 50
percent. Douglas lowered ticket prices, but attendance continued to
drop, despite games with teams such as the Visitations and Original Celtics. As a result, very few home games were scheduled.
Though the team had traveled to the midwest since 1928, they were
forced to barnstorm after 1932 to remain financially solvent. This
was obviously a disappointment to Harlem fans and occasionally
the Rens drew capacity crowds when they returned to Harlem, especially for traditional games at Thanksgiving, Christmas, and
Easter.[54]

Douglas sought markets for his team in Philadelphia, Pittsburgh, and midwestern cities in the early 1930s. For the first time
in January 1933, the Rens toured the south, playing black college
and club teams. Though seating was segregated in the south, white

college coaches attended Rens games and diagrammed the Rens' plays.[55]

The depression also brought changes in the structure of the Rens basketball organization. In January 1933, Douglas became the manager of the Renaissance Ballroom. He no longer traveled with the Rens on the road but instead appointed a road manager, Eric Illidge, and Fats Jenkins became a player-coach. Douglas booked games for the Rens from the ballroom. He demanded a guarantee and a percentage of the proceeds from opposing teams.[56] The Rens traveled by bus and centralized their operation in a large city, commuting to small cities and towns to play games. Initially, the team problems encountered on the road included obtaining halls or gymnasiums to play in and continuing to draw smaller crowds at the games. On the road, the Rens stayed at the homes of private black citizens or at black college dorms. When they returned to Harlem, Douglas greeted them with special dinners and signs outside the ballroom that read, "Welcome Rens."[57] In summer of 1936, Douglas redecorated the Renaissance Ballroom, spending $15,000 for improvements, which included an outdoor thirty-foot neon sign said to "command the avenue."[58]

Though offers were made from as far away as California, Douglas kept the Rens in the eastern half of the country. By the mid-1930s, the Rens were drawing several thousand fans at games against the Indianapolis Kautskys and National Basketball League teams. Literally thousands of fans, black and white, patronized Rens games on the road, and games against the Original Celtics in Washington, D.C., became an annual event in the spring.[59] By the late 1930s, basketball enjoyed big business in the midwest.

As noted earlier, in the 1940s, during World War II, several changes affected the Rens and the business of basketball. Douglas lost players to both retirement and the war effort, yet he continued to market his team. He was admired for maintaining his team regardless of travel problems and a loss of players. Douglas planned for his Rens to play at the ballroom every Sunday night, as well as on holiday nights.[60] Games on Thanksgiving and Christmas night drew the largest crowds, especially when the Rens played the SPHA or the Visitations, because of the holiday, the seasonal visitors to Harlem, and the return of servicemen on furlough.[61]

In the fall of 1941, the Colored Intercollegiate Athletic Association banned college teams from playing professional teams. The Rens no longer barnstormed in the south.[62] Buses were banned as transportation for basketball teams. Nonetheless, basketball continued, as teams traveled by train.[63] The Rens continued to barnstorm the midwest during World War II but chiefly reverted to their pre-depression schedule of Sunday-night games in Harlem.

After the war, integration provided great hope for Bob Douglas and his dream of obtaining league affiliation for his team. When the Basketball Association of America (BAA) organized in the fall of 1946, however, no black teams or black players were included. The BAA wanted to use black teams to draw crowds but would not sign black players or black teams to the league. When the opportunity to play preliminary games for BAA presented itself, Douglas took the bait. He believed his Rens could be admitted to the league if BAA owners saw their basketball talent and ability to draw crowds. Douglas agreed to have his Rens play preliminary games to the BAA games, since he believed that eventually doors would open and the Rens would walk through.[64] When the Rens played the preliminary games, two to three times as many spectators attended. This was not enough, however, either to convince the BAA to change or to give professional black basketball a solid position on its own. Professional black basketball needed a larger facility than the Renaissance Ballroom, one that could hold more spectators. Ned Irish, long known for refusing to contract with black teams to play in Madison Square Garden, continued his racist attitude. Black teams like the Rens were forced to barnstorm to remain in business. This prevented fans in New York City from seeing them. Douglas made plans for his team to play in arenas in Washington, Philadelphia, and Baltimore in the spring of 1948.[65]

Tired of the financial struggle, Douglas put his Rens up for sale after the Chicago professional tournament in May 1948. When no acceptable offers came forth, he leased the team to Eric Illidge, the longtime Rens road manager, for the 1948–49 season, while Douglas himself maintained ownership.[66] Under Illidge, the Rens finally gained entrance into a league, the National Basketball League, in late 1948. But the team's troubles were far from over. Representing the town of Dayton, local white citizens boycotted the all-black team. The Rens finished the NBL season in last place, partly because they took on the losing record of the Detroit Vagabonds, and their NBL contract was revoked in March 1949.[67] Douglas realized he could no longer compete financially with the top white teams, and in May 1949, he leased his Rens to Abe Saperstein for a two-year period. For the next two years the Rens served as the undercard team for the Globetrotters, and there was little news about them. In the fall of 1951, management of the Rens returned to Bob Douglas.[68] Much like the Negro Leagues of baseball, however, with integration, the Rens declined in importance and eventually went out of business.

The legacy left by Bob Douglas remains enormous. Referred to as "the fox of 138th Street" and "the man who put Negro Basketball on the Map" by sportswriters of the time, Douglas's genius as a businessman kept the Rens afloat financially over a twenty-six-year period through times of depression and war. Romeo Dougherty noted of Douglas in 1929, "He is one of the finest and squarest men that ever did business in this community," and the sentiment was echoed nearly a decade later by Chester L. Washington Jr. of the *Pittsburgh Courier*.[69] Washington highlighted Douglas's business savvy, especially his ability to book games and draw crowds in hard times. While over 50 percent of his fellow black citizens in Harlem lacked a job in the 1930s, Douglas found ways to keep his Rens in business and earn a middle-class income. When World War II caused a loss of top players to retirement and the war industry, Douglas maintained the Rens by recruiting young players and allowing his top players to revolve to various teams. Honesty and integrity permeated every transaction Bob Douglas made. His handshake was as good as any contract.

When asked to write a letter supporting the nomination of Bob Douglas for the Naismith Memorial Basketball Hall of Fame in 1969, longtime friend and colleague Nat Holman wrote eloquently, saying:

No man's life has been more dedicated to the game of basketball for more than half a century. . . . His contribution to basketball isn't measurable. The tendency is to look back at the record of achievement, but no applicant, I am sure, has made greater

progress under greater odds. When one considers the exhaust-
ing, back breaking pace his teams had to go through, having been
the target for discrimination in the early days of the sport—his
leadership, his integrity, his intelligence qualifies Bob Douglas
for a place in the Hall of Fame. His greatest reward is written on
the heart of his players. His influence on the black community on
both amateur and professional players will remain long after he
and the rest of us are forgotten and he will not be forgotten for
a long time.[70]

Renaissance basketball player Bill Yancey also wrote on behalf of
his former coach: "First if Bob gave you his word or a handshake it
was better to me than any contract I have ever signed . . . he made
us go first class and he kept basketball alive for a number of years
when it was really on the rocks . . . if any man belongs in the HALL,
that man is Bob Douglas."[71] It took two years, but in 1971, Bob
Douglas was inducted into the Naismith Memorial Basketball Hall
of Fame as a contributor. Though his 1932–33 Renaissance team
achieved Hall status eight years earlier in 1963, Douglas was the
first black individual inducted. The "Father of Black Basketball" had
finally received his just reward, forty-eight years after organizing
a professional basketball team in Harlem, New York.

While much of Douglas's legacy remains, many opportunities
for professional basketball teams, coaches, and owners to build
community have fallen by the wayside. On the court, Douglas
stressed teamwork over individualism. In the 1990s NBA, the reverse holds true. Individualism comes first, and fans and the media
idolize individual players. Douglas knew that giving back to the
community was important for building community support. The
Rens played numerous games during their tenure, with proceeds
from the games donated to charity causes in the community. NBA
teams and owners today make millions of dollars, much more than
the Rens ever made, but there are no games between NBA teams
where a large portion of the profit for the night is given to charita-
ble causes. Although minor basketball leagues, such as the Continental Basketball Association, exist, the loosely developed farm
system that Douglas set up has yet to be attempted by the NBA.
The New York Knicks have no B teams, youth basketball leagues, or

youth programs in New York City; nor do any of the NBA teams. As an owner, Douglas made personal financial sacrifices in order to keep his business thriving, something no NBA owner would do today. Fans and spectators were charged a fair admission for Rens games. When the depression caused a decrease in attendance in Harlem, Douglas sought other venues in which to play but still maintained a connection to the community with games during the holidays. Players earned a middle-class income and learned the value of hard work. Today, in the NBA, the owners and players are constantly battling for more and more money, as witnessed by the 1998–99 lockout. Costs of the game are passed down to the consumer, and only the wealthy can consistently attend NBA games.

Douglas's greatest legacy, that of black ownership in basketball, remains unattained in league play today. When the Rens went out of business, A. S. "Doc" Young, sportswriter for the *Chicago Defender*, felt that the loss of black ownership of the Rens was the greatest tragedy. Like the Negro Baseball Leagues, black basketball lost out when integration stepped in. Today, there are no majority black owners in the NBA. While Bob Douglas would likely approve of the high salaries currently earned by NBA players, he would also believe a lack of progress had been made in black ownership of teams. Perhaps if current and recently retired black players reviewed the history of the Rens and Douglas's example of black ownership, they would discover possibilities of replicating Douglas's efforts today in the professional game. Then, Douglas's dream of total equality on the basketball court would be attained.

NOTES

1. Bruce Newman, "Yesterday," *Sports Illustrated*, October 22, 1979, p. 101.

2. James Weldon Johnson, *Black Manhattan* (New York: Alfred A. Knopf, 1930), pp. 152–153.

3. Gilbert Osofsky, *Harlem: The Making of a Ghetto* (New York: Harper & Row, 1963), pp. 132–134, 137.

4. *New York Amsterdam News*, 12 June 1948, p. 26.

5. Ibid.; and *Pittsburgh Courier*, 5 July 1930, sec. 2, p. 6.

6. David Johnson, interview with Susan Rayl, New York, 5 July 1994.

7. *New York Amsterdam News*, 25 February 1925, p. 4.

8. See, for example, *New York Amsterdam News*, 22 December 1926, p. 11; 29 December 1926, p. 12; 5 January 1927, pp. 12–13.

9. *New York Amsterdam News*, 5 March 1930, p. 12.

10. See *New York Amsterdam News*, 14 September 1927, p. 10; and September and October issues generally in the 1920s and 1930s.

11. *New York Amsterdam News*, 10 February 1926, p. 6.

12. *New York Amsterdam News*, 23 December 1925, p. 6.

13. *New York Amsterdam News*, 15 March 1933, p. 9.

14. John Wooden, letter to Susan Rayl, 27 September 1994; Richard Lapchick, phone interview with Susan Rayl, 10 January 1996.

15. *New York Amsterdam News*, 9 December 1925, p. 7.

16. *New York Amsterdam News*, 10 November 1926, p. 12.

17. *Pittsburgh Courier*, 11 February 1928, sec. 2,, p. 4; *Interstate Tattler*, 14 December 1928, p. 12.

18. *New York Amsterdam News*, 18 April 1928, p. 19.

19. *Pittsburgh Courier*, 29 March 1924, p. 6.

20. *Pittsburgh Courier*, 10 January 1925, p. 7; 31 January 1925, p. 7.

21. *New York Amsterdam News*, 11 January 1941, p. 15; 1 February 1941, p. 14; 8 February 1941, p. 19; 15 February 1941, p. 18; 3 February 1945, p. 8A; *Pittsburgh Courier*, 1 February 1941, p. 17; *The Afro-American*, 22 February 1941, p. 20.

22. *Pittsburgh Courier*, 10 April 1943, p. 19.

23. *The Afro-American*, 18 December 1943, p. 23; *New York Amsterdam News*, 11 December 1943, p. 5B; *People's Voice*, 11 December 1943, p. 32.

24. *New York Amsterdam News*, 16 December 1925, pp. 6–7.

25. *New York Age*, 23 April 1932, p. 6; 7 May 1932, p. 6.

26. *Pittsburgh Courier*, 17 March 1934, sec. 2, p. 4; *New York Amsterdam News*, 24 March 1934, p. 10.

27. *New York Times*, 24 December 1935, p. 19.

28. *New York Amsterdam News*, 2 March 1940, pp. 1, 7; 23 March 1940, p. 18; 30 March 1940, p. 14.

29. *The People's Voice*, 1 March 1947, p. 29; 15 March 1947, p. 28; 22 March 1947, p. 28.

30. *New York Amsterdam News*, 23 December 1925, p. 6; 30 December 1925, p. 6; 26 March 1930, p. 12; 15 October 1930, p. 17.

31. *New York Amsterdam News*, 5 January 1927, pp. 12–13; *Pittsburgh Courier*, 5 February 1927, sec. 2, p. 6.

32. *New York Amsterdam News*, 19 January 1935, p. 11; 2 February 1935, p. 11; 9 February 1935, p. 1.

33. *New York Amsterdam News*, 27 November 1937, p. 17; 8 January 1938, pp. 14–15; 19 March 1938, p. 17; 15 February 1941, p. 18; 22 November 1947, p. 3; 10 January 1948, p. 10.

34. See Richard Lapchick, *Five Minutes to Midnight: Race and Sport in the 1990s* (New York: Madison Books, 1991).

35. *Pittsburgh Courier*, 11 January 1936, sec. 2, p. 4.

36. *New York Amsterdam News*, 4 December 1929, p. 14; *Pittsburgh Courier*, 18 January 1930, p. 15.

37. *Pittsburgh Courier*, 10 March 1934, sec. 2, p. 5.

38. See, for example, *New York Amsterdam News*, 27 January 1926, p. 6; *Pittsburgh Courier*, 8 January 1938, sec. 2, p. 16.

39. John Isaacs, interview with Susan Rayl, New York, 14 May 1994.

40. *New York Amsterdam News*, 30 November 1927, p. 8; *Chicago Defender*, 3 December 1927, part 1, p. 12; *Pittsburgh Courier*, 3 December 1927, sec. 2, p. 6.

41. See, for example, *New York Amsterdam News*, 1 December 1934, p. 11; *Chicago Defender*, 6 February 1937, p. 13; 13 February 1937, p. 15.

42. *Chicago Defender*, 22 February 1936, p. 14; *Pittsburgh Courier*, 7 January 1939, sec. 2, p. 17; 21 January 1939, sec. 2, p. 17; *New York Amsterdam News*, 27 March 1948, p. 26; James Douglas, telephone interview with Susan Rayl, 26 June 1994.

43. *Pittsburgh Courier*, 18 March 1939, sec. 2, p. 16; *Chicago Defender*, 18 March 1939, p. 9.

44. *Sheboygan Press*, 27 March 1939, p. 16; 28 March 1939, p. 12.

45. *Oshkosh Daily Northwestern*, 21 March 1940, p. 23.

46. Isaacs, interview with Rayl, 14 May 1994.

47. *New York Amsterdam News*, 5 October 1927, p. 8; 12 October 1927, p. 10; 8 October 1930, p. 17; 15 October 1930, p. 17; 14 October 1944, p. 6B.

48. *New York Amsterdam News*, 11 September 1929, p. 15; 23 October 1929, p. 12.

49. *Pittsburgh Courier*, 18 January 1930, sec. 2, p. 15; *The Afro-American*, 18 April 1942, p. 23; John Isaacs, interviews with Susan Rayl, 14 May 1994 and 17 August 1995.

50. *New York Age*, 29 December 1923, p. 6.

51. *New York Amsterdam News*, 2 September 1925, p. 5.

52. *New York Amsterdam News*, 19 October 1927, p. 9; 18 December 1943, p. 5B; 5 February 1944, p. 5B; 3 March 1945, p. 12A; 4 January 1947, p. 17.

53. *New York Amsterdam News,* 17 October 1928, p. 8; 24 February 1932, p. 12; 25 October 1933, p. 8.

54. *New York Age,* 10 December 1932, p. 6; Robert L. Douglas, letter to Frank O'Connell, 23 November 1932, Robert L. Douglas file, Naismith Memorial Basketball Hall of Fame, Springfield, Massachusetts.

55. *Pittsburgh Courier,* 24 January 1931, sec. 2, p. 5; 21 November 1931, sec. 1, p. 7; 24 December 1932, sec. 2, p. 4; Isaacs, interview with Rayl, 14 May 1994. 56.

56. *Pittsburgh Courier,* 14 January 1933, sec. 2, p. 5.

57. *Pittsburgh Courier,* 4 February 1933, sec. 2, p. 4; Isaacs, interview with Rayl, 14 May 1994.

58. *Pittsburgh Courier,* 19 September 1936, sec. 2, p. 6

59. *New York Amsterdam News,* 14 February 1934, p. 7; 24 January 1934, p. 8.

60. *New York Amsterdam News,* 14 October 1944, p. 6B.

61. *People's Voice,* 26 December 1942, p. 37; 5 January 1946, p. 34; *New York Amsterdam News,* 26 December 1942, p. 14.

62. *Pittsburgh Courier,* 13 December 1941, sec. 2, p. 17.

63. *People's Voice,* 13 March 1943, p. 29.

64. *New York Amsterdam News,* 21 December 1946, p. 12; *People's Voice,* 15 February 1947, p. 28; *Pittsburgh Courier,* 15 February 1947, sec. 2, p. 16.

65. *New York Amsterdam News,* 6 March 1948, p. 26; 13 March 1948, p. 27.

66. *Pittsburgh Courier,* 1 May 1948, sec. 2, p. 11; *New York Amsterdam News,* 23 October 1948, p. 29.

67. *Dayton Journal,* 18 December 1948, p. 19; *Oshkosh Daily Northwestern,* 1 April 1949, p. 11; *Chicago Defender,* 28 May 1949, p. 15.

68. *N.Y. Rens vs. Eastern College All-Stars Program,* 4 November 1952, p. 4, Johnny Walker file, The Schomburg Center for Research in Black Culture, Harlem, New York.

69. *New York Amsterdam News,* 23 October 1929, p. 15; *Pittsburgh Courier,* 7 January 1939, sec. 2, p. 17.

70. Nat Holman, letter to the Hall of Fame Honors Committee, 25 June 1969, Robert L. Douglas file, Naismith Memorial Basketball Hall of Fame, Springfield, Massachusetts.

71. Bill Yancey, letter to Lee Williams, 25 June 1969, Robert L. Douglas file, Naismith Memorial Basketball Hall of Fame, Springfield, Massachusetts.

9

incivility and basketball

EARL SMITH

The institutional arrangements required for the freedom of expression of beliefs and the representation of interests and ideals—both of which can be divisive—can function effectively in society if those who use them for their own particularistic ends are at the same time restrained by an admixture of civility.

—Professor Edward Shils, "Observations on Some Tribulations of Civility" (1997)[1]

It has been said that the problem with many modern athletes is that they take themselves seriously and their sport lightly.

—George F. Will, Men at Work[2]

Introduction

The white world—specifically the white community in the United States—finds it difficult to accept blacks as being best in anything, except basketball and popular music.

—Herb Snitzer, "The Realities of Cultural Change"[3]

The American people, this amorphous grouping of individuals who encompass all characteristics, yet none exclusively, of race, class, and gender, have asked a very interesting question. It is, I believe, of enormous importance. The question is this: What social arrangements best suit African American males? This question has been especially persistent since the days of the "Great Society" social-programming experiments.[4] The answer to this befuddling question is this: None. Well, none other than that with which Herb Snitzer so eloquently presents us—the freedom to pursue basketball.[5]

Many believe that it is there, on any basketball court, indoors or out, that these men can do whatever they like. The same Americans still believe that off the court the African American basketball players do not know how to behave, and they ultimately despise them. Professor Elijah Anderson captures this sentiment when he says, "An overwhelming number of young black males . . . are committed to civility and law-abiding behavior. They often have a hard time convincing others of this, however, because of the stigma attached to their skin color, age, gender, appearance, and general style of self-presentation."[6] It is, after all, so much about the style of self-presentation. The ability to survive in a multicultural world is a relentless, day-to-day task. It is a world in which race/ethnicity and gender still matter. That world, too, encompasses the institution of sports, especially in American society.[7]

It was after Pee-Wee League basketball practice, in the comfort of their home, that a young boy sat on his father's lap in front of the color television set, watching the game highlight clips on ESPN cable sports channel. Most of the clips were of men running, shooting, or throwing a basketball. The clip that kept them both riveted to the set was an argument between a player and the referee. The player clearly was not getting his way and had already lost his temper. In slow motion, the player head-butted the referee. The scene was played over and over on the instant replay sequence. The boy's father explained to the child that the player was being bad and was thrown out of the game for his behavior, but the boy had seen it. One of the most popular basketball players, a professional, got mad at the referee and, in a fit of anger, head-butted him. This was not an isolated incident.[8]

Bad behavior has always had a part in collegiate and professional sports. A generation ago, I was sitting in the stands at Dodger Stadium the day Juan Marichal clubbed John Roseboro with his bat. A generation before that, Ty Cobb was notorious for spiking opposing players and beating up heckling fans. It is only recently, though, that this news of Cobb's uncivil behavior has become widely known. In this revelation, we also learn that Cobb was a racist.[9]

But a line has been crossed. Bad sportsmanship and uncivil behavior are now a big part of the story of commercial sports. It is the same line crossing that worries a club of neoconservative social thinkers, whose members include William Bennett, Irving Kristol, Robert Bellah, Shelby Steele, and James Q. Wilson. They are concerned that a shared American Dream is disappearing, and along with it the power to guide relations among us.

The diagnosis can be accurately simplified: too much individualism. It is a clarion call that was sounded at least as long ago as Alexis de Tocqueville's early-nineteenth-century work *Democracy in America.*[10] Individualism means that people think of themselves in isolation from others and "imagine that their whole destiny is in their own hands"—with the implication that it is up to others to manage their own destinies. Tocqueville worried that it made us a restless people, never satisfied with what we have, always thinking about the good things we do not yet have. On those occasions when individual yearnings must be subjugated to larger public purposes, Tocqueville believed the limits could come from religion and republican government.

But there is more to maintaining a society than religion and republican institutions. Robert Putnam has applied the ideas from his decades-long study of Italian civic institutions[11] to the American situation in his impressive article "Bowling Alone."[12] The starting point of the argument is that Americans are bowling more than ever, but they are doing it alone; sometimes with family and friends, but not in wider groups such as organized clubs and leagues. As he found in his Italian study, the effectiveness of political institutions, the amount of social trust, and the prevalence of other-regarding behavior are functions of the amount and quality of civic participation by citizens. Membership in clubs and associations, in brief, makes people better neighbors and makes collective institutions work better. Putnam considers the private and individualistic trends, illustrated by the eye-catching title "Bowling Alone," to be *a loss of social capital.*[13]

In his book *Making Democracy Work: Civic Traditions in Modern Italy,* Putnam pursued several hypotheses for the loss of civic engagement. Among the independent variables he tested were (1) the notable 1970s increase in the proportion of women in the workplace, (2) an increase in the number of hours Americans work each week, and (3) the increasing amount of time

Americans spend on a couch that is parked in front of a television set. By far, the strongest explanation seems to lie in the habit of watching television.

Though some could consider this attitude cliché, it is important to note that a line has been crossed in regard to the social behavior of both professional and collegiate players.[14] This chapter is an analysis of civility, or the lack thereof, among athletes at the intercollegiate and professional levels of the team sport of basketball.[15] The underpinning for the essay is the 1990s sentiment that social behavior in American society has gone awry, that is, the outwardly manifested behavior of the American people is no longer held in check by the reciprocal nature[16] of the normative structure of the American value system.[17] Something, surely, has changed, and much of this change can be traced to the impact that television has over daily lives, for both children and adults. Hence, I begin with television.

The Impact of Television on Civil Society

The societal impact of TV on the behavior of Americans is central to the understanding of the social behavior of collegiate and professional basketball players. Concern is justifiably warranted. Who, for example, can ignore the bizarre behavior of the performers in World Championship Wrestling, televised almost nightly and regularly appearing at local stadiums? Athletes—real and imaginary—are now seen by more people and more often than ever before, solely because of the new, advanced technologies that are now part of the American home. The most obvious advancement is television. Putnam put it thus:

> There is reason to believe that deep-seated technological trends are radically "privatizing" or "individualizing" our use of leisure time and thus disrupting many opportunities for social-capital formation. The most obvious and probably the most powerful instrument of this revolution is television. Time-budget studies in the 1960s showed that the growth in time spent watching tel-

evision dwarfed all other changes in the way Americans passed their days and nights. Television has made our communities (or, rather, what we experience as our communities) wider and shallower. In the language of economics, electronic technology enables individual tastes to be satisfied more fully, but at the cost of the positive social externalities associated with more primitive forms of entertainment.[18]

Furthermore, according to research findings by Judith Van Evra,[19] especially applied to the generation of Americans known to us as baby boomers, television not only is an available instrument of entertainment but has become paramount as an instrument of socialization. Television is undoubtedly the greatest disseminator of information as we head toward the twenty-first century. It has an ability to mold and shape public opinion unparalleled in the history of this nation. And, since some 98 percent of all American households have at least one television set, it can be deduced that TV has had a big impact on the American value construct.[20] This deduction is consistent with survey data, collected since 1968, on the impact that TV has on American society.[21]

An astute professional observer of the American sporting scene today may conclude that it is no wonder that so much of the uncivil behavior we are witnessing comes at this point in time, that is, at the height of mass consumption of television programming, and especially negative programming, which has engulfed our society. And while not all uncivil behavior can be fairly blamed on TV, a good portion of it comes from the socialization effect TV has on so large a part of the American population. This is especially true of lower-class youth and members of underrepresented minority groups, many of whom go on to play collegiate and professional basketball.[22]

As the enormous revenues generated from television sports programming[23] seem to keep growing, so do the frequency and acrimony of the contractual negotiations between athletes and their teams. The money and freedom to pursue options in basketball today are exponentially greater than in the 1960s when professional basketball players like Connie Hawkins (Phoenix Suns) had no rights that NBA coaches and owners had to respect.

Hawkins, coming into the sport from a troubled past and implicated in several college basketball scandals, was essentially banned from playing in the newly rising and commercially oriented NBA. Hawkins was placed in a position where he had to choose either to stay with the Suns (and play less) or to jump back to the American Basketball Association (ABA), where promises of more money and playing time tempted him to break his contract and effectively end his career, playing in a small market.[24] The choices players are making today are essentially the same as those Hawkins faced. It is only the conditions that have changed.

Give Me the Money

The next point in my understanding of uncivil behavior in American sports—but not the least important—involves the escalating levels of money being awarded to all professional athletes, not just the superstars. Even benchwarmers have multimillion-dollar contracts, with incentives. Yet those who benefit the most from increased dollars for playing sports are the families of the athletes, the coaches, and, of course, the players' agents.[25] The overall worth of athletic talent is now measured by individual athletes' appeal outside the games they play, rather than by the efficiency of their game as it is played on the court or field.[26]

In the popular culture, this situation is best expressed in the 1996 movie *Jerry Maguire*.[27] The resounding line in the film comes from Cuba Gooding Jr.—"Show me the money!" The real portrait, though, of the amounts of money being tossed around emerges when one looks at the most recently available data on salaries for the most highly paid NBA players.

What is not shown in Table 1 is that even rookies right out of college—most playing less than the full four years of what was once customary for college basketball players—earn a big paycheck. The average salary for the first five picks, for a three-year contract, is $7.65 million. In this august group was high school star Kobe Bryant, who commanded $3.5 million from the Los Angeles Lakers.[28]

Table 1. National Basketball Association Most Highly
Paid Players, 1997 Season

Player	Team	Salary (in millions)
Michael Jordan	Chicago	$33.14
Patrick Ewing	New York	$20.5
Horace Grant	Orlando	$14.28
Shaquille O'Neal	Los Angeles	$12.85
David Robinson	San Antonio	$12.39
Alonzo Mourning	Miami	$11.25
Juwan Howard	Washington	$11.25
Gary Payton	Seattle	$10.51
Dikembe Mutombo	Atlanta	$9.81

SOURCE: *USA Today,* June 6, 1998.

Table 2. Most Highly Paid Athletes, 1997–1998

Player	Team	Sport	Contract (in millions)	Years
Kevin Garnett	Minnesota Timberwolves	Basketball	$126	6
Shaquille O'Neal	Los Angeles Lakers	Basketball	$120	7
Alonzo Mourning	Miami Heat	Basketball	$112	7
Shawn Kemp	Cleveland Cavaliers	Basketball	$107	7
Kevin Brown	Los Angeles Dodgers	Baseball	$105	7
Juwan Howard	Washington Wizards	Basketball	$100.8	7
Terrell Davis	Denver Broncos	Football	$56.1	9

SOURCE: ESPN Network (http://espnnet.sportszone.com), Dec. 17, 1998.

Table 2 shows the most recent data on the most highly paid athletes in American sports in general.

Notice that the baseball and football players lag far behind the multiyear salaries of NBA players. Many a commentator has come to the conclusion that this escalating money was at the heart of the 1998 NBA lockout, a conclusion that seems to be accurate.[29]

Though, logically, highly paid athletes should no more be scrutinized than highly paid celebrities in other professions, such intense scrutiny is invited by both the expectations that come with the privileged status of being an athlete and the outward aberrant behavior of so many of the athletes, particularly in basketball.[30] I do not mean that other celebrities do not commit indiscretions and even violent crimes (both in and out of sports), only that male basketball players seem to lead the way in this arena.

Uncivil Behavior in Sports

One reason this seems true is that sports[31] remain a bastion of
male privilege. In essence, it is a male reservation. The British
sports sociologist Eric Dunning[32] notes that sports are sites for
the inculcation, expression, and perpetuation of masculine habits,
identities, behaviors, and ideals. As such, male athletes harbor
and later develop a specific male psyche geared toward patriarchal supremacy over women. This carryover from earlier days
into our time may be viewed with surprise as we close out the
twentieth century.[33]

The exercise of patriarchal supremacy is particularly evident
in places frequented mostly by males—that is, taverns, gambling
dens, the political meeting hall, and sports venues. To be sure, the
sports hijinks occur in the male bastions of sports: semi-pro and
professional ice hockey, professional football (as we define it in
America and as it is played overseas, as soccer), professional
baseball, the spectacle of professional wrestling, and the National Basketball Association are places where male prowess is on
display.

To be sure, women are not permitted into the ring or onto their
male counterparts' playing fields. Where they are merely decorous
bangles or sexual complements to the measured excellence of muscled men practicing their trades, women are welcome as singers of
the national anthem, cheerleaders (or what Bissinger calls Pep-
pettes),[34] ball girls, even trainers—until the actual play gets underway. They then move aside, for these contests take place in a man's
world.

The bonds between men and women are completely dissolved
by the solvents of television and money in a sporting context.
Men and women become unable, even to co-exist in a civil way.
Research shows that when men are watching or participating in
brutal sporting events, for example, boxing matches or football
on Super Bowl Sunday, and the "home team" or the favorite
gladiator loses, women, too, are losers. They are losers to batter-
ing and other forms of domestic violence. In her book *The
Stronger Women Get, the More Men Love Football*, Mariah Burton Nelson, former Stanford University basketball star, has

shown a strong correlation between men's watching aggressive sports on television (e.g., boxing matches and the Super Bowl) and violence against women in their lives. She notes:

> During the game, reports of domestic violence were lower than usual, but the number of calls soared in the first four or five hours after Denver lost the game. . . . Women are beaten daily, but Super Bowl Sunday seems particularly dangerous for American women. Though some battered women's shelters report no correlation between football and wife beating, shelters in Philadelphia, Los Angeles, and Marin County, California, have reported receiving more calls from distraught, bruised, and threatened women that day than on any other day of the year.

This has been underscored in a venue apart from the playing fields: A centerpiece of the O. J. Simpson trial was the fact that he had battered his former wife Nicole Simpson on Super Bowl Sunday in 1988.[35] Furthermore, in empirical research done by sociologist David Phillips, we have direct evidence that violent acts rise after aggressive sporting events. In his research, Phillips demonstrates that aggressive male behavior (in his example, homicide) increases within a span of two to five days after boxing matches take place.[36]

Bad Sports

Sportsmanship is the mantra on which the American Sports Creed turns.[37] The dominant belief in our society is in the positive effect that sports has on our individual lives and on the nation. Sports columnist Robert Lipsyte of the *New York Times* put it best when he said:

> For the past one hundred years most Americans have believed that playing and watching competitive games are not only healthful activities, but represent a positive force on our national psyche. In sports, they believe children will learn courage and

self-control, old people will find blissful nostalgia, and families will discover new ways to communicate among themselves. Rich and poor, black and white, educated and unskilled, we will all find a unifying language. The melting pot may be a myth, but we will all come together in the ballpark.[38]

Yet the many examples of "bad sportsmanship" cause us to wonder about what scholars and journalists alike have overlooked. We know today, for example, that in the past the "marriage" between sportswriters and teams and or between sportswriters and players allowed for bad deeds, even violent crimes by athletes to go unreported. Today, these deeds are commonplace, widely reported but rarely examined.

Heretofore, these accounts have been discussed only in a limited number of sports journals and newspaper articles. In this chapter, even with a generous allowance of space, it is impossible to be exhaustive or definitive with an analysis of incidents of uncivil behavior in sports. In conducting my research, I mined many and varied accounts of such behavior. The sources included but were not limited to research articles, newspaper stories, and Web pages on the Internet.

The list I came up with runs long and ranges from Marge Schott to Denny McClain, from Michael Irvin to George Steinbrenner, from Jimmy Piersall to Doc Gooden, from Sandy Alomar Jr. to Wilfredo Cordero, from Barry Switzer and Mike Tyson to Dennis Rodman and Latrell Sprewell. Even longtime NBC sports announcer Marv Albert (who grosses over $2 million per year in base salary alone) has been indicted and convicted by a Virginia grand jury for biting, raping, and sodimizing a former girlfriend. Albert makes the "uncivil behavior in sports list" not only because he pleaded guilty but, mainly, because he told a national TV audience that he was innocent of all charges (*USA Today*, September 2, 1997). He lied.

One conclusion of this research is that, across the sports landscape, television exposure and big money contracts have changed the way in which both players and fans behave, even how they act toward one another.[39] The case is no longer the case as it was in 1986, when CBS sports director William MacPhail announced that "sport is a bad investment ... we're doing great if we break even."[40] Today, sports do much better than just break even; sports have developed into multibillion-dollar-a-year businesses, and growth continues. This is especially true for the new all sports television networks; some stations, such as ESPN and the Fox network, are running sporting events twenty-four hours every day.[41]

Several illustrations here help to establish my point that athletes at the college/university level (as well as the institutions themselves, in their treatment of student-athletes) and professional level have turned to a behavior mode that is unacceptable. Several recent and very public examples demonstrate what, exactly, "bad sports" has come to represent in American society. The examples are known to both the sporting community and the general public because of the high profiles provided by the mass media. The first "case" itself demonstrates how bad all of this has become.

Case One: Dennis Rodman

On June 12, 1997, National Basketball Association commissioner David Stern levied a punitive fine against Chicago Bulls superstar forward Dennis Rodman. The monetary fine, totaling some $1 million, was said at the time to be the largest fine in sports history.[42] The path that led to this massive fine was a long one. Rodman had assumed a "bad boy" persona while a member of the Detroit Pistons, and his visibility became even greater when he joined the world champion Chicago Bulls. His behavior both on and off the court fueled the wrath of the commissioner and the Chicago Bulls team owners, players, and fans.

Rodman had already crossed the uncivil behavior line on several occasions: making gestures to Utah Jazz fans, calling them names, speaking in an unflattering way about the Mormon religion; headbutting referees; and throwing temper tantrums on and off the basketball court. But when Rodman kicked an on-court cameraman in the groin, Stern exploded. This act set off the NBA credibility alarm. The NBA knew it had to do something in this instance that would surpass all the other fines levied against Rodman. The fan fallout over the incident was immense, and so the NBA levied the blockbuster fine.

Case Two: Kermit Washington

It was a balmy night outside; inside the Forum, the Los Angeles Lakers were getting set to play the Houston Rockets. It is hard to remember if the rest of the game was of any consequence, for the events in the third quarter overshadow all else and are etched in professional basketball history.

Laker forward Kermit Washington was struggling for a loose ball while running upcourt when Houston player Kevin Kunnert got into a shoving match with Washington. Looking back, it seems that Kunnert threw two punches at Washington and "things happened." Washington (six feet eight inches and 230 pounds), seeing from the corner of his eye a Houston Rocket player heading in his direction, turned and landed a right cross to the jaw of Houston player Rudy Tomjanovich. The rest is history. NBA commissioner Larry O'Brien suspended Washington for sixty days (at a cost of $50,000) and fined him an unprecedented amount of money for the time, $10,000.

Tomjanovich, a forward for the Rockets, was sent to the hospital for fifteen days with a broken jaw, fractured skull, broken nose, cracked eye socket—and a ruined career. Lisa Olson, writing for the *New York Daily News*, said:

> Tomjanovich was felled in one punch, his skull and cheekbone fractured, his jaw and nose sinking back into his head like bloody pulps. [Kareem] Abdul-Jabbar said it sounded like a watermelon being dropped on cement.[43]

While it may be hard to corroborate that Kermit Washington's right against the jaw of Rudy Tomjanovich forever changed the game in the NBA, it came at a time when the NBA was beginning to have trouble with its players and the image of the game.

Case Three: Latrell Sprewell

The case of Latrell Sprewell makes it abundantly clear that the issues of power, money, and control are causing some major sportsmanship problems for the NBA.

Many athletes become frustrated with their coaches. Coaches make you work hard. They do things that pique athletes. No coach can be as irritating as Indiana's Bobby Knight, yet he survives: even requests made of former Indiana basketball players such as Quinn Buckner, Isiah Thomas, and Steve Alford to talk about the rules the autocratic Knight invokes and the legendary games he plays with his players' minds do not get a response.[44] Yet, while most college and professional athletes, like those coached by Knight, do nothing about their frustrations with their coaches, Latrell Sprewell is different.

Golden State Warrior Latrell Sprewell crossed the bad-sport line and may still be paying the price. In a fit of anger (how else to describe it?) during a practice session on December 1, 1997, Sprewell threatened and choked his coach, P. J. Carlesimo. Other players witnessed the act. Why did he do it? Carlesimo was "in his face." Phil Taylor of *Sports Illustrated* put it thus: "When he [Sprewell] assaulted and threatened to kill his coach, P. J. Carlesimo, . . . he committed one of the most outrageous acts on the court or field of play that American professional sports in the modern era has known, and that act will surely follow him for the rest of his life."[45]

Almost anywhere except in the NBA, says *New York Times* columnist Ira Berkow, such an act would have meant immediate dismissal.[46] Sprewell initially was stripped of his four-year $32 million contract (with a loss also of all endorsement revenues, estimated at $500,000 with Converse) for his behavior. Furthermore, Commissioner David Stern suspended Sprewell for a year from the NBA. But on March 3, 1998, Sprewell was reinstated to the Warriors after lodging a grievance against the team and the league that was favorably heard by arbitrator John Feerick, dean of the Fordham University Law School.[47]

To be sure, Sprewell's behavior has become the standard by which bad sports will be measured.

Case Four: Educational Malpractice

The fourth and final case addresses the issue of institutions of higher learning that fail to provide for the proper education of their student-athletes. Student-athletes[48] are a valuable form of social capital[49] in institutions of higher learning. They provide a type of entertainment that allows these institutions to compete in athletic contests that have increasingly become commercialized.[50] The contested nature of the status of student-athletes (Are they students? Are they athletes?) has always been and remains problematic.[51] This conflicted status even caught the attention of the immortal coach from Alabama, Paul "Bear" Bryant, who once said:

> I used to go along with the idea that [athletes] on scholarship were "student-athletes," which is what the NCAA calls them. Meaning a student first, an athlete second. We were kidding ourselves, trying to make it more palatable to the academicians. We don't have to say that and we shouldn't. At the level we play, the boy is really an athlete first and a student second.[52]

Although my proposition is broad, my claim is for a case of educational malpractice and/or "systematic educational malfeasance" on the part of Division I basketball programs.[53] The increased commercialization of college sports has had a negative effect on student-athletes.[54] And while the NCAA continues to push the line of student-athletes being amateurs, this is simply not true.

This especially can be seen with regard to African American basketball players.[55] The data available show that many, if not most, of these athletes stake their whole future on intercollegiate basketball, as being the ticket out of surroundings of despair. This takes us to the flip side of participation in college basketball: The student-athlete very often does not receive, in return for his athletic performances, the quality education that is promised.

Each year we learn that several institutions have failed to graduate any of their male basketball players, and that those institutions that did graduate their athletes for the most part fell behind both the institution's own average for graduation and the national average for graduation. In headlines from the most recent data

Table 3. Institutions with High and Low Graduate Rates—1998

Institution	Graduated	%	Grad Rate for Overall Student Body
Xavier	30/30	100	67%
Howard	24/24	100	54%
N. C. Asheville	6/6	100	45%
Duke	69/71	97	92%
Manhattan	25/26	96	73%
Lehigh	73/78	94	81%
San Francisco	12/13	92	61%
Georgetown	33/36	92	89%
William & Mary	47/52	90	89%
Dayton	16/18	89	71%
Texas-El Paso	15/54	28	22%
New Orleans	12/45	27	24%
Alabama State	5/19	26	18%
Jackson State	8/34	24	29%
Bethune-Cookman	3/13	23	38%
Texas Southern	10/44	23	8%
Fullerton State	10/55	18	40%
Miss. Valley State	7/43	16	25%
Maryland Eastern Shore	3/60	5	32%

SOURCE: Adapted from USA Today, November 9, 1998 (article by Steve Wieberg).

available, we see the following: "In men's basketball, a sport that annually scores poorly, the [graduation] rates dipped to a seven-year low of 41 percent."[56] For African American men, the new rate is 37 percent, down two percentage points from 1997. What is instructive from these new data is how poor institutional behavior is when it comes to carrying out the mandated missions for colleges and universities. We learned that for the period from 1991 to 1997—thus giving the scholarship basketball players approximately six years to graduate—ten institutions on the list graduated their basketball players at rates below 30 percent.

Data from Table 3 reveal that some institutions do better than others, and that one of the unanticipated consequences of basketball competition at the Division I level is that many of the smaller schools and historically black institutions (HBIs) fare very poorly. All this, of course, is the price paid for high-level competition. (And, so that I am not misunderstood, graduation rates are at the far end of the continuum: they represent, at best, the "tip of the iceberg" of both educational malpractice and educational malfeasance.)[57]

The portrait that Professor Timothy Davis paints of student-athlete basketball player Terrell Jackson is not unfamiliar to me.[58] For twelve years I was a professor at Washington State University in Pullman, Washington. Much of the time my introductory sociology classes and African American Studies classes (as well as my upper-division Sociology of Sport course) were filled with student-athletes from baseball, football, male and female gymnastics, women's and men's basketball. Most, if not all, of the problematic cases that I remember over this long period of time were male basketball players—both African American and white. Many were not academically eligible for college, and most whom I had in class were admitted to the institution by way of the Academic Development Program (ADP).

Other Cases: A Brief Review of Impacts

In the early 1990s, in Lakewood, California—a town where the "Youth Sports Hall of Fame is not at the high school and not at City Hall but in the McDonald's at the corner of Woodruff and Del Amo"[59]—adolescent athletes from a street sex gang that goes by the name of Spur Posse made use of their athletic popularity in high school to terrorize their local neighborhoods. These scholastic athletes raped, pillaged, and inflicted fear on Lakewood residents, fellow students, and almost everyone who lived in the town. The saddest part of their behavior is that they got away with the terrorizing.[60]

The crowning youth-related bad-sport incident, though, received national and even international media attention and is the subject of a new book. The incident, which will forever label the young lady involved, took place in a white middle-class suburb located in Glen Ridge, New Jersey on March 1, 1989. There, four young athletes—Kyle Scherzer, Bryant Grober, Kevin Scherzer, and Chris Archer—all white males, gang-raped with a baseball-bat handle a young white female who is said to have an IQ in the neighborhood of 76. These "boys" intentionally degraded the girl and received notoriety for their debasing behavior.[61]

One final display of incidents related to my subject: On Saturday, June 28, 1997, in a much anticipated and touted World Boxing Association heavyweight title fight, "Iron" Mike Tyson twice bit the ear of Heavyweight Champion of the World Evander Holyfield. This behavior was an all-time low, even for professional boxing, and an international audience saw it on pay-per-view television.[62]

As much as we have come to expect the unanticipated in boxing—who can forget George Foreman taking on five opponents in one fight?—it is not as if uncivil behavior is confined to that sport. The larger problem, it seems, is that the behavior of athletes and fans is just as bizarre outside the ring or arena as it is inside.

Events that top the list are the stalkings and attacks that have recently taken place in figure skating (the Tonya Harding–related assault on Nancy Kerrigan) and on the women's tennis tour. One of the top female tennis players,[63] Monica Seles, was stabbed on April 30, 1993, while playing in a tournament in Hamburg, Germany. Gunther Parche, the assailant, was a fanatical fan of tennis player Steffi Graf and did not want Seles around for competition. For his crime, Parche was given a two-year suspended sentence.[64]

Conclusion

To bring this essay to a close, I pose a question (as it came from Professor Robert Putnam): "Whatever happened to civic engagement?"[65] Indeed, there is a tradition of *civility* in sport: it manifests itself in the ideal of fair play in games as well as a willingness simply to participate in the contest. Yet there is another side to this story. Another tradition is at work in the arena of modern sport—openly avowed, assiduously cultivated, and zealously carried out—which was succinctly defined in football Coach Woody Hayes's statement that "I'd rather die a winner than a loser" and was nicely demonstrated in the testimony of ex-professional lineman Alex Karras that "I hated everyone on the football field and my personality would change drastically when I got out there. . . . I had a license to kill for sixty minutes a week. My opponents were all fair game, and when I got off the field I had no regrets. It was like going totally insane."[66] To again pose the question, and to put the matter slightly differently: What has happened to our collective concern for fellow Americans, in this instance both on and off the playing fields? Consider, for instance, basketball player Latrell Sprewell in a fit of anger placing his hands around the neck of his coach and choking him. What does an act like this symbolize? Even if the coach went beyond the boundaries in imposing stricter work requirements, employers and bosses do this all the time.

Is it folly to assume that friendliness, getting an autograph[67] from a professional athlete (without getting spit on), or attending a game without having beer[68] dumped down your shirt remain only as figments of the sports sociological imagination?[69] In answering this question, I am sure I bump up against the larger one of just what we stand for as a society, a people, and as athletes entering the twenty-first century.[70] As it stands now, not very much.

For many people, the sports world is one of the few places where none of the problems of the real world exist. It is, for sure, a world described by the late commissioner of baseball A. Bartlett Giamatti,[71] in his posthumously published essay "Take Time for Paradise: Americans and Their Games" (1989), as a fantasy world. In this chapter, though, I have shown that many of the problems of uncivil behavior we encounter in the world at large are, in fact, quite present in the real world of sports. And, theoretically speaking, while it is close to impossible to try to account for the complexities of human social behavior,[72] there is something to the fact that the outward manifestations of this uncivil behavior in the sports world have become visible to us largely with the advent of TV.[73]

Would our society's situation, in relation to sports, have been the same had television been available to document both the sporting prowess and the uncivil, racist behavior of the legendary Ty Cobb? Outside the scholarly sports community, the public still knows Cobb best for his baseball abilities, rather than for his public displays of drunkenness or his virulent racism.[74] Under the lights of

TV, Cobb's behavior would have been exposed, similar to that of the infamous Cincinnati Reds owner Marge Schott. There is then, a value to TV and investigative reporting that is apparent here, as it relates to uncovering uncivil behavior of athletes.

In a paper co-authored with the sports sociologist Wib Leonard, I argued that the reason for a lack of sociological theory in stacking research needs to be found[75] if we are interested in explaining that phenomenon. I underscore that argument here. I am noting that, conceptually, we still have a long way to go when we try to explain the social behavior that unfolds in and around sport activities in our society at all levels.[76] This is especially true when at issue is the behavior of individual superstar athletes.

Francis Fukuyama, in his immensely important book *Trust*,[77] demonstrates that where the community ethos dissolves and folkways disappear, you end up in a situation wherein citizens can no longer trust in one another. When this happens in American society, says Fukuyama, you begin to see the rise of violent crime and civil litigation; the breakdown of family structure; the decline of a wide range of intermediate social structures, such as neighborhoods, churches, unions, clubs, and charities; and the general sense among Americans of a lack of shared values and community with those around them. Civility needs to be restored. It has been lost in many areas of our society, and we suffer for it. I refer to what has been lost as the Norms of Civility, and presently in sports, we lack these norms. This problem is not new. It was given sociological clothing in the work of the French sociologist Émile Durkheim, first articulated in his treatise *The Division of Labor in Society*.[78] According to Durkheim, societies are best conceived of as a coterie of individuals. Under the most favorable conditions, humans strive to work together toward an agreed-upon "end" that, in the final analysis, satisfies all within the group. The French sociologists put it this way: Society is not alone in its interest in the formation of special groups to regulate their own activity, developing within them what otherwise would be anarchic; but the individual, on his or her part, finds joy in it, for anarchy is painful to him. The individual also suffers from pain and disorder whenever interindividual relations are not submitted to some regulatory influence, that is, in states of *anomie*.[79]

In this chapter, I argued that to successfully observe and understand the significance of uncivil behavior in sports—here the example has been basketball—we must expand on our overall understanding of the nature of empirical science. This way, we are in a better position to accommodate the multidimensional nature of the sporting world.

In conclusion, it is important to reiterate that what we are now seeing in the form of uncivil behavior in sports in general and in basketball in particular goes beyond sports and the people who inhabit this arena. Sports are a microcosm of society. The behavior athletes, coaches, and fans exhibit only reflects the society in which we live.[80] And because of the high status and prestige placed on and associated with sports, we can expect that the money which goes to the owners of franchises; the equipment outfitters; the media magnates who own and control CBS, NBC, FOX, CNN, ESPN; the concessionaires; the elected officials who run cities where teams play; and the players themselves will drive individualism and greed to the extreme. Related to all this is the conflicting role the media have come to play in sports. While the mass media have the power to uncover injustices, racist attitudes, and incivility for the good, in our daily lives they also contribute to the lack of norms and the rise of incivility by bringing negative behavior directly to us on a daily basis.

NOTES

1. Edward Shils, 1997, *The Virtue of Civility* (Indianapolis: Liberty Fund Books).

2. George F. Will, 1990, *Men at Work: The Craft of Baseball* (New York: HarperCollins), p. 3.

3. Herb Snitzer, 1991, "The Realities of Cultural Change," *Reconstruction* 1, 1:33.

4. Wherein most, if not all, of the twentieth-century legislation was passed, everything from open housing to free, unintimidating voting. See, especially, John A. Andrew III, who summarizes most of this legislation in his 1998 book on Lyndon Baines Johnson entitled *Lyndon Johnson and the Great Society* (Chicago: Ivan R. Dee Publishers).

5. This is the major theme for two basketball "documentaries" I have recently seen, *Hoop Dreams* (1994) and *Soul in the Hole* (1997).

6. Elijah Anderson, 1990, *Streetwise* (Chicago: University of Chicago Press).

7. The best treatment of the meaning of race in sports is in Kenneth Shropshire's 1995 book titled *In Black and White: Race and Sports in America* (New York: New York University Press). The broad focus of the book—treating issues from players' unequal access to management positions, to the role and meaning of sport agents—makes it a must for sport scholars interested in unequal justice. See my 1997 review in the *Sociology of Sport Journal* 14:198–200.

8. See Troy Cross, 1996, "Assaults on Sports Officials," *Marquette Sports Law Journal* 8:441. Dennis Rodman, in a game between the Chicago Bulls and the New Jersey Nets (March 16, 1996), head-butted the referee and was handed a six-game, $20,000 fine.

9. Geoffrey Ward and Ken Burns, 1994, *Baseball: An Illustrated History* (New York: Alfred A. Knopf).

10. Alexis de Tocqueville, 1945, *Democracy in America*, 2 vols. (New York: Doubleday).

11. Robert Putnam, 1993, *Making Democracy Work: Civic Traditions in Modern Italy* (Princeton: Princeton University Press).

12. Robert Putnam, 1995, "Bowling Alone: America's Declining Social Capital," *Journal of Democracy* 6:65–78.

13. Ibid.

14. I could extend the analysis to both Little League sports and interscholastic sports, and I do so in my forthcoming book, *The Sporting World of African American Athletes: From Jackie Roosevelt Robinson to Eldrick "Tiger" Woods*. See also, especially, H. G. Bissinger, 1990, *Friday Night Lights: A Town, a Team, a Dream* (New York: Harper-Collins).

15. While this concentration on basketball does not allow me the space to examine other interesting problems that exist in different individual and team sports (such as auto racing, American football, and even soccer, the last of which is often the major concern of sports scientists in other countries), the scope of the project would be overwhelming if I tried to branch outward. See, especially, E. Dunning, 1997, "Sport and Racial Stratification." I thank Prof. Dunning for sharing a copy of his chapter with me as it will appear in his forthcoming book *Sport Matters* (New York, Routledge).

16. See, especially, Alvin Gouldner, 1960, "The Norm of Reciprocity." *American Sociological Review* 25:161–178.

17. Jennifer L. Hochschild, 1995, *Facing Up to the American Dream* (Princeton: Princeton University Press).

18. Putnam, "Bowling Alone," p. 75.

19. Judith Van Evra, 1994, *Television and Child Development* (Hillsdale, NJ: Erlbaum).

20. Ibid., p. 6.

21. Many of these surveys are summarized in the Internet version of *Advertising Age*, http://www.adage.com. See also S. Barnett, 1992, "*TV World* Special Report: Sports—The Price of Admittance," *TV World* (April):17–27.

22. H. G. Bissinger, in his 1990 book *Friday Night Lights*, (a portrayal of Odessa, Texas, and its Permian High School football team), and Wake Forest University legal scholar Timothy Davis, in his 1992 work "Ross v. Creighton University: Seventh Circuit Recognition of Limited Judicial Regulation of Intercollegiate Athletics," *Southern Illinois University Law Journal* 17 (Fall 1992):85–115 (portrayal of abuses suffered by intercollegiate athletes, especially those of minority status), provide two good examples of my point here in Boobie Miles and Kevin Ross, respectively, both of whom were used as fodder for their sports teams.

23. The NFL landed a $17.6 billion deal with ESPN, CBS, ABC, and FOX. The NBA has a $2.6 billion deal with NBC, and the NCAA recently sealed a deal with CBS for $6 billion to televise the NCAA tournament. See Jack McCallum, 1997, "Foul Trouble," *Sports Illustrated*, December 15, pp. 68–69; and Stefan Fatsis, 1998, "NBA Bravely Plans for Post-Jordan Era," *Wall Street Journal*, February 6.

24. David Wolf, 1972, *Foul! The Connie Hawkins Story* (New York: Warner Books).

25. See, especially, Bob Cousy, the NBA Hall of Famer, in his remarks criticizing high-profile player agents (such as David Falk) who have "done so much damage to the game we all love, just for the sake of unbridled greed, ego and control" ("Cousy Blasts NBA Players Union," CNN/SI, December 12, 1998, http://cnnsi.com/basketball/nba/news).

26. Obviously, this does not apply to Chicago Bulls superstar Michael Jordan. Jordan has appeal among all Americans as well as international appeal. (Consider also his box-office smash movie *Space Jam* [1996], co-starring Bugs Bunny). Jordan still rates as one of the best basketball players in the world.

27. To date the film has grossed $150 million, making it the second most successful TriStar Production film in history (behind *Sleepless in Seattle* [1993]).

28. These figures pale, of course, when compared to the $12 million shoe deal (Adidas) for high school star Tracy McGrady (Mt. Zion Academy, Durham, North Carolina), who commanded this figure even before he was drafted by the Toronto Raptors (ninth in the first round).

29. Players should be paid what they are worth. Owners who bemoan this and say the league is in "financial distress" must be looking past the multimillions paid to Commissioner David Stern. Stern is said to be making $40 million over five years. See, Andrew Zimbalist, 1998, "A Masterpiece of Obfuscation." *New York Times,* December 13, 1998, p. 56. See also Robert Lipsyte, 1998, "What's Really behind This NBA Lockout?" *New York Times,* December 13, p. 55.

30. I do not concern myself here with the issue of whether or not excessive scrutiny is wrong. On this, see Merrill Melnick, 1992, "Male Athletes and Sexual Assault," *Journal of Physical Education, Recreation and Dance* 63:32–35.

31. A lot of talk about the "progress of women in sport," especially with the inauguration of the Women's National Basketball Association (WNBA), accompanied the twenty-fifth anniversary of Title IX 1997. See, especially, Mariah Burton Nelson, 1997, "Women Take the Court, Playing for Peanuts," *New York Times,* June 21. I am surprised to hear the same talk coming from Donna Lopiano, executive director of the Women's Sport Foundation. Much of the talk is utter nonsense and does not stand up to empirical scrutiny. For an updated analysis of Title IX, see Timothy Davis, 1998, "Student-Athlete Sexual Violence against Women: Defining the Limits of Institutional Responsibility." *Washington and Lee Law Review* 55 (1):55–116.

32. Eric Dunning, 1986, "Sport as a Male Preserve," pp. x–xx in Norbert Elias and E. Dunning, eds., *Quest for Excitement* (Oxford: Blackwell).

33. Tim Curry, 1991, "Fraternal Bonding in the Locker Room." *Sociology of Sport Journal* 8:119–135. "Although seldom defined explicitly, the fraternal bond is usually considered to be a force, link, or affectionate tie that unites men. . . . Some of the activities around which men bond are negative toward women" (pp. 119–120). The denigration of women in places like locker rooms was evident in the case of sportswriter Lisa Olson, who was allowed in the locker room of the New England Patriots football team. The players harassed her with lewd behavior and aggressive sexual talk. She was "modeled for" and asked if she "wanted some of this" ("A Woman Sports Reporter in the Men's Locker Room," *USA Today,* November 28, 1990, p. 7A). At an earlier time, when women were first allowed in the locker room, the New York Yankees baseball team displayed a two-foot-long cake designed in the form of a penis to their female

reporters. See William Nack and Lester Munson, 1995, "Sports' Dirty Secret," *Sports Illustrated*, July 31, pp. 62–65.

34. Bissinger, *Friday Night Lights*, chap. 7, "School Days."

35. Mariah Burton, *The Stronger Women Get, the More Men Love Football* (New York: Harcourt), p. 133.

36. David P. Phillips, 1983, "Mass Media Violence and U.S. Homicides." *American Sociological Review* 48:560–568. See also Lawrence Schoen, 1996, "Out of Bounds: Professional Sports Leagues and Domestic Violence." *Harvard Law Review* 109:1048–65.

37. Harry Edwards, 1973, *The Sociology of Sport* (New York: Dorsey).

38. Robert Lipsyte, 1984, "Sportsworld," p. 3 in Stanley Eitzen, ed., *Sport in Contemporary Society* (New York: St. Martin's Press).

39. Professor Phoebe Weaver Williams has done some of the best work on how fans interact with players, in her 1996 research presentation "Performing in a Racially Hostile Environment," *Marquette Sports Law Journal* 6:287–314.

40. Quoted in Howard Nixon, 1976, *Sport and Social Organization* (Indianapolis: Bobbs-Merrill), pp. 61–62.

41. These innovations have also benefited men's college basketball. It is not uncommon for the Final Four basketball tournament each spring to generate gross revenues in the range of $76 to $80 million. See Monica Emerick, 1997, "The University/Student-Athlete Relationship: Duties Giving Rise to a Potential Educational Hindrance Claim," *UCLA Law Review* 44:875, wherein she notes the following: "Applications for admission at Georgetown University increased thirty-three percent after Patrick Ewing joined the basketball team and led the team's ascent to becoming a basketball powerhouse. Additionally, it is estimated that Ewing generated $12.3 million for the university through increased attendance, television, and NCAA tournament revenues during his four years at Georgetown. At North Carolina State University, private donations grew thirty percent, from $9.4 million to $12.27 million, during the year following the school's NCAA basketball championship."

42. Fines in the amounts of $50,000, $25,000 and $7,500 had also been levied against Rodman during the 1996–97 basketball season. Rodman lost this $1 million in salary in conjunction with the eleven-game suspension he received after kicking a courtside photographer. See CBS SportsLine, June 12, 1997 (http://www.sportsline.com); and Terry Pluto, 1995, *Falling from Grace: Can Pro Basketball Be Saved?* (New York: Simon and Schuster).

43. Three stories were consulted here: Sam Goldaper, 1977, "Lakers Kermit Washington Fined $10,000," *New York Times*, December 14, p.

C30; Harvey Araton, 1993, "An Elbow, Followed by a Punch: Washington Began Violent NBA Era," *New York Times*, April 11, p. A24; Lisa Olson, 1997, "Shattered in Time," *New York Daily News*, December 21, p. 103. For an account that takes into consideration the issue of race, Washington's feelings about "the punch," and the turn his career took after the suspension, see David Halberstram, 1981, *The Breaks of the Game* (New York: Alfred A. Knopf), pp. 54–56.

44. Bobby Knight is a coaching legend, having won the coveted NCAA Men's Basketball Tournament three times. He has also won the basketball title at the Olympics and the Pan-American Games, as well as the National Invitational Tournament (NIT) and scores of Big Ten titles. Yet, Knight is known widely for his ability to challenge his players' manhood, their maleness. He has been known to hang sanitary napkins in the lockers of players whose maleness he is challenging. In the profession, he is considered a tyrant. See Nack and Munson, "Sports' Dirty Secret," p. 62–65.

45. Phil Taylor, 1997, "Center of the Storm," *Sports Illustrated*, December 15, p. 62.

46. Ira Berkow, 1998, "Go Ahead, Choke the Boss—Only in the NBA," *New York Times*, March 5.

47. See, especially, Mike Lopresti, 1998, "No Winners, Too Many Losers from Sprewell Reinstatement," *USA Today*, March 5, p. 2C; and Sam Smith, 1998, "Choke Artist Latrell Sprewell Shares Some of the Blame for Lockout," *Chicago Tribune*, December 4.

48. "Student-athlete refers to college students who attend post-secondary institutions on athletic scholarships" (Timothy Davis, 1992, "Examining Educational Malpractice Jurisprudence: Should a Cause of Action Be Created for Student-Athletes?" *Denver University Law Review* 69:58, n. 7).

49. To define *social capital*, we note it is "the aggregate of the actual or potential resources which are linked to possession of a durable network of more or less institutionalized relationships of mutual acquaintance or recognition." This is how Pierre Bourdieu defined the term in "The Forms of Capital," in John G. Richardson (ed.), 1986, *Handbook of Theory and Research for the Sociology of Education* (Westport, Conn.: Greenwood), pp. 241–58. It should be noted, however, that social capital is imbedded in the nature of social relationships. To possess social capital, a person must be related to others; hence the applicability to institutions of higher learning. See, especially, Alejandro Portes, 1998, "Social Capital: Its Origin and Applications in Modern Sociology," *Annual Review of Sociology* 24:1–24.

50. "The largest financial rewards of athletic success derive from participation in postseason events such as bowl games in football, and the

NCAA Men's Basketball Tournament. . . . In 1982, the NCAA Basketball Tournament sold its broadcast rights for $14,000,000; by 1995, the price was $152,000,000, an increase of more than 1,000%" (Brian Porto, 1998, "Completing the Revolution: Title IX as a Catalyst for an Alternative Model of College Sports," *Seton Hall Journal of Law* 8:357).

51. Timothy Davis, 1991, "An Absence of Good Faith: Defining a University's Educational Obligation to Student-Athletes," *Houston Law Review* 743:751–59.

52. Emerick, "University/Student-Athlete Relationship," p. 877.

53. Melvin Braziel, 1997, "United We Stand: Organizing Student-Athletes for Educational Reform," *Sports Lawyers Journal* 4:82–111.

54. Walter Byers, 1995, *Unsportsmanlike Conduct: Exploiting College Athletes* (Ann Arbor: University of Michigan Press). Byers's book is not to be taken lightly. He is the former, long-term executive director of the NCAA. His text represents, overall, a change of heart reflected in his personal and professional break with the official line of the NCAA on the issue of amateurism.

55. I do not remember any significant recommendations from the much-publicized Knight Committee Report in relation to African American athletes. See *Report of the Knight Foundation Committee Report on Intercollegiate Athletics*, 1993 (Charlotte, S.C.: Knight Foundation).

56. Steve Wieberg, 1998, "Drop in Graduation Rates Appears in Every Category," *USA Today*, November 8, p. 12C.

57. When you think about it, the graduation rate is at the end of the scale. Just as or more important are the day-to-day, year-after-year activities (or the lack thereof) of basketball student-athletes who are kept eligible with "Mickey Mouse" courses, tutoring that borders on the brink of educational fraud, and summer school courses that would not meet regular academic muster. All represent the true meaning of educational malpractice and educational malfeasance. See, especially, Rick Reilly, 1998, "Class Struggle at Ohio State," *Sports Illustrated*, August 31.

58. Davis, "Examining Educational Malpractice Jurisprudence," pp. 57–96.

59. Joan Didion, 1993, "Trouble in Lakewood," *New Yorker*, July 26, pp. 46–65. Quote is from p. 55.

60. Earl Smith, forthcoming, *The Sporting World of African American Athletes: From Jackie Roosevelt Robinson to Eldrick "Tiger" Woods*.

61. See the new work by Bernard Lefkowitz, 1997, "The Boys Next Door," *Sports Illustrated*, June 23, p. 76. Also, Harvey Araton, 1997, "A Misguided and Warped Value System," *New York Times* June 28, p. C36.

On July 1, 1997, *USA Today* reported that the former athletes received prison sentences for their rape.

62. The initial action taken by the Nevada Boxing Commission was to hold up Tyson's reputed $35 million purse. Tyson was suspended for a year, and when the hearing took place a year later, he was reinstated as a professional boxer. See Michael Ventre, June 28, 1997, "An Animal's Despicable Act of Cowardice," special to MSNBC (http://www.msnbc.com/news/83284.asp) and Nick Charles, June 29, 1997, "Tyson's Last Stand," CNN/SI, http://www.cnn.com/SPORT.

63. Ms. Seles was ranked number one at the time.

64. Robert Lipsyte, 1997, "The Dangerously Thin Line of Fanaticism," *New York Times*, June 29, p. 17.

65. Putnam, "Bowling Alone," pp. 65–78.

66. Cited in Ashley Montagu and Floyd Matson, 1983, *The Dehumanization of Man* (New York: McGraw Hill), p. 195.

67. On July 24, 1993, Vince Coleman, a New York Mets outfielder, tossed a live firecracker—equal to a quarter of a stick of dynamite—into a crowd of autograph-seeking fans at Dodger Stadium. Several people in the crowd were injured, including a two-year-old girl. Coleman never apologized for his behavior. See Richard Scheinin, 1994, *Field of Screams* (New York: Norton), p. 396.

68. A big part of the curtailment of the sale of alcohol at athletic events (collegiate and pro) comes from the fan behavior that ensues from a long afternoon and/or evening of drinking at the game. See, especially, the accounts of the June 4, 1974 "Ten Cent Beer Night" in Cleveland, wherein twenty-five thousand Cleveland Indians fans consumed sixty thousand ten-ounce beers and attacked the players of the baseball game between the Cleveland Indians and the Texas Rangers.

69. Araton mused about this deterioration in social behavior after finally coming to grips with the fact that his seven-year-old son had no interest in the local traveling soccer team. See Harvey Araton, 1997, "A Misguided and Warped Value System," *New York Times*, June 28, p. C36.

70. The question is brilliantly asked, by the way, by the social philosopher Francis Fukuyama in his 1995 book *Trust: The Social Virtues and the Creation of Prosperity* (New York: Free Press).

71. Giamatti was also a former president of the prominent Ivy League school Yale University.

72. Frank Sulloway, in his 1996 book *Born to Rebel: Birth Order, Family Dynamics, and Creative Lives* (New York: Pantheon Books), seems to imply that a considerable part of explaining this behavior is found in sibling birth order. See, especially, chap. 3, "Birth Order and Personality."

73. Obviously, this is not to say that no uncivil behavior existed in the sports world before TV. Sportswriters just did not report such matters in the time when reading newspapers was one of few communications options open to society.

74. Ward and Burns, *Baseball,* p. 323.

75. Earl Smith and Wilbert Leonard, 1997, "Twenty-Five Years of Stacking Research in Major League Baseball: An Attempt at Explaining This Re-occurring Phenomenon," *Sociological Focus,* 30:321–331.

76. This does not exclude the uncivil behavior being reported in the Little League games young children play, be the sport football, soccer, or baseball. See Gary Alan Fine, 1987, *With the Boys: Little League Baseball and Preadolescent Culture* (Chicago: University of Chicago Press).

77. Fukuyama, *Trust.*

78. Émile Durkheim, 1933, *The Division of Labor in Society* (New York: Macmillan).

79. Ibid., p. 15 (my emphasis). See also Earl Smith and K. Wong, 1989, "Durkheim, Individualism and Homicide Rates Re-examined," *Sociological Spectrum* 9:269–283.

80. The "sport as a microcosm of society" metaphor is used by almost everyone who conducts sociological, psychological, legal, and economic research on sports, but it is hardly ever fully analyzed. That task is beyond the scope of the goals set for this chapter. See, generally, Stanley Eitzen and George Sage, 1997, *Sociology of North American Sport* (Madison, Wis.: Brown and Benchmark); Richard Lapchick, 1986, *Fractured Focus: Sport as a Reflection of Society* (Lexington, Mass.: Lexington Books); and Timothy Davis, 1997, "Who's In and Who's Out: Racial Discrimination in Sports," *Pacific Law Journal* 28:341–372.

10

attacking the rim
the cultural politics of dunking

DAVIS W. HOUCK

But what if the fast break
doesn't materialize
and there is no open man to
take the shot?
When the twenty-four second
clock has run out
somebody will have to take
the ball to the basket.
Baby, you've got to put it up!
Twenty four seconds
is all you get! Shit, Hubie, we
ain't
had nothin' to do with
deciding this hard ass,
arbitrary time: we just play
by the rules
that somebody else made.
Say what? Hell, man,
we ain't had no responsibility
to abdicate.
—Raymond Fleming,
"Basketball Jones" [1]

AT FIRST GLANCE, THE JUXTAPOSITION
between Ray Fleming's vernacular prose poem and
the lifeless, committee prose of the NCAA is jar-
ring. At closer inspection, though, the stylistic in-
congruity recedes into a thematic coherence: rules
and race. The racial identity of Hubie Brown's in-
terlocutor is not in doubt: the collective "we" has
no power to create and govern—except during the
ebb and flow of the basketball game. And even this
ebb and flow is carefully regulated by an "arbitrary
time" stipulated by an impersonal white "somebody." The NCAA statement is clearly about rules,
specifically rule 9, section 11, which banned dunking in intercollegiate men's basketball for nearly
ten years, from 1967–1976. But what of race? Can

Henceforth, the ball cannot be
thrown into the basket. It will be
a violation for the offense to
touch the ball or basket when
the ball is in or on the basket
and to touch the ball when any
part of the ball is in the cylinder
above the basket.
—National Collegiate Athletic
Association, "Digest of
Committee Action
for 1967–68" [2]

such desiccated prose possibly contain racial overtones? Kareem
Abdul-Jabbar, among others, believes so: "The dunk is one of basketball's great crowd pleasers, and there is no good reason to give it
up except that this and other niggers were running away with the
sport."[3] That the NCAA deliberately targeted Abdul-Jabbar the
UCLA junior was reflected in the no-dunk rule's popular designation—the Alcindor rule.[4]

As the aforementioned suggests, there's much more to dunking
a basketball than the physical act and the corresponding two points.
Dunking is a far more symbolic and rhetorical act, one that impli-
cates a complex cultural politics and a corresponding commodity
culture. In addition to an overtly racial dimension, dunking impli-
cates matters of violence, gender, and the marketing of professional
basketball. As such, the "value" of dunking far transcends its os-
tensible "worth" as two points. Advancing such a reading of the
dunk continues a line of inquiry that treats basketball as a "contemporary field where cultural politics are often at work, but seldom fully appreciated."[5]

To discuss dunking in terms of politics and economics runs
against the grain of common wisdom. Such wisdom typically argues that, at least since 1976, dunking has been largely a matter
of aesthetics. Beginning with Julius "Dr. J" Erving and David
Thompson in the first dunking contest, held in 1976, through
such notables as Michael Jordan, Dominique Wilkins, Anthony
"Spud" Webb, Shawn Kemp, Dee Brown, and Kobe Bryant, dunking has been staged as theater. Often accompanied by a heavy
musical beat, contestants have been numerically judged by a pan-
elist of "experts" for originality, difficulty, force, and execution.[6]
Fans, of course, also participated informally in offering their
scores from the sidelines. Such contests were, until 1998, carried
live by major cable companies to a sizable audience. The "point"
of dunking before a live national audience was not to score two
points but to put one's body and basketball skills on display. Thus
do seemingly impossible moves such as dunking from the foul
line (à la Erving, Jordan, and Brent Barry), blindfolded dunks (à la
Cedric Ceballos), and dunks by players short in stature (à la, the
five-foot seven-inch Webb) come into sharper relief. Dunking
contests were designed to push the body to its physical limits—

and, not surprisingly, the accompanying visuals for such a physical test were often spectacular.[7]

Bodies and body-based performances, though, are far from "mere" aesthetic phenomena. Beginning largely with Michel Foucault's critique of prisons and sexuality and extending into the present, bodies have been seen less as natural or biologically given and more as historically determined, socially situated, and culturally constructed. Thus have the body and body-based performances become an object of inquiry for the sociologist, the historian, and the rhetorician. Perhaps more than any other basketball-related phenomenon, dunking is about disciplined, controlled, and productive bodies; as such, it invites interrogation and critique, not naturalization or what one writer calls "hypnotic fascination."[8]

Dunking, Violence, and Masculinity

Most observers of the National Basketball Association (NBA) would likely agree that violent behavior on the part of players reached its zenith in the late 1980s and early 1990s. While the league has always had its share of goons and hatchet men, the success of the Detroit Pistons showcased a physical, intimidating style of play that eventually earned them the nickname Bad Boys. Intimidation and confrontation greatly assisted the Pistons, led by Rick Mahorn, Bill Laimbeer, and Dennis Rodman, in their back-to-back championship seasons. The Bad Boys, though, represented only one type of on-court violence—and while perhaps the most visible and obvious, it is but one among several. Dunking represents another form of violence, one that appears bound up with issues of identity and masculinity.

On the surface, dunking, especially as practiced by such luminaries as Erving and Jordan, seems to be less about violence than about artistry, grace, and athleticism. A closer look, though, reveals a culture of violence attending the dunk. In videotape from the 1960s and early 1970s, most players seem almost polite about their dunks. There is no hanging on the rim, no bent rims, no collapsed baskets, and few primal screams. Nowadays, in stark contrast, when players dunk, the force with which they slam is unmistakable; the rim is often quite literally attacked, frequently leaving hands, wrists, and forearms bloodied and bruised. The most obvious manifestation of such violence is when players literally destroy the rim and the backboard with the sheer force and power of their dunks. To "accomplish" such a feat is to scale the Olympus of dunking, and no small bravado attends such a demolition. Then a junior at the University of Pittsburgh, in 1988, Jerome Lane slammed with such force off a fast break against Providence that the backboard exploded into thousands of glass shards. His on-court reaction was most telling: instead of a look of astonishment or even gravity, Lane strutted around his team's bench, "high-fiving" his Pitt teammates. Off the court, Lane stated, "It was like a dream come true. I never believed I could do that. . . . Oh well, there goes another fantasy."[9] A similar reaction occurred when Texas Tech's Darvin Ham demolished a backboard in a 1996 NCAA tournament game against the University of North Carolina. After the game Ham revealed, "I thought, 'Yes . . . finally.' I felt so good I just wanted to rip off my shirt and start flexing like Hulk Hogan."[10] Oklahoma State center Bryant "Big Country" Reeves responded a bit differently. After shattering a backboard in practice before a 1995 NCAA tournament game in Seattle, Reeves carefully selected several shards of glass to display in his trophy case. Shattered glass, cut by one's own power, is indeed a prize worth displaying.

Of course, to discuss the violence attendant in breaking a backboard is also to discuss the player who popularized the "genre"— Philadelphia 76ers man-child Darryl Dawkins. In the span of twenty-one days in 1979, "Chocolate Thunder" shattered two backboards. For the dunk-happy Dawkins, such an event required poetic memorialization; thus the infamous "Chocolate Thunder Flying, Robinzine Crying, Teeth Shaking, Glass Breaking, Rump Roasting, Wham Bam, Glass Breaker I am Jam." The second demolition somehow muted the loquacious inhabitant of "Love-Tron" (Dawkin's claimed personal planet); he named it the Candy Slam.

Only the true NBA aficionado would recognize the second adjective in Dawkins's designation—"Robinzine Crying"—but its significance to the culture of violence attending the dunk is hard to overestimate. The adjective refers to Kansas City Kings player Bill Robinzine, whose misfortune it was to be on the receiving end of Dawkins's thunderous dunk. Beyond receiving a cut on his hand from a glass projectile, Robinzine had been dunked on, and to be dunked on, perhaps now more than ever before, is to be a passive recipient of violence. It is to be humiliated, embarrassed, to be "faced," "used," "dissed," and shown up. As former Philadelphia 76ers coach Jim Lynam notes, "But now guys stick fingers in guys' faces [after dunking] while millions are watching on TV, which is an embarrassment. It's almost a challenge to one's manhood. You're forced to respond."[11]

Ironically, in light of NBA commissioner David Stern's largely successful attempts to eradicate violence in the league, the NBA's official web site seems to celebrate the violent nature of dunking. It does this principally through description. In the "Theater" section of the web site, viewers will find the "top 10 dunks of the 1997–98 season."[12] It's apparently not enough for the league to have Quick-Time Video for each of the dunks; in addition, the league sees fit to describe each dunk. Their rhetorical choices are most revealing: Antonio McDyess "tears into the paint" for a "rim-rocking dunk"; Ray Allen "crushes the thundering right-handed slam"; Shaquille O'Neal "throw[s] down a vicious slam"; Michael Jordan "tears into the key" and "slams it home"; Kevin Garnett "hammers down the right-handed tomahawk jam"; Glenn Rice "deposits an awesome two-handed rip"; and Grant Hill "flushes a wicked dunk." Nearly all the award-winning dunks are described unequivocally in violent terms. And, more to the point of Bill Robinzine and his importance to Dawkins, six of the ten dunks featured on the site are described in terms of being *done to* someone. To dunk with violence apparently isn't enough; that violence isn't directed solely at an inanimate metal sphere but at an opposing player. To dunk at the highest levels is thus to do violence to another player, so suggests the NBA.

The point is really a simple one: whether done by a "good guy" or a "bad guy," dunking speaks a universal language understood by those who play the game. Such language is reflected in the prose of Nelson George, whose insightful analysis of what he terms the

African American basketball aesthetic features this Jordanesque account of dunking: "It [dunking] is the unstoppable weapon that, when done with the rim-bending authority . . . establishes a player's physical mastery of an opponent."[13]

Yet an invocation of simplicity doesn't get us off the hook. As Foucault, among others, advises, cultural critics should always attempt to make seemingly facile gestures difficult. And even though the dunk sometimes masquerades as a facile gesture, it is far more than just an efficient method of scoring. It is rather, as several have suggested, the ultimate "weapon" on the basketball court, an expression in the literal sense of the word. But why an expression accompanied by the vernacular of violence? And why has that vernacular only recently emerged?

To raise such questions is to sense immediately their recalcitrance; they simply cannot be answered in a definitive manner. I would, however, suggest one possibility among several, one whose origin dates to a seeming throwaway line from former Denver Nuggets star Dan Issel. Recounting the style of play in the American Basketball Association (ABA), Issel states, "The dunk was a bigger play in the ABA than it is in today's NBA; it was a statement of your *manhood* and your talent."[14] Issel's invocation of manhood, of masculinity, is perhaps the thread that leads right back to O'Neal, Karl Malone, Hill, Jordan, and Larry Nance: to exert physical and mental control and dominance over another basketball player is, perhaps lamentably, an index of masculinity in late twentieth-century American culture.

In the early years of the NBA, though, dunking was often avoided because of its aggrandizing tendency. Dunking called attention to the dunker, and the team, not the individual, was the focal point of the game. Former Boston Celtic great Bob Cousy speaks for many of his era: "It [dunking] wasn't a featured thing when we played. (Bill) Russell could do it easily, but he held it in disdain. He'd never do it in practice or warmups. To him it was showing off."[15] Perhaps it shouldn't surprise us that dunking literally took off during the post-Russell "Me Generation" of the 1970s and continued to soar with the valorization of individualism during the Reagan years—to say nothing of the imperiled status of black masculinity over the last three decades.

Brent Barry and Rex Chapman notwithstanding, dunking in today's NBA is largely a black phenomenon. Some might ground this claim along genetic lines, others simply on the large majority of black players in the league. And while both possibilities have plausible evidentiary warrants, Richard Majors and Janet Billson suggest a third possibility with the notion of "cool poses." For many young black men, access to means to "fulfill their dreams of masculinity and success" has simply been unavailable, if not outright denied. To compensate and survive, many young black men "have adopted and used cool masculinity."[16] The cool pose involves "the construction of a symbolic universe. Denied access to mainstream avenues of success, they [young black men] have created their own voice. Unique patterns of speech, walk, and demeanor express the cool pose. This strategic style allows the black male to tip society's imbalanced scales in his favor." Dunking is no stranger to the "cool pose." According to Majors, dunking "accentuates the self and brings attention to the self. It neutralizes the social pressure."[17] The self needs such attention precisely because it is imperiled.

Some might object along the following lines: superstar athletes such as Michael Jordan shouldn't need to engage in such expressive, aggrandizing behavior; their sense of self, after all, is buttressed by a large bank account and transcontinental fame. In his eloquently written and revealing look at Jordan, *Hang Time*, Bob Greene poignantly captures the motivating force behind Jordan's unparalleled success—a fear of failure and loss of respect.[18] In an era when individualism continues to reign supreme, and when the individual identities of so many young black men are threatened, one begins to understand why dunking with force on someone else is a forceful rhetorical expression of one's own identity.[19] Nowadays, NBA stars simply don't need the soloist's aestheticism of the dunk contest—in fact, the league as a whole doesn't. Such display offers little personal satisfaction beyond recognition. That said, dunking remains the single most important shot in the game—in part because of the identity politics that it enacts. Thus, while the league has suspended the dunk contest, it will certainly not suspend the dunk; in fact, it will continue to market the dunk as its signature rhetorical gesture.

Dunking, Marketing, and Commodity Culture

Even though Julius Erving and a host of his talented brethren
jumped from the ABA to the NBA in 1977, the league was far from
profitable and popular. Its reputation was such that its marquee
event—the league finals—was often televised to the nation only by
tape delay. With the *Los Angeles Times* reporting that more than 70
percent of NBA players were drug users, the credibility and marketability of the league was seriously imperiled as the 1970s closed.
According to popular legend, two players from the Midwest
"saved" the league: Earvin "Magic" Johnson and Larry Bird. Magic
was an opposing coach's worst nightmare and a camera's best
friend: a six-foot nine-inch point guard bordered on the absurd,
while Magic's showtime game and charisma played to full houses
in the Forum.[20] Playing on the other coast, in Boston, Bird proved
as anomalous as his name: slow-footed and lacking much "lift,"
Bird was still able to dominate a game with his no-look passes, his
uncanny touch from long range, and his physical play on the
boards. He was also white—a fact not lost on a league whose large
white audience was increasingly alienated from players and a style
of play that it no longer recognized. The Lakers and Celtics, Magic
and Bird—together they defined each other for nearly a decade.
Their identificatory rivalry led the league to experience exponen-
tial popularity and revenues.

Of the many things that Magic and Bird were, they were not
dunkers; their games were much more horizontal than vertical.
Bird's gravity-bound ways were particularly conspicuous: the
metaphorical acceptance of "white man's disease" paralleled Bird's
rise to fame. Even today, several years removed from the league,
Bird's dunk in a Miller Lite beer commercial elicits the laugh line
"Bird dunks?!"

The NBA aggressively marketed Bird, Magic, and their bicoastal
rivalry, but their "value" to the league began to wane in the late
1980s. Simultaneously, a new star was born, one whose breathtak-
ing vertical game inspired the nickname Air. Michael Jordan arrived
in the NBA in 1984—as did new commissioner David Stern. Unlike
Magic and Bird, Jordan had no equal or alter ego—at least, not on
the court. Off the court, many have designated Stern as the Michael

Jordan of NBA marketers—and with good reason. In Stern's relatively short tenure, the league has gone from an unstable sell in the
United States to a multibillion-dollar international conglomerate.
Stern's front man has been Jordan, and with Jordan has come the
hegemonic rhetorical icon of the dunk. The league has quite literally sold itself, its players, and its game to the world largely on the
basis of Jordan and his above-the-rim style of play.[21] In the NBA's
own words, "together Jordan and the dunk became international
sensations."[22] One need only look at a pickup game at the local gym
or to the NBA All-Star Game to witness Jordan's suasive appeal.
The Air Jordan shoes are only the most obvious manifestation of
this; the low socks, baggy shorts, and closely cropped, if not shaved,
hairstyle are Jordan signatures—to say nothing of "23" jerseys and
T-shirt likenesses.[23] The Jordan look, as Todd Boyd accurately notes,
"emphasizes the physical attributes of its practitioner."[24] If Darryl
Dawkins's dunks changed the physical architecture of basketball,
then Jordan's dunks and style of play have changed its corporeal
architecture.

Many Jordan-affiliated corporations have contributed to these
changes, Nike being only the most conspicuous. Yet the NBA has
taken a backseat to no one when it comes to marketing Jordan. The
league's entertainment arm has seemingly created its own Jordan
video division. Videocassettes such as *Come Fly with Me, Michael
Jordan's Playground, Air Time,* and *Above and Beyond,* while all
featuring Jordan, also feature the full panoply of his dunking *oeu-
vre.* This is to say nothing of other NBA-produced dunking fare,
such as *Super Slams of the NBA* and *NBA Super Slams 2*—both of
which give Jordan star billing. Much like Erving before him, popular signification of Jordan on the court has often been limited to
dunking, spectacular as it might be.

While it was Gatorade that introduced the "Be Like Mike" jin-
gle, the NBA has sold its own version of it. Just one proof of the success of the NBA's rhetorical campaign is the migration of the Jor-
dan-popularized dunk from the court to other NBA-sponsored
events, places, and programming. The league's traveling publicity
arm is known as the NBA Jam Session, which tours the world to
hype the league and its players. The Jam Session, which originated
at the 1993 All-Star weekend in Salt Lake City, uses interactive

events to communicate the sights, sounds, and actions of the NBA. Given its name, it should not surprise us that one such event is a slam-dunk competition for patrons.

The league's official web site features dunking in fairly promi-nent ways.[25] In the site's "Theater" section, viewers can watch the top ten dunks of the 1997–98 season in QuickTime Video. Yet this isn't the only part of the site that features dunking. NBA executives have designated six of the top ten plays of the season as dunks. Sim-ilarly, nine of the ten top rookie plays of the year were dunks. In total, viewers can click on twenty-five different icons to watch the NBA's finest execute its most rhetorically important shot. As if to underscore the point that dunking sells, viewers are encouraged to "visit" the NBA store, where dunking paraphernalia exist in abun-dance. Fans can purchase a wide assortment of posters featuring top dunkers; they can "become" their favorite dunkers through a jer-sey acquisition; and they can also purchase a wide assortment of dunking-related videos.

The NBA's rhetorical arm, though, reaches even further than the traveling carnival and cyberspace. The league, in cooperation with NBC, also produces its own weekend magazine show, featuring Ahmad Rashad and Willow Bay. Perhaps not surprising, the league punningly calls its weekly program *Inside Stuff*. That dunking fea-tures prominently in its programming is attested by the "Jam Ses-sion" segment, in which the week's most spectacular dunks are showcased with the hottest music.

While dunking has added immeasurably to the NBA's "bottom line," it has also had a direct effect on certain marginal players' marketability. The case of Vancouver's Dee Brown is instructive. In the 1990–91 season, then a rookie with the Boston Celtics, Brown was toiling largely in obscurity as Bird, Kevin McHale, and Robert Parrish monopolized nearly all the media attention outside the Boston area. The only "recognition" that Brown had received dur-ing his rookie campaign stemmed from a much-publicized racial in-cident with Wellesley, Massachusetts, police officers. In the summer of 1990, as Brown and his white fiancée, Jill Edmonds, sat in a car outside a Wellesley post office, police ordered the suspected bank robber out of the car at gunpoint. Little did the officers realize that their loaded weapons were trained on the Celtics' number-one draft choice and not the light-skinned black male described by a bank employee.

Brown's publicity (and financial status) changed for the better in February 1991. With a series of spectacular dunks, including the final "cover your eyes, look out below" slam, Brown won the NBA's Slam-Dunk Contest, defeating Seattle's Shawn Kemp in the finals. Just as significant as Brown's dunks was what he did before each dunk. In an unabashed show of commercialism, Brown "pumped up" his Reebok hightops. Much like the Spike Lee/Mars Blackmon exclamation ("It's gotta be the shoes"), the pumped-up shoes, the visual logic suggested, enabled Brown to complete his gravity-defying slams. The results of Brown's dunking success were predictable and immediate: within a week, Brown had a million-dollar endorsement deal with Reebok and plans for his own sneaker commercial—all because of a few nationally televised dunks.[26] Thus, in many respects, Brown's $20,000 winner's check was pocket change; the real payoff occurred only after the television lights went dark.

Given the ubiquity and aggressive marketing of the dunk, it shouldn't surprise us to see just how successful the NBA has been. Popular culture has seemingly devoured the dunk and the manifold profits that attend it. Take, for example, the relatively new basketball slick, *Slam*.[27] The hip-hop, trash-talking style of the magazine serves as a bulletin board for the virtues of dunking. Featuring sections such as "In Your Face," "Trashtalk," "Slamups," "Slamadamonth," and "Stuff," the magazine highlights the vertical game popularized by Jordan—whose visual and textual presence is a constant in its pages. Equally interesting are the products that get advertised in *Slam*. The NBA's Jordan trilogy is just one of many dunking-related consumer products. "Rim Rattler," for example, advertises hoop gear for the player. "Rim Rocka," though not explicitly about clothing apparel, features a Bulls-clad player dunking and ducking as the backboard above him shatters into small shards. Little could Dawkins have known twenty years ago that his dunking legacy would be appropriated for, of all things, commercial appeal in a clothing line!

Perhaps even more interesting than the clothing companies who advertise in *Slam* is a line of products with which I was, until recently, completely unfamiliar. In a recent issue, no fewer than nine different companies advertised jumping technologies designed to increase one's vertical leap—for the express purpose of dunking. Strength, whose plyometric training shoe retails for $124.95; Jump USA; SkyFlex; Air Alert; Vertical Power; and Strength Through Science—these companies and others offer a dizzying array of claims and visual "evidence" for increasing one's vertical leap. The point, of course, is not to debate the merits of the product—though adding ten inches to a vertical leap in two months seems to beg credulity. The point rather is to observe the intense competition for the dunking dollar—and the unsurprising fact that a magazine called *Slam* would be underwritten, in part, by this competition.

In addition, the singularity and individuality associated with dunking is "eloquently" reproduced in SkyFlex's full-page ad: "You got SkyFlex shoes. You trained in them. There's only one thing left to do . . . SLAM." (The final word takes up nearly a third of the page.) If young basketball players are being weaned on a steady diet of dunking's importance, this serves as an important context for many players', coaches', and analysts' complaints regarding the increasingly one-dimensional games of today's players. According to the hype, there's only one thing to do—not to win, have a jump shot, be a good passer, or be a team player but to *slam*.

Hegemonic Masculinity and the Dunk

The hegemony of the dunk, fomented in no small degree by the NBA and its marketers, also comes with its own gender politics. The NBA-sponsored Women's National Basketball Association (WNBA) and the now-defunct American Basketball League (ABL), while in many respects trying to create their own identities, have thus far failed to distance themselves from dunking. To the contrary, and perhaps to their long-term detriment, the new women's leagues have attempted to promote themselves, in part, to a vertically obsessed audience by showcasing players who can dunk. No small irony attends the fact that the ABL staged its first-ever dunk contest during the same year that the NBA suspended its version. What was a novelty in the ABL was, by 1998, banal in the NBA.

One is left to surmise that the pivotal variable in the comparison is the gender of the dunker.

More insidious is the notion that female players might have to "prove" their abilities by mimicking their male peers—thereby reinscribing an age-old adage in feminist circles that women are co-erced into becoming "manlike" in the workplace. By attempting to play above the rim, by co-opting the NBA's style of play, both women's leagues implicitly reinscribe the dominant male order—in this case, the hypermasculinized world of dunking. "I don't know that we should be so obsessed with when the dunk is going to come into the women's game," warns University of Washington coach Chris Gobrecht. "I guess it always has bothered me that there is a belief that our game won't be up to the level of the men's game until we can do things the men can do. That's always rubbed me the wrong way."[28]

In his masterful look at the NBA, David Halberstam "acciden-tally" broaches the issue. Regarding then Portland Trail Blazer Li-onel Hollins and his attempt to come back from an injury, Halber-stam asks, "When he went for an open basket, . . . if he could not stuff, was he truly a professional player?"[29] Halberstam's question cuts to the heart of the matter: despite the contract with a profes-sional team, is the non-dunking female really a professional bas-ketball player? Michael Jordan obliquely attempts a diplomatic an-swer: "A few years ago you couldn't fathom the idea of women dunking. Now you see it and it continues to improve. That's one of the highlights the fans miss that the men have. If they had it, I think you'd see people flocking to see women's basketball."[30] Jor-dan's diplomacy, at closer inspection, proves misleading. The equa-tion is quite simple: no dunking translates into sparse attendance. Some dunking will bring more people (men?) to watch games. WNBA star Lisa Leslie seems to agree: "It [dunking] would change the men's outlook on the women's game."[31]

Leslie has carried around the burden of dunking since at least her freshman year at the University of Southern California (USC). Much like her predecessor Cheryl Miller, Leslie arrived at USC to huge expectations after a high school career that featured, among other accomplishments, an astonishing 101-point outburst in one half. Many of those expectations, though, hinged on dunking during an intercollegiate game, a feat that only one female collegian has ever accomplished. With thirty onlookers, West Virginia University's six-foot seven-inch Georgeann Wells dunked late in a game against the University of Charleston on December 21, 1984. Said Wells nearly seven years later, "It's always on my mind. It will never go away. I'm surrounded by it. It was the greatest thing that ever could have happened as far as my basketball career is concerned."[32] That an untelevised dunk in a largely meaningless game could mean so much is profound proof of the cultural capital attending the dunk. That capital has never been lost on Leslie. As sportswriter Filip Bondy notes, "Lisa Leslie knows what is at stake. She understands that a single dunk in the Olympics would echo through the ages, would rocket the sport with videotape highlights for fuel."[33] Bondy, no doubt, is correct in his assessment: dunking would be worth a great deal to women's basketball generally and Lisa Leslie specifically. The more important issue, though, is: Should the dunk "mean" so much to women's basketball? I agree with Gorbrecht: as long as the fixation with dunking remains a media focal point for the women's game, both leagues will simply reproduce a somewhat disingenuous style of play, one premised more on the imitation of a male ideal than on the individual strengths that a woman brings to the court.

I also agree with Abigail M. Feder in her brilliant look at the gender politics in men's and women's figure skating. She argues that when physical abilities no longer distinguish men and women in a given sport, femininity is "overdetermined" by the media in order to keep female athletes from being labeled as masculine or lesbian.[34] One can witness such overdetermined femininity already at work with the player once dubbed the "Michael Jordan of women's basketball," Sheryl Swoopes. In her advertising campaign with Discover, Swoopes adopts the archetypal image of overdetermined femininity—the self-confessed "shopaholic." And while this represents but one instance, one wonders about the potential backlash for a league that promotes itself, in part, by visually challenging men on the playground and by verbally proclaiming, "We got next"—to say nothing of dunking. Such an overt attempt at equalization requires, according to Feder's logic, a corresponding "safe" image of the female athlete, especially for a heterosexual male viewing audience. And what can be less threatening than a domesticated woman stuck safely in the malls of America? So while Scott Hamilton uses his Discover card to buy golfing paraphernalia and Michael Chang uses his card to buy fishing equipment and gas for his boat, Swoopes buys lots of shoes—and not of the basketball variety.

Whither Dunking?

When he set the first peach basket at ten feet, Dr. James Naismith not only set a goal for players to shoot at, but he also "created" dunking. Of course, "the other doctor" didn't dunk, nor did the early players of the game; but by setting the goal at this height, Naismith created the possibility for numerous ways to score—the dunk being one of them. That it took several generations for dunking to evolve into a method of scoring does not diminish his "discovery." From day one, the dunk was always latent, waiting to be discovered, a possibility created simply by the act of hanging a basket at a certain height. Naismith would no doubt be surprised at his creation: the dunk has become the most important shot in basketball, a shot whose seeming simplicity belies a complex and dynamic set of cultural and economic practices.

This initial examination of these practices no doubt raises more questions than answers. To specify just a few: Can't a dunk, to paraphrase Freud, be just a dunk? Can't it simply be a strategic shot best suited to a given situation on the court? If an identity politics is expressed and enacted in dunking, isn't this a positive expression, one that should be cultivated? And if an identity politics is linked with dunking, what of the many white players who dunk? If dunking is coded along race and class lines, how are we to understand its appeal to white players? Similarly, should dunking always be coded as male, simply by virtue of the fact that men were the first to do it and see its possibilities? Hasn't the WNBA succeeded, by its existence alone, without the dunk? Is dunking just a violent action rather than a form of violence? Isn't the NBA marketing more than a particular shot, indeed an ethos intimately bound up with players and personalities? Given these and many other questions raised by the analysis, it's clear that dunking critics have their work cut out for them.

One question that deserves particular attention arises from the adjective most frequently used to describe dunking: *spectacular.* The term is particularly apt: dunking, perhaps above all else, is spectacle. It should come as no surprise that dunking's popularity parallels the growth of televised sport. The dunk seems like it was meant to be viewed—repeatedly. Long-term lucrative network deals have ensured that television will continue to disseminate the dunk to future generations around the world. Not only will viewers be able to watch more games and dunks through the wonders of satellite technology, but dunking will also remain a staple of shows featuring sports highlights. During basketball season, programs like *Sportscenter* will continue to capitalize on the dunk's rhetorical appeal. As long as dunking translates into large audiences and, hence, advertising revenues, it will remain a featured part of any highlight reel.

The NBA, though, is not putting all its eggs into the television basket. It is also actively cultivating a large presence in cyberspace, one in which dunking figures prominently. That presence will only grow with better digital technology and increased computer use. Already the NBA has its own dunking database, endlessly repeatable based on the click of an icon. Such interactivity holds interesting implications for the dunk. It seems clear that the dunk will be increasingly divorced from its most important context—a game in which there is a winner and loser. Instead, it will continue to proliferate simply as a virtual image, one whose appeal seems increasingly far removed from real players in real games at real points in time. Thus, perhaps have we arrived at dunking in postmodernity: dunking as pastiche, dunking as fluid in space and time, and dunking as the only meaningful or "real" act of signification.

We have come a very long way in less than forty years, from the urban playgrounds of renegade dunkers such as Earl "The Goat" Manigault, Connie Hawkins, and Herman "Helicopter" Knowings to a domesticated dunking suburbia of digitized images and video-game caricatures. We have also come a long way in how we treat the dunk, from the NCAA's ban on it from 1967 to 1976 to its valorization and commodification in the present. Finally, regardless of how the dunk is mediated and how it continues to accrue meanings, it will remain basketball's most important and most valuable shot.

NOTES

This essay is gratefully dedicated to Ray Fleming, who, despite his gravity-bound ways on the court, inspires his students to make soaring moves on life's playground. For reading earlier drafts, thanks to Chris Scodari, Beni Tsurumi, Debra Kain, and Andy Furman of Florida Atlantic University; Caroline J. S. Picart of the University of Wisconsin, Eau Claire; and Jim Malek of Ithaca College. Thanks also to Marty Benson for locating archival materials on the NCAA's ban and eventual reinstatement of the dunk.

1. Raymond Fleming, "Basketball Jones," in *Ice and Honey* (Ardmore, PA: Dorrance & Company, 1979), 3.

2. National Collegiate Athletic Association, *Digest of Committee Action for 1967–68*, NCAA, 1.

3. Quoted in Nelson George, *Elevating the Game* (New York: HarperCollins, 1992), 145.

4. Before converting to Islam, Abdul-Jabbar's name was Lew Alcindor.

5. Todd Boyd, ". . . The Day the Niggaz Took Over: Basketball, Commodity Culture, and Black Masculinity," in *Out of Bounds: Sports, Media, and the Politics of Identity*, ed. Aaron Baker and Todd Boyd (Bloomington: Indiana University Press, 1997), 125.

6. In the first dunking contest, held by the American Basketball Association (ABA), contestants were judged on "artistic ability, imagination, body flow as well as fan response." See Michael Murphy, "The ABA Way," *Houston Chronicle*, 4 February 1996, 17.

7. Perhaps a similar logic underlies the cultlike celebrity attending Dennis Rodman. But, instead of a performance aesthetic based on leaping, Rodman's is a body aesthetic premised largely on a fluid or chameleon-like body.

8. George Will, "The Athletic Jazz of Michael Jordan," *Newsweek*, 18 October 1993, 90.

9. Quoted in John Feinstein, "Pittsburgh's Master Rebounder Has a Shattering Experience," *Washington Post*, 1 February 1988, C2.

10. Quoted in Steve Zipay, "Smashing Backboard Makes You Media Icon," *Newsday*, 19 March 1996, A75.

11. Quoted in Phil Velasquez, "Trash Talk Getting Out of Control," *Chicago Sun-Times*, 29 May 1994, 7.

12. http://www.nba.com/theater/00742568.html

13. George, *Elevating the Game*, xvii.

14. Terry Pluto, *Loose Balls: The Short, Wild Life of the American Basketball Association* (New York: Simon & Schuster, 1990), 26, emphasis added.

15. Quoted in Sam Smith, "The Stuffs That Dreams Are Made Of," *Chicago Tribune*, 5 February 1988, 12C.

16. Richard Majors and Janet Mancini Billson, *Cool Pose: The Dilemmas of Black Manhood in America* (New York: Lexington, 1992), 2.

17. Quoted in Peggy Peterman, "The Cool Look: It's a Way of Displaying Pride," *St. Petersburg Times*, 4 January 1988, 1D.

18. Bob Greene, *Hang Time: Days and Dreams with Michael Jordan* (New York: St. Martin's, 1993).

19. For a captivating account that painfully details the extent to which young black men are imperiled, see John Valenti and Ron Naclerio, *Swee'-pea and Other Playground Legends: Tales of Drugs, Violence and Basketball* (New York: Michael Kesend, 1990).

20. For an overtly racialized reading of Johnson's marketability, see Cheryl L. Cole and Harry Denny III, "Visualizing Deviance in Post-Reagan America: Magic Johnson, AIDS, and the Promiscuous World of Professional Sport," *Critical Sociology* 20 (1994): 123–47.

21. Jordan's unrivaled popularity both on and off the court has not escaped the attention of cultural critics. Perhaps predictably, much of their critical attention focuses on matters of race and class; see Michael Eric Dyson, "Be Like Mike? Michael Jordan and the Pedagogy of Desire," *Cultural Studies* 7 (1993): 64–72; David L. Andrews, "The Fact(s) of Michael Jordan's Blackness: Excavating a Floating Racial Signifier," *Sociology of Sport Journal* 13 (1996): 125–58; Norman K. Denzin, "More Rare Air: Michael Jordan on Michael Jordan," *Sociology of Sport Journal* 13 (1996): 319–24.

22. *NBA Super Slams 2*, executive producer Don Sperling, CBS/FOX, 1995.

23. For an informative and entertaining reading of the "23" and "45" jersey signifiers, see Edward G. Armstrong, "The Commodified 23, or, Michael Jordan as Text," *Sociology of Sport Journal* 13 (1996): 325–43.

24. Boyd, ". . . The Day the Niggaz Took Over," 136; see also Dyson, "Be Like Mike?" 64–72.

25. The site's address is http://www.nba.com.

26. Reebok, unfortunately, relied on grossly stereotypical representa-

tions of the black male to sell its shoes: Brown's penultimate dunk was rendered as the "King Kong Slam." As Nathan McCall notes, "For whites, the glossy TV images of brothers as superathletes have a completely different effect. Their sense of supremacy is fed by seeing us portrayed as leaping monkeys, more closely related to beasts of the field than to human beings." See Nathan McCall, *What's Going On* (New York: Random House, 1997), 13–14.

27. All references to *Slam* are taken from the August 1998 issue.

28. Quoted in Dick Rockne, "Lisa Leslie—To Dunk or Not to Dunk," *Seattle Times*, 3 February 1991, C1.

29. David Halberstam, *The Breaks of the Game* (New York: Ballantine, 1981), 84.

30. Quoted in Julie Deardorff, "Slam against Women's Game—No Dunks—May Change Soon," *Chicago Tribune*, 18 January 1993, N1.

31. Quoted in ibid.

32. Quoted in Rockne, "Lisa Leslie," C1.

33. Filip Bondy, "Leslie Dunkin' for Dollars: U.S. Player Ready to Slam," *New York Daily News*, 15 April 1996, 57.

34. Abigail M. Feder, "'A Radiant Smile from the Lovely Lady': Overdetermined Femininity in 'Ladies' Figure Skating," in *Women on Ice: Feminist Essays on the Tonya Harding/Nancy Kerrigan Spectacle*, ed. Cynthia Baughman (New York: Routledge, 1995), 22–46.

11

retelevising a revolution
commercial basketball and a chat with gil scott-heron

JAMES PETERSON

The revolution will not be televised.
—*Gil Scott-Heron,*
"The Revolution Will
Not Be Televised"

The revolution is about basketball.
—*KRS One (1996–97*
Nike commercial)

The revolution will be televised! televised!
—*Papa Wu and Uncle Pete,*
"Wu Revolution"

THE CONVERSATION THAT INITIATED THIS entire piece arose from a discussion about a paper that I presented to a group of fellow aspiring scholars. In this paper, I begin to establish some practical and theoretical connections amongst various formations of the concept of the underground throughout African American cultural history. To demonstrate some of the conceptual overlap between Ralph Ellison's *Invisible Man* and KRS One's "Hole," a dark and eerie tale rapped by a nameless narrator whose mental and physical poverty facilitate his criminal-mindedness, I played "Hole" and some of KRS's other tunes.

One of the first questions asked was what my opinion was on KRS's voiceover for the (in)famous

Nike commercial, in which he performs an arguably capitalistic re-
vision of Gil Scott-Heron's "The Revolution Will Not Be Televised." Before I could formulate a complete response, two notable
black scholars began to debate the "authenticity" of KRS One and
Gil Scott-Heron. One scholar argued that KRS One disrespected
the politically charged content of the original, authentic Heron version. I could sense nostalgia for the "revolutionary sixties" gripping
the audience. How could KRS One, in cahoots with Nike, suggest
that the revolution will be televised or that the revolution is about
basketball?! The other scholar argued that perhaps we aren't critical enough in our understanding of Black History. He challenged
the authenticity and/or revolutionary praxis in the publishing, production, sale, and distribution of the original recording. I thought
that both scholars made valid points, so I went through the normal
journalistic routes to secure an interview with Gil Scott-Heron
about the commercial, the revolution, and basketball. The following
are excerpts from our conversation, recorded on July 7, 1998.

JP: Can I tell you a little bit about myself and about the project?
GSH: Yeah. If you feel that that would enhance it.
JP: Yeah. I think it will. My name is James Peterson. I'm from
Newark, New Jersey, and I'm at the University of Pennsylvania. I'm working on a Ph.D.
GSH: OK.
JP: My dissertation is about the concept of the underground;
from the Underground Railroad in slavery, through the underground of jazz, to the underground of hip-hop. One of my professors here asked me to do a piece on basketball and hip-hop.
And I immediately thought of KRS One and the Nike commercial, and I wanted to talk to you about that Nike commercial,
about your work, and about what you think about hip-hop culture and basketball and how those things are starting to come
together in some ways today. So, I just wanted you to talk
freely about any of those things. My main, specific question is,
have you spoken to KRS One at all about the commercial or
what your thoughts are about that Nike commercial.
GSH: I worked with him on it.
JP: Can you tell me about that process?

GSH: We were in the studio on Green Street.

JP: OK.

GSH: I was called and made aware of the fact that the music from that tune was gonna be used for a Nike commercial that would be produced down there and then I would be involved with it. People thought I should be involved with it since they were rewriting the words.

JP: [Laughter]

GSH: See, that particular tune does not belong to my publishing company. So I did not have an option one way or the other in terms of whether or not it was used. But since it was gonna be used, I had an option as to whether or not I should be involved to see how it was gonna be used. A copy of the script was sent to me. I went over it. Took a look at it. And [I] played basketball both in high school and college.

JP: Oh! OK.

GSH: And followed the people (particularly in the Washington area) because I lived there for so long and taught at Federal City College and at Johns Hopkins before I left there. And [I] knew Coach [John] Thompson and some of the other people down there. And [I] saw how it was being put together and really admired the cats they were puttin' on the commercial.

JP: That's right.

GSH: As young . . . as a whole new squad [that] I believed they would develop to be with Jason Kidd, Joe Smith . . .

JP: I think Kevin Garnett was on there.

GSH: Right. That's going to be the All-Star Five in a couple of years.

JP: No question.

GSH: Kris [KRS One] is not that familiar with basketball. And he does not keep up with it like that and so what he needed more than anything else was some way to work the names and the attitude that they were trying to put together to syncopate the shit. And that's what I tried to help with.

JP: So you actually worked on the commercial. You know, a lot of people don't know that. So when you first saw the script, what was your response to it? You were positive about it?

GSH: I was positive they were going to do it because it was not my publishing. But it was nice of the people who published it to call me.

JP: No question.

GSH: And tell me that it was going to be done.

JP: Did you get a chance to meet KRS One?

GSH: We worked with them in the studio. We were there and [we] saw how it was done and tried to help shape it. Since it wasn't my words, I didn't have that much of an attitude towards it at all, other than the fact that I enjoy basketball and I like the cats that they were talking about and [I] like KRS.

JP: Let me reproduce for you some of the conversations that have happened in response to the commercial. Some people (who may not know that you were involved with the production) think KRS One was out of control using those words to talk about basketball. They say the revolution is not about basketball.

GSH: Well . . . young folks are about revolution and basketball is a part of their culture. And a lot of the people that they admire and will admire and have admired were basketball players . . . from the time Kareem Jabbar was the best man at my wedding. [Laughter] He introduced me to my wife. There's nothing alien as far as I'm concerned about basketball at all. It's ours. We let them play every once in a while. [Laughter]

JP: Another question: Is basketball more like hip-hop or more like jazz?

GSH: Basketball is a separate thing altogether. My father was a professional soccer player. I don't consider soccer as a part of the culture he was livin' in. He played for the Celtics and was the first black player to play in Scotland.

JP: Wow.

GSH: I think that we have to learn to separate our art and our athletics and our disciplines because we go different ways. That's what freedom is. Having the choices to go and . . .

JP: . . . do different things.

GSH: You know, they wasn't lettin' nobody like us in the University of Pennsylvania not too long ago. [Laughter]

JP: That's right.

GSH: So now we can jam on it together if we want to, but if we do it negates the things that a lot of folks did to make those things possible. We ignore the sacrifices that were made to make certain things possible if we do not acknowledge them as such. So what we're doing with our academic potential, athletic potential, and artistic potential, all of that is owed to various people who made certain sacrifices to make it possible, but they're not the same thing.

The most intriguing information that I learned from this interview was that Mr. Scott-Heron does not own the publishing rights to arguably his most famous tune, "The Revolution Will Not Be Televised." For whatever reasons, "The Revolution" had to be sold. I am not interested in this irony because I think that it undermines revolutionary thought or action in the 1960s and 1970s; it doesn't. For all intents and purposes, this commercial was an unauthorized remake. Mr. Scott-Heron *consulted*, but he couldn't halt the reproduction of his previously owned work. For that matter, KRS One could not have done this either.[1] His voice certainly confounds the issue, because he is considered by many to be a seminal voice for revolution by and in hip-hop culture. But I don't think that this commercial fooled anyone. The revolution is not about basketball when we are 80 percent of the players and 0 percent of the owners. The revolution is not about basketball when players don't invest time and resources in their (former) communities.

At best, the Nike-induced re(tele)vision of Mr. Scott-Heron's work provides all of us with the opportunity to be critical in our memories of African American activism in the sixties and right now. The revolution is about basketball when its commercials force us to rethink our history and challenge those who would misrepresent it. The revolution is about basketball when young black men and women earn wealth and resources and reinvest in their own communities. Critical memory in the Black Public Sphere does not allow for a comfortably nostalgic remembrance of the revolutionary sixties. Instead, it challenges us to rethink and intensely evaluate homely notions of the past in conjunction with the dynamic elements of the present and the future.

Finally, we are left to contemplate the meaning of revolution. The simplest definition of revolution is "the overthrow and replacement of a government."[2] African Americans have not ever overthrown the American government. We have engaged in revolutionary struggles (slave revolts, the Underground Railroad, boycotts, sit-ins, etc.). We have had many revolutionaries (i.e., people who have seriously challenged the American government with the intent to overthrow, replace, or reform). Reformation now appears to be the struggle in which most "revolutionary" activists are engaged. Gil Scott-Heron suggested to me that we "learn to separate our art and our athletics and our disciplines because we go different ways. . . . We can jam on [these things] together if we want to, but if we do it negates the things that a lot of folks did to make those things possible." If we are invested in reforming America, then we will need revolutionary reformers in all our "disciplines."[3]

NOTES

1. I made repeated attempts to contact KRS One, his publicist, and/or his management for an interview. I spoke with several people, was promised (at least) a response to my questions, but I never received this response.

2. *The American Heritage College Dictionary*, 3d ed.(Boston: Houghton Mifflin Company, 1993), p. 1169.

3. Renee T. White, "Revolutionary Theory: Sociological Dimensions of Fanon's *Sociologie d'une revolution*," in Lewis R. Gordon, T. Denean Sharpley-Whiting, and Renee T. White, eds., *Fanon: A Critical Reader* (Cambridge, MA: Blackwell Publishers, 1996), p. 100.

SOURCES

The American Heritage College Dictionary. 3d ed. Boston: Houghton Mifflin Company, 1993.

The Black Public Sphere Collective, eds. *The Black Public Sphere*. Chicago: University of Chicago Press, 1995.

Kelley, Robin D. G. *Yo' Mama's Disfunktional: Fighting the Culture Wars in Urban America*. Boston: Beacon Press, 1997.

McCall, Nathan. *What's Going On: Personal Essays*. New York: Random House, 1997.

White, Renee T. "Revolutionary Theory: Sociological Dimensions of Fanon's *Sociologie d'une revolution*." Pp. 100–109 in Lewis R. Gordon, T. Denean Sharpley-Whiting, and Renee T. White, eds., *Fanon: A Critical Reader*. Cambridge, MA: Blackwell Publishers, 1996.

12

sheroes over the rim

a brave new women's basketball world

TINA SLOAN GREEN AND ALPHA ALEXANDER

Introduction

Both authors have been involved in the struggle for equality in women's athletics for over thirty years. With the emergence in the 1990s of two new professional basketball leagues, women's basketball has finally arrived in the United States; but what does this really mean? In looking beyond the year 2000 at women in professional basketball, we have chosen to examine how professional women's basketball came to fruition; to look at how the professional ranks are doing now, after their second season of play; and, most important, to look at the direction in which women's professional basketball is heading in the new millennium.

Background

Historically, the Association of Intercollegiate Athletics for Women (AIAW), established in 1971, played a major role in collegiate competitive women's sports. Marian Washington, Vivian Stringer, Carole Oglesby, Vivian Acosta, and Tina Sloan Green were members of the first Committee on the Status of Minorities in the AIAW. There we fought for racial representation and fair treatment. Men were content to allow women to have their own leagues until the AIAW Women's Basketball Championships became profitable. When the male-dominated universities saw the potential of economic revenue in women's basketball and faced the threat of sanctions under Title IX, an interest emerged in the NCAA to create women's championships.

Eventually, the NCAA, with its vast resources and influence, won the political and legal battle against the AIAW that resulted in the NCAA assuming control of women's intercollegiate sports and the eventual demise of the AIAW, in 1982. Thus, the male-dominant NCAA kept control over the profits, the rate of growth, and the leadership of women's basketball. By 1995, with the sellout crowds and national television exposure of NCAA women on the road to the Final Four, female basketball stars were in the limelight and a target of interest for promoters of the 1996 Olympic women's basketball team. Attendance at the NCAA women's basketball games rose for the seventeenth straight season to nearly 7.4 million, an increase of 9.7 percent. The NCAA tournament drew a record crowd of 285 million fans. The championship game received a 3.7 rating from ESPN.

It is amazing to think that just three years ago women basketball players who wanted to continue playing after college were playing professionally in Europe and Japan for lack of opportunities here in the United States. As a result of the U.S. women's basketball team's gold-medal performance in the 1996 Olympics in Atlanta, the team's commercial attraction, and the commercial success of women's college basketball, women's professional basketball finally became a reality in the United States, with not one but two leagues taking center stage.

Businesspeople saw the profitability in women's basketball and created the American Basketball League (ABL) in the fall of 1996.

Nine cities were chosen as sites for competition. Each ABL team played a forty-four-regular-game schedule, with playoffs during the traditional basketball season, which lasts approximately six months. Players averaged salaries of $80,000, with top players commanding as much as $150,000. Many of the U.S. Olympic team players, such as Dawn Staley, Theresa Edwards, and Nikki McCray, signed agreements to play with the ABL. In the first season, however, the American Basketball League lost $4 million, double its initial projected losses. In the off-season it received a $6 million infusion. In the end, though, none of this was enough, and the league dissolved and filed for federal bankruptcy protection in December 1998.

The National Basketball Association (NBA) responded to the ABL's formation in late 1996 by launching its own league, the Women's National Basketball Association (WNBA). Unlike the ABL, the WNBA played in existing NBA arenas in eight cities during the summertime. Given its shortened season—only twenty-eight games over a ten-week period—salaries ranged from $15,000 to $50,000, with a league average of $35,000. Top-ranked national players, including Ruthie Bolton-Holifield and Sheryl Swoopes, received $250,000 in their first year, while Lisa Leslie allegedly signed a two-year, $1 million contract.

Two very competitive, committed, and successful leagues in their own right; yet the question circulating among fans of both leagues between 1996 and 1998 was whether the two leagues would survive. The ABL, with its exclusive contracts, small city teams, fewer but loyal fans, and high salaries, struggled under little publicity of its athletes, few sponsors, and minimal media coverage. And without a major TV deal or another major investment from another source, it could not go on.

The WNBA was the favorite to last from the start. The league is strong financially, and its games and playoffs are played in NBA venues during the NBA off-season. Although the WNBA athletes' salaries are lower than those in the ABL were, they have a large number of sponsors, and their games are televised nationally three times a week on NBC, ESPN, and Lifetime, averaging 1.4 million households per game. Thanks to the NBA's clout with NBC (the major carrier of NBA games), the WNBA received a great deal of promotion during the NBA playoffs.

From the beginning, there was one key difference between the two women's leagues. The ABL spent more on salaries and less on promoting their athletes and was basically supported by private investors and profits. The WNBA, by contrast, is simply an extension of the NBA that utilizes NBA resources. The WNBA spends millions on advertising to promote their teams because they are focused on creating stars.

There exists enough talent to stock two professional leagues and enough public support for both to have coexisted. Players, agents, and fans alike had a vested interest in the survival of two leagues. Now we are left with one, and we must ask ourselves what the future will hold for women in professional basketball. What will it take to keep professional women's basketball alive and thriving in the United States? What programs, influences, and issues will play a key role in the survival or demise of the women's game? What opportunities will arise?

The Role of Grassroots Programs

When we interviewed Frank Green, a basketball media pioneer who was responsible for the first televised women's basketball game in 1975, he told us,

> Grassroots programs and professional women's basketball are in the minority. They will, however, have a greater impact on each other in the year 2000 because many of today's professional female basketball players came from a grassroots program. The identification with both comes from believing in yourself and realizing you can achieve. (June 24, 1998)

Dawn Staley, who played for the ABL's Philadelphia Rage and who serves as a role model to African American girls, came from a grassroots program in Philadelphia. She has said:

> These programs will continue to serve as a launching pad for young girls into sports and will help develop and raise the necessary skill levels of girls. They will also help to identify and nurture new talent. Supporting these grassroots programs is vitally

important for many inner-city girls—especially girls from diverse backgrounds—whose low economic status has historically prevented them from participating in games or sports. However, unless neighborhood grassroots programs can compete in quality with the more established programs, it is doubtful that significant numbers of female champions will emerge during the next decade. (October 10, 1998)

When we interviewed Jay Norman, former assistant basketball coach at Temple University and past director of the Temple University National Youth Sports Program (NYSP) for over twenty years, he said, "We need more basketball programs for girls. To do this, funding is required" (June 10, 1998).

For many girls, sports programs offered at their local YWCA, Girls Scouts, and Girls Incorporated are their first exposure to sports. They may also be the place where a young girl picks up a basketball for the very first time. For example, the YWCA has a grant program sponsored by Nike's P.L.A.Y. (Participate in the Lives of America's Youth) that provides seed money for balls and other basketball equipment to YWCAs across the country, so that they can start up basketball and volleyball programs for girls between the ages of nine to fourteen years of age. Started in the 1995–96 season, these programs focus specifically on skill development, building self-esteem, and having fun. Having fun is key to endearing girls to the game of basketball and getting them to, as the WNBA has marketed the phrase, "join in."

With the success of professional women's basketball, groups of girls are being taken to games by their coaches, mothers, fathers, friends, and relatives. The girls become "hooked" as they begin to identify with the players.

Promotion and Media Coverage of Women's Professional Basketball

Greater prominence through media exposure is an advantage that the upcoming generation of collegiate professional women athletes can and will enjoy as the game becomes more successful. For example, Nike's financial support for the travel, training, and promotion of the U.S. women's basketball team prior to the 1996 Olympics had a dramatic impact on the commercial and spectator value of these athletes after their gold-medal finish.

Conversations with high school–aged African American females revealed that when it came to women's basketball, young girls were familiar with the names and faces of the stars of the game. A mere five years ago, this would not have been the case. This is partially due to such efforts as ESPN's investment of millions of dollars for the exclusive rights to televise the NCAA Women's Basketball Tournament, which came about mainly because many felt that as more women participated in sports, they would become both spectators and viewers of women in sports. This potential market of viewers has the kind of purchasing power that makes television executives take notice. If girls have the opportunity to watch any highly skilled athlete on television, their motivation to pursue the sport as participants may also increase.

Jay Norman said, "I find it more enjoyable to watch women because they are more fundamentally sound. Because of the height and power of the guys they spend much more time in the air. Women have to depend on the fundamentals of passing and shooting."

Leadership Is the Key

Leadership in the form of shared power will be crucial for women in professional basketball in the new millennium. It is necessary for the owners and leagues to realize the importance of the athletes and be willing to delegate some decision making to them. If owners and top administrators in women's basketball are not willing to share power, players will join unions for protection and autonomy.

Currently, women are seen at all levels of management in professional basketball leagues. Comparing the NBA with the ABL, for example, during the 1997 basketball season, women comprised 44 percent of NBA league management and 38 percent of NBA front-office management (Richard Lapchick and Kevin Matthews, "1997

Racial Report Card," Northeastern University's Center for the Study of Sport in Society). In comparison, women held 56 percent of the ABL league management positions and 68 percent of the ABL team management positions (Terese Stratta, "The Status of Black Women in Professional Sports," paper presented at the 1998 Black Women in Sports Foundation [BWSF] Conference in Philadelphia). When Terese Stratta investigated the WNBA, she discovered that existing employees from the NBA held a disproportionate number of management positions in the WNBA. Given the overlap in employee duties and the fact that the WNBA did not resemble a true start-up league with equal opportunities for employment, as did the ABL, management data for the WNBA were not recorded.

Just as we have seen a decrease in the numbers of female coaches over the years, the overall numbers of females in sports-related fields are likely to decrease if certain affirmative action measures are not taken. Since men do and will control the infrastructure of women's basketball on the collegiate and professional levels, and since women's basketball now promises lucrative financial gains, men will be reluctant to give up power. They will retain control by creating a few visible female positions in the organization while retaining male leadership in the power roles. There are also great disparities in the racial makeup of the coaches, and these disparities need to be addressed. For example, when comparing the head and assistant coaches of the two professional women's leagues, Stratta found very different pictures related to representation by race. Of the nineteen ABL coaches, only two women and one man were Black (16 percent representation), whereas fifteen women and one man were Caucasian (84 percent representation). Of the twenty-six coaches in the WNBA, six women and three men were Black (35 percent representation), ten women and six men were Caucasian (62 percent representation), and one woman was Asian (4 percent representation).

There has also already developed a trend toward hiring young, inexperienced women with potential for success, in order to avoid huge salaries and to bring fresh faces before the audience. Young women who are hired in these roles must do their homework; they must investigate and understand the history of women's sports, specifically basketball, so that they can intelligently respond to the challenges faced in the workplace with regard to hiring and affirmative action. Often, many who have been hired as a result of affirmative action tend to deny its importance once they get the job. To advance the case for more female sports administrators, we must cultivate male allies and also support qualified women when appropriate, not turning our backs on the continuing need for affirmative action (as the states of California and Washington did in 1997 and 1998).

In summary, we are anxious to see what the future holds. Young people, both boys and girls, will grow up appreciating talent regardless of the gender of athletes. The son of one of the writers, Frankie Green, who is fourteen years old, can name and give stats on most of the WNBA players. Female basketball players may become household names among the youth. Consequently, men may become a considerable part of the spectator market in another decade. What will need to occur to allow professional women's basketball in the United States to continue to thrive and take off beyond the year 2000? As in most cases in this country, economic profit has been and will continue to be the motivation behind the growth and promotion of women's basketball.

After fighting for so many years for female equity in sports, we are excited that we are still alive to see athletes benefiting from our struggles.

13

who's got next?
gender, race, and the mediation of the wnba

TARA McPHERSON

*The acknowledged Other must
assume recognizable forms.*
—*bell hooks*

A WHILE BACK, I WAS VISITING A FRIEND
and noticed that her young daughter was playing
with Christie, the African American version of the
WNBA Barbie. As a six-foot-tall failed basketball
player, I've been intrigued by the recent high visibility of women's sports, a rise to popularity Mat-
tel certainly hasn't failed to capitalize on. I asked
my friend's daughter how she liked the doll, and
she said it was "pretty fun" but looked a lot more
like part-time model and Los Angeles Sparks player
Lisa Leslie than like Teresa "T-Spoon" Weatherspoon, since the WNBA Barbies don't have "any
muscles" or T-Spoon's signature cornrows. Personally, she liked T-Spoon better as a player "because
she's really physical; all those muscles are the
bomb." She went on to explain that sometimes she

pretended the Christie doll was T-Spoon anyway (though all attempts at cornrowing her hair had failed); at other times she imagined *she* was T-Spoon and the doll was both of them, and they both
had more muscles than any of her Barbies did.

I was intrigued by this girl's description of her play, partly because of the ease with which she projected herself into other forms,
using the WNBA Barbie as a kind of avatar, a screen for virtual pro-
jection, and also because, in imagining herself elsewhere, she actively took her body along for the game. She knew that this skinny-
assed Barbie wouldn't last long in a real WNBA game and loved the
well-muscled bodies of her favorite players, T-Spoon and Cynthia
"Coop" Cooper. This body awareness was closely wed to her awareness of race, for her dissatisfaction with basketball Barbie reflected
her knowledge of all Barbies' basic whiteness, despite WNBA
Christie's politically correct chocolate-hued tone.

With her buxom figure, Anglo features, and permanently arched
feet, WNBA Barbie might seem worlds away from the sweaty,
muscled arenas of women's basketball, but the issues of femininity,
race, and embodiment that coalesce around her plastic form are
equally pertinent to understanding the WNBA, or more important,
its mediated representations. Since its inception, the league has
struggled to image its players as both skilled and feminine, a representational double bind that has yielded complex and troubling figures of racialized women's bodies. In an era many (including Los
Angeles's hip hop radio station, 92.3 Beat) hail as "color-blind,"
such questions of race, the body, and representation are crucially
important, even as we (unevenly) move toward increasingly digital
modes of representation that seemingly leave the flesh behind.[1]
Bodies matter, even (perhaps more so) in the jacked-in age of
ESPN.com. Fans may be flocking to sites like www.nba.com, but
basketball's still better live and sweaty.

B-Ball in the Digital Domain

I guess you could call me a basketball fan now that the WNBA has
established itself on the sports scene. Here in Los Angeles, I try to

catch a live Sparks game whenever I can; but, despite my love of the live, my fandom mostly revolves around frequent excursions to www.wnba.com. As I surfed the site over the past couple of years, I started thinking about much of the recent academic theory on cyberspace that I had been reading, and I came to realize that most web sites do not really sync up with these theories.

In her recent book *How We Became Posthuman,* Katherine Hayles notes that "the 30 million Americans who are plugged into the Internet increasingly engage in virtual experiences enacting a division between the material body that exists on one side of the screen and the computer simulacra that seem to create a space inside the screen" (20). In *Virtualities,* Maggie Morse describes the "oral logic of incorporation" that drives virtual systems, systems with "the power to erase the organic [body] from awareness" (141). Both Hayles and Morse go on to underscore the importance of remembering the body in an era of digital reproduction, of reinscribing the corporeal into the virtual, and I am sympathetic to their urgings. Yet my own experience of Internet sites, particularly those addressed to women, does not support the now almost clichéd view that virtual life disavows the material body.[2] Grand claims are not very useful in understanding the nuances of cyberspace, particularly as we work to try to discern the links between old (say, print and TV) and new (read: the web) forms of representation and their racial logics. Indeed, some web sites serve as powerful spaces of imagined racialized embodiment that directly and overtly reference the material world, weaving the physical body and the digital corpus together. Furthermore, these digital explorations of physical embodiment do not always provide cause for celebration or evidence of an "improved" cyberspace, for simply "remembering" the body or ushering it into the digital era is not enough. Bodies bear history in very particular ways, and many of these histories might be better transcended.

In what follows, I turn to the specific example of the WNBA, the Women's National Basketball Association, in order to trace the traffic between the material and the virtual and between old and new representations of the body, of race, and of femininity. While I devote some time to an examination of www.wnba.com, the official WNBA web site, I situate this analysis in a broader context that includes both televisual and print coverage of not only the WNBA but also its brother league, the NBA, in order to compare the gendered and racialized modes of address structured by means of these various representational modalities. And, for reasons I hope will soon become apparent, gender first emerges as a central term of analysis.

We Got Next: Women and Basketball

The WNBA began its first season in the summer of 1997, building on the success and popularity of the 1996 gold-medal-winning Olympic women's team and the trailblazing of the American Basketball League (ABL), a now-defunct women's league formed in 1996. The WNBA's first year (played in the NBA's off-season in the same stadiums) saw a higher attendance at games than had been predicted, partly due to the massive marketing power of the NBA, which hyped the organization with the "We Got Next" slogan during the NBA playoffs. The nascent league also scored a great television deal, with Fox, NBC, and Lifetime all signing on to broadcast games, a televisual seal of approval that had largely eluded the ABL. Viewer turnout was better than hoped for as well, with audience shares roughly equal to those for men's hockey or many regional telecasts of Major League baseball. NBC averaged 2 million households per game.

Feminist scholars writing on the gendered representation of women athletes have noted that "stereotyped media framings of the female athlete ... increasingly undermine any potential threat" she might pose to cultural systems of meaning, particularly by sexualizing women sports figures or by reinscribing them within fairly traditional notions of feminine appeal and appearance (Kane/Lenskyj 188).[3] Put differently, muscle is recoded by means of stylized femininity and beauty. One could certainly make such an argument vis-à-vis the early marketing of WNBA stars, particularly Lisa Leslie and Rebecca Lobo, two players featured extensively in early advertising and publicity. Slim and well coiffed, neither woman epitomizes what Laurie Schulze, in reference to female bodybuilders, has termed "a radical female body that interrogates gender" (76), and each was neatly packaged within fairly mainstream definitions of femininity in talk-show appearances, *Glamour* magazine copy, and print and television advertisements.

Much was made of Leslie's modeling contract with the Wilhelmina Agency, and magazine spreads from *Vogue* to *Elle* to *People* to *Sisters in Style* offered lavish spreads of the elegant Leslie posed in high-end fashions, small U.S. flag bikinis, and glamorous locations. An early television advertisement for Reebok opens in grainy black and white with a quick pan up Rebecca Lobo's shapely legs, moving from high-heeled pumps to waist height before cutting away. Other quick shots of Lobo in the ad include one close-up in which she wears pearls. The WNBA's early marketing worked vigorously to contain the threat of the muscled woman (and, implicitly, of the sports dyke) through a soft-focus view of the female.

Of course, given the recuperative power of mass media when faced with alternative images of femininity, none of this is all that startling. In the age of the *Sports Illustrated* swimsuit issue, I am hardly shocked to see Lisa Leslie decked out in a bikini. If basketball players (Dennis Rodman included) want to explore their feminine side, more power to them. Lisa's looking pretty good in *Vogue*. In fact, a certain mediated knowingness is reflected in much of the press, indicating that the women are fully aware of the feminization of their images. One of my favorite ads has Lobo, wearing her uniform and looking cocky, spinning the signature orange and white ball of the league, intoning "It's no fairy tale. . . . It's *pro* women's basketball. . . . Welcome to the ball, Cinderella." But if these early ads dealt heavily in feminine beauty, more interesting is the relatively quick way in which these images of what we might call "femme-y femininity" were supplanted by a more muscular, physical femininity, figured in the shift of focus from preseason league celebrities Lobo and Leslie to a pair of players who emerged as the league's true MVPs and fan pleasers, Cynthia Cooper and Teresa Weatherspoon.

The representational strategies that frame these players turn more to the muscular and the physical, away from posed girly shots toward action-filled images that threaten to spill free from the space of the frame. Cynthia Cooper sweats and bench-presses her way through a television spot promoting awareness of breast cancer, wearing a weight belt and baggy workout clothes, suggesting that the image of the muscled female may not be so threatening to mainstream media as to necessitate its elimination. Even the high-heeled Reebok ad discussed earlier intercuts shots of Lobo as femme with action sequences of Lobo playing ball. Furthermore, the televising of actual game play foregrounds the physical, using framing, slow motion, and instant replays in forms not unlike male basketball (a noted departure from the televising of women's NCAA games earlier in the decade).[4]

Still, more traditional discourses of femininity, particularly those tied to notions of the familial and the domestic, do work to re-contextualize the women of the WNBA, structuring a feminine mode of address that sometimes knocks roughly against the more aggressively shot game play, wedding, as we shall see, embodiment to the familial in precise, if masked, ways. Pretaped interview segments aired during the games usually focus on the family-life of the players, working to frame them within the normative hetero-sexual family, and much was made of the pregnancies of several players, as well as the battle with breast cancer of Cynthia Cooper's mother, Mary Cobbs. Opening shots of the first championship game featured Houston Comet Sheryl Swoopes with her nine-week-old son, while much of the game's commentary regarding Coop also detailed her nurturing and caretaking qualities. One announcer noted that Coop's season was "made all the more remarkable by the personal struggles she's had this year . . . not only looking after her mom but raising nieces and nephews . . . somehow she has juggled it all." Many of the players emerge as superwomen, able to excel at both "traditional" and exceptional femininity.

At a more symbolic level, the various franchises are relentlessly narrativized as "teams" in several senses of the word. Each is represented as a kind of family, full of—in the buzzwords of one WNBA promo—"spirit/trust/expression/teamwork." Shots of the teams during time-outs focus relentlessly on the "closeness" of the players, with an emphasis on hand holding and group hugs. One broadcast tidbit discussed the role Houston coach Van Chancellor's wife, Betty, played in the extended family of the Comets, pointing out that she was integral in urging Chancellor to address Cooper's need to care for her mother. Advertising for the league underscores that this is *family* entertainment—both affordable and accessible, interweaving the WNBA family and the families of America. A *Sports Illustrated* article (Wolff 1997) opined that the WNBA proves that "women players can connect more intimately" than men (56) both among players and between players and fans, though the homoerotic dimensions of this comment were not, of course, explored. In fact, the WNBA carefully elides any overt references to its family of lesbian fans (or players), a distinct marker of difference between this league and the more queer-friendly (and now bankrupt) ABL.[5]

The WNBA web site also evidences this mix of the physical and the familial, though its modes of address seem more resolutely feminine, borrowing as they do from such conventional forms as the advice column, the woman's magazine, and the talk show (especially in the Oprah-inspired "book club" section, featuring New York's Coquese Washington). Here, the web displays its ability to merge print and broadcast, creating an illusion of liveness (flashing text and scrolling banners promote a sense of urgency and an ontology of "the new and the now") while also exploiting the database capacities of the Internet so loved by stats fans. Featured components of the site include "Ask Olympia" and "Tammi's Tips" as well as "diary" entries for several players and a "family photo album" for Rebecca Lobo. A "Personal Notes" section provides the interested surfer with details of each player's hobbies, home life, and family. All these formats function as threshold or liminal devices that work to ease the transition from older mediated forms into digital modes of information delivery. And, because they're activated by a click of the mouse and harbor the promise of interactivity and hypermedia, the world of the web imbues these familiar discursive modes with the promise of the new.

Interactivity in the site is largely confined to clicking your way through a wealth of information, e-mailing the players, or engaging in frequent but heavily orchestrated "live chats" with different players and coaches. Yet these chats also reveal that interactivity occurs at more a metaphorical level, as the fans engage the players and actively imagine themselves as part of the WNBA. Much as my friend's daughter saw herself as both T-Spoon and WNBA Barbie, female fans of the league project themselves into the positions of players, repeatedly asking "how it feels" to play pro ball, how a gal can improve her game, and how to audition for the league. And, though we do not need the Internet to fantasize ourselves onto the hardwood, the mode of address structured by the web site—particularly what we might call its more feminine modes of address—actually facilitates this transformation, encouraging and structurally underwriting what I have previously termed a kind of volitional mobility, creating the mise-en-scène for imagining transformation, imagining possibility.[6]

This transformation is very much tied to the physical body, returning us to our discussion of embodiment in virtual realms. Fans visiting the WNBA web site do not seem, to use Hayle's terminology, particularly susceptible to the "condition of virtuality," to the deep rift between the world of embodied materiality and the world of digital data. Rather, the game—the game of basketball—mediates between embodiment and the virtual, as players offer up tips on improving your game and your body while also detailing at great length the physical stakes of tough play, from sprained ankles to sore muscles to being too tall for the boys. The video highlights provided on the site also foreground physicality, through both their imagery and their captions, almost fetishizing hard-hitting action, spinning bodies, and the beauty of a jump shot. They also mobilize physicality, moving the spectator through space on the axis of the body. If television coverage of sports addresses the viewer as a "you" or as part of a "we," the interactivity of this web site encourages the user to participate as an "I," structuring a dynamic of connected presence. Rather than just being *at* the game (the promise of television: we take you there), we're suddenly *in on* the game, interacting with the players by means of live chats or fan forums. There is a sense of volitional mobility, an experience of presence, that makes us one of the team, one of the family. Both the structural experience of moving through the site and the feminine forms of address it deploys help underwrite this sense of the familial and of physical presence.

Thus, sites such as this one function as a realm in which materiality and embodiment are present in virtual life, where the body is neither disavowed nor totally recuperated by means of traditional and hegemonic narratives of feminine beauty. But we might also ask, What precisely about the WNBA and its material reality would serve to underwrite this turn from beauty to a muscular embodiment that is still framed by discourses of the family?

Blackness and Basketball

If I have proceeded throughout the previous section as if oblivious that the word *race* is a central part of this chapter's title, it is largely because there is little overt discourse about race in either the traditional or the digital mediation of the WNBA. In the league's official public relations and in most of the press coverage, race—particularly race as blackness—is both invisible and hypervisible. Todd Boyd has argued that, in men's basketball, "blackness has been normalized through performance" (121); but this does not, of course, mean that racialized and racist discourse is absent from sports media. Rather, Boyd and others argue that class politics mediate race in basketball coverage, underwriting a representation of the young black male as urban, aggressive, violent, and out of control. This figure can be linked to that of the gangsta in rap, an image conversant with yet overdetermined by the historical representations of black masculinity.

Certainly, the WNBA's portrait of its two-time MVP Cynthia Cooper as a dedicated daughter, foster mother, and team player seems worlds apart from the figure of the gangsta, and there is little about the mediation of the WNBA that parallels the urban "street" image of the NBA. But the figuration of racialized femininity in the WNBA has everything to do with both the historical representation of the black female body and the current demonization of the NBA player.

In an article analyzing the media representations of Anita Hill, Wahneema Lubiano asks, "What is being coerced when 'woman' is used in specific ways—especially when categories like 'black woman' are not expressly articulated but are, nonetheless, over-whelmingly present?" (357–58)—a question we might equally ask of the WNBA. If the NBA mediates black masculinity by means of the "new jack" image, the WNBA's manipulations of black femi-ninity turn on the familiar figure of the black lady: street culture is replaced by the mantra of "caring, cooperation, and spirit."

From the careful, Miss Manners tone of the "Ask Olympia" col-umn to the spirit of uplift reflected in Coquese's virtual book club, the WNBA through its web site and other public relations, as well as the wider press coverage, presents black women as "good colored folk," as simultaneously accommodating and accommodated. In the endless stories detailing Cynthia Cooper's dedication to both her ailing mother and her adopted nieces and nephews, and in her "es-cape" from Watts to suburban Houston, Coop is portrayed as over-coming blackness and urbanness, an acceptable image of black fem-ininity for an era of conservative multiculturalism. Lubiano high-lights that in the case of Anita Hill, the black lady was demonized and threatening, but here she functions differently. Contextualized within the sports stadium, an arena largely ceded to blackness and where black success is, within limits, culturally sanctioned, the image of the black lady tips in another, reassuring and domesticated direction, more like "good help" than like the scheming Hill; the black lady as a part of the team, a part of the family.

Thus, we can also read the familial narratives that populate dis-cussions of the WNBA as more than simply attempts to recontex-tualize muscular women within the space of domesticity. While they may be that, they are also racialized narratives, intent on em-bracing a domesticated and embodied version of black femininity at the expense of the agency and histories of actual women and to the detriment of black masculinity. The familial discourse also helps stabilize the player's sexuality as heterosexuality even as it locates femininity in a muscular, physically active corporeality: tough, yes; dykes, no.

Writing in *Sports Illustrated*, Alexander Wolff, celebrating the differences between the WNBA and the brasher NBA, commented that "there's a story behind [the success of the league]—of fans sick of athletes and owners whose loyalties are shorter-lived than mayflies, and of kids and parents nauseated from having to accept as heroes male pros who buy drugs and sell autographs" (56). Others noted that viewers "would be drawn by the chance to see a version of the game that emphasized teamwork, passing and proficient shooting—virtues often conspicuously lacking in the slam-dunking, trash-talking, chest-thumping men's game" (Green 27). These frequent discussions in the press of the WNBA as "a kinder, gentler basketball" and as a return to the purity and origins of the sport are direct attacks on the high visibility of black masculinity in the NBA. The logic of the team or family stands in sharp contrast to the popular representation, especially post-lockout, of the male players as greedy, ego-driven, and brash. Much as in the pages of the infamous Moynihan Report, dominant culture wields black femininity against black masculinity by way of a narrative and visual logic that simultaneously functions to deny racism (the women are "successful") through a seeming embrace of multiculturalism.

So, given the "sedimented histories" that different bodies bear, simply championing an embodied virtuality is never enough. In examining the televisual construction of black male athletes, Stephen Michael Best notes that "television works to maintain a grip on the flesh," (230) particularly black flesh; and we would do well to remember that other, embodied modes of virtuality can be equally binding, and that there are often high costs associated with our virtual skins. As we move from the televisual to the digital era, it matters how the body enters cyberspace and how agency is facilitated in the overlapping of the material and the digital.

This question of agency is an interesting and important one, particularly if we are to avoid falling prey to the cultural myth of black technophobia, a myth that usually works in the service of the powers that be, denying the degree to which women of color have always talked back to (and with) technology. Hazel Carby, Angela Davis, Hortense Spillers, and others have noted the historical struggle black women have waged against various ideologies of womanhood, taking up the technology of the pen to define themselves in the face of powerful forces framing them narrowly, and it is important to consider the WNBA players' and their fans' own strategic evasions of the overdetermined marker of the black lady. Though the official discourse of the WNBA site strives to normalize blackness in basketball by domesticating it, occasional cracks surface in this kinder, gentler story. For instance, in the fan mail responding to Coquese Washington's book selection, *Beloved*, one woman wrote:

> I would have done the same thing to protect my children from the white man's hand. I'd rather let my child lay six feet under than endure the hatred, humiliation, disrespect and pain our people went through. I was disappointed with our own for the way they treated Sethe and Denver. Just like today, we as a black community do not stand together, which makes it easier for the white man to walk over us. (letter by Juanita Davis, 1999)

Here, the black body resurfaces in an embodied context, cognizant of the weight of history, by means of a mediated publicness that addresses race and refigures the black lady. Likewise, in a video web chat, Coop answers a young black girl's questions about basketball, encouraging her to see both basketball and education as tools with which she can confront the world and survive the inner city. In the five-second space of the grainy video, we see Coop imagine a different public where black women and girls work together to "raise the roof," taking their game to a higher level and defining the lady on their own terms.

NOTES

For their aid with this chapter, I thank my research assistants, Elizabeth Ramsey, Miae Choi, and Ethan Thompson. Thanks are also due to my very tall parents, Brad and Kay McPherson, for their love of basketball and their encouragement, whether on or off the court.

1. I explore the impact of such ideas of "colorlessness" in the digital realm in my "I'll Take My Stand." See also the rest of the volume that contains that essay, Rodman, Kolko, and Nakamura, eds., *Race and Cyberspace*.

2. Morse and Hayles do recognize that virtuality is not a "total" condition; that is, both recognize that embodiment can take many forms in cyberspace. Still, the tendency of cybertheory to focus on virtual reality environments, MUDs (Multi-user dimensions), and CD-ROMs operates to

the exclusion of the more everyday applications and experiences of the web. Proclamations about the erasure of the body from cyberspace are fairly common; many popular accounts go on to celebrate this possibility, provoking the understandable ire of feminist theorists.

3. A substantial body of research exists detailing the images of women in sports media. Collections by MacClancy, Wenner, and Messner and Sabo are good examples of this work. Many of these essays focus on the biased nature of women's sports coverage, noting the tendency of the media to sexualize or to feminize female athletes. While interesting, much of this work remains descriptive and fails to investigate how these mediated images circulate within larger cultural narratives of race, gender, and class.

4. For a description of the difference in production techniques in men's and women's basketball in the early 1990s, see Duncan and Messner 1998. Based on my examination of televised WNBA games, I would have to say that many of the differences in the shooting of actual game play have evaporated (although some of the WNBA's cameras are placed closer to the court, ostensibly because the women are smaller). However, many of the "extra-game" materials—canned segments, time-out close-ups, etc.—are different, a point I will return to.

5. For an interesting commentary on the relative "queerness" of both leagues, see the *Advocate* article by Michele Kort. In her piece, she notes that "the ABL has directly marketed to gay women by advertising in lesbian newspapers and setting up booths at gay pride festivals" but goes on to underscore that "lesbianism still isn't locker room chatter" (60).

6. I first introduced the idea of "virtual mobility" in "Television Predicts Its Future," as a way of theorizing the specificity of the web in relation to what I see as one of its most important predecessors, television.

WORKS CITED

Best, Stephen Michael. 1998. "Game Theory: Racial Embodiment and Media Crisis." In *Living Color: Race and Television in the United States*, edited by Sasha Torres. Durham: Duke University Press.

Boyd, Todd. 1997. *Am I Black Enough for You? Popular Culture from the 'Hood and Beyond*. Bloomington: Indiana University Press.

Duncan, M. C., and M. A. Messner. 1998. "The Media Image of Sport and Gender." In *MediaSport*, edited by L. A. Wenner. New York: Routledge.

Green, Daniel. 1997. "Toss Up." *Working Woman*, vol. 22 (April 1997): 26–29.

Hayles, N. Katherine. 1999. *How We Became Posthuman: Virtual Bodies in Cybernetics, Literature, and Informatics*. Chicago: University of Chicago Press.

hooks, bell. 1992. *Black Looks: Race and Representation*. Boston: South End Press.

Kane, Mary Jo, and Helen Jefferson Lenskyj. 1998. "Media Treatment of Female Athletes: Issues of Gender and Sexuality." In *MediaSport*, edited by Lawrence Wenner. New York: Routledge.

Kort, Michele. 1997. "The Girls in the Bleachers: Phantom Fans." *Advocate* (September 9, 1997): 59–60.

Lubiano, Wahneema. 1992. "Black Ladies, Welfare Queens, and State Minstrels: Ideological War by Narrative Means." In *Race-ing Justice, Engendering Power*, edited Toni Morrison. New York: Pantheon Books.

MacClancy, Jeremy, ed. 1996. *Sport, Identity, and Ethnicity*. Oxford: Berg Press.

McPherson, Tara. 2000. "I'll Take My Stand in Dixie-Net: White Guys, the South, and Cyberspace." In *Race and Cyberspace*, edited by Gil Rodman, Beth Kolko, and Lisa Nakamura. New York: Routledge.

———. 2000. "Television Predicts Its Future: On Convergence and Cybertelevision." In *Virtual Publics*, edited by Beth Kolko. New York: Columbia University Press.

Messner, Michael, and Donald F. Sabo, eds. 1990. *Sport, Men, and the Gender Order: Critical Feminist Perspectives*. Champaign: Human Kinetics Publishers.

Morse, Margaret. 1998. *Virtualities*. Bloomington: Indiana University Press.

Moynihan, Daniel P. 1965. *The Negro Family: The Case for National Action*. Washington, D.C.: U.S. Department of Labor. Reprinted in Lee Rainwater and William L. Yancey *The Moynihan Report and the Politics of Controversy* (Cambridge, Mass.: MIT Press, 1967).

Rodman, Gil, Beth Kolko, and Lisa Nakamura, eds. 2000. *Race and Cyberspace*. New York: Routledge.

Schulze, Laurie. 1990. "On the Muscle." In *Fabrications: Costume and the Female Body*, edited by Charlotte Herzog and Jane Gaines. New York: Routledge.

Wenner, Lawrence, ed. 1998. *MediaSport*. New York: Routledge.

———, ed. 1989. *Media, Sports, and Society*. London: Sage Publications.

Wolff, Alexander. 1997. "Won for All." *Sports Illustrated* (September 8, 1997): 56.

14

view the world from american eyes

ball, islam, and dissent in post-race america

SOHAIL DAULATZAI

The same man that was colonizing our people in Kenya was colonizing our people in the Congo. The same one in the Congo was colonizing our people in South Africa, and in Southern Rhodesia, and in Burma, and in India, and in Afghanistan, and in Pakistan.

—Malcolm X

THE GLOBAL FLOWS OF CAPITAL THAT characterize our current moment in history have had a major impact in defining social, cultural, and national identities. Of the many forms of transnational popular culture, sports has come to occupy a prominent position in the contemporary global landscape due to the interplay of international marketing conglomerates, the synergistic relationships among multinational corporations, and the mobilization and interlinking of diasporic publics. Though the Olympics and the World Cup soccer tournament are prominent in this regard, basketball—and especially the NBA—is becoming increasingly global. The movement of players from Europe and Africa into the NBA is growing.

The popularity of the league overseas is undeniable, what with the Dream Teams, the McDonald's Open, and the ability of the league to market its players within a global imaginary. But this popularity must be underscored by the fact that the NBA is a cultural expression of the marginalized in American society—namely, African Americans—and it is also very much a commodity, with its systems of production and distribution firmly rooted in Western capitalism. Like literature, film, or any other cultural form, the NBA must be viewed as a mediated expression that can, and often does, reproduce dominant Western discourses. Like these other forms, it must be interrogated as a system of meanings that not only reproduces and constructs hegemonic discourses in the United States but also those between the United States and the rest of the world.

The traditional narratives in the NBA concerning race, masculinity, and cultural politics have to be reconfigured as the game becomes a larger part of global commodity culture. As race came to be normalized within the NBA,[1] effacing earlier discourses of difference, new narratives have emerged that have invoked notions of otherness that constructed identities for colonial and postcolonial subjects. One of these narratives involved Mahmud Abdul-Rauf, an All-Star guard who refused to stand for the national anthem during the 1995–96 NBA season. Formerly Chris Jackson, Abdul-Rauf—an African American—converted to Sunni Islam, the largest sect of Muslims in the world, covering parts of Africa, Asia, and the Middle East. Abdul-Rauf claimed that the American flag was a "symbol of tyranny and oppression." In addition to the mainstream criticism of his resistance, another Muslim player, Hakeem Olajuwon, criticized Abdul-Rauf's refusal to stand. As can be expected, the media and public backlash was severe. The criticism aimed at Abdul-Rauf served not only to position the debate as one in which he was viewed as an ungrateful athlete with a multimillion-dollar contract but also to animate a series of discourses regarding "Islam" and American national identity. By constructing the discourse around Islam, the NBA was able to situate itself in a broader configuration in which conceptions of nationhood and patriotism were starkly contrasted with the anti-Americanist and anti-democratic characterizations popularly associated with Islam. Had Abdul-Rauf been Chris Jackson (the Christian) and refused to stand, the implications and significance of his act would have changed the contours of the debate.

But because he was a Muslim, and considering the recent historical relationship between America and Islam, the Abdul-Rauf incident is a compelling text through which to examine the American national project—with its inclusions, exclusions, and elisions—and the manner in which sports, as an expression of that project, animates and legitimates dominant national myths. The xenophobic and racialized Orientalist discourses that have served to essentialize Muslim identity in the United States have appealed to the core of what it means to be "American" (rational, democratic, compassionate, virtuous, progressive, etc.), at the same time subsuming the national, racial, and ethnic differences that comprise the United States so as to mobilize a discrete national identity that is defined against Islam.

The current rhetoric surrounding Islam and the West is no doubt informed by historical confrontations between Christianity and Islam that date back to the seventh century. But it is the recent conflicts between the United States and the Islamic world—the Iran hostage crisis; the Persian Gulf War; the confrontations with Muammar Qaddafi, Osama bin Laden, Saddam Hussein, and many others—coupled with the downfall of the Soviet Union that has led to the construction of Islam as the new ideological menace that is challenging the New World Order. The rhetoric surrounding Islam has been one in which the West and Islam are on an inevitable collision course—a clash of civilizations that pits one believed to be democratic and progressive against one characterized as oppressive, violent, and archaic. As a result, Islam has been reductively used to describe a multiplicity of changes, economic, political, social, and cultural, that the decolonizing Islamic world is experiencing.

The flag incident involving Abdul-Rauf and the NBA enacted a similar discourse regarding Islam, one that has discursively controlled and undermined the complexity and heterogeneity within the Islamic world. This historically informed notion in the West of what Islam is has essentially maintained a monolithic conception of the Muslim subject without regard to notions of race, nationality, and cultural politics. The media backlash and the dynamic between Abdul-Rauf and Olajuwon situate the debate in a context in which the ideologically constructed signifier "Islam" has become extremely problematic. As a result, I want to use the flag incident not only to examine the cultural politics of the NBA but also to create an engaged critical discourse that attempts to understand the social, political, cultural, and ideological terrain in which the western notion of Islam has been constructed and resisted in mainstream discourse. I am not so much interested in the textual power of the Qur'an or in Islam as religious doctrine as in the uses and meanings associated with the term *Islam*. In addition, I am interested not only in Abdul-Rauf and Olajuwon the men but also in Abdul-Rauf and Olajuwon as social and cultural representations—their respective media images. My interest is in their public images and the power and politics of these images.

Keep Your Friends Close, but Your Enemies Closer

In *Orientalism* (1978), Edward Said examines the relationship between the West and the Muslim East and argues that the West "produced" the East not as a variety of cultures and societies that functioned on their own but as an imaginary One that served to define the West in opposition to it. Said asserts that this trope served to construct the West as democratic, rational, moral, and progressive, because the East was created as exotic, irrational, despotic, and backward. The power dynamics inherent in this construction have led to an understanding of Islam as static and eternal, so that these descriptions continue to resonate today in American political and cultural discourse.

The NBA and the mainstream media configured the Abdul-Rauf incident within a similar formation that foregrounded Islam at the expense of the more complex and compelling issues that were central to Abdul-Rauf's refusal to stand. The historical place that race has occupied in African American conversion to Islam and the empowered subject position that results from such a transformation were obscured by the league and its media apparatus. Instead, Islam became the NBA's whipping boy as the league's demonization of a foreign "threat" served not only to highlight the NBA's subtle refusal to engage with its own racial politics but also to undermine Abdul-Rauf's resistance to America's historical and continuing racial formation.

Abdul-Rauf, who was an All-Star guard with the Denver Nuggets at the time of the episode, was subsequently traded to the lowly Sacramento Kings, where his playing time was limited. He then signed a contract to play professional basketball in Turkey—not having received a significant offer from any NBA team for his services—and subsequently retired from basketball, still in the prime of his career. That he had gone from an NBA All-Star to no longer playing in the league and then to retirement in three-plus seasons raises some compelling questions regarding the NBA and its racial politics. It is important in this regard to mention that Craig Hodges, a former player on the Chicago Bulls championship teams of the early 1990s, has sued the NBA, claiming that he was black-listed by the league and not offered a contract because of his politics and his associations with the Nation of Islam. Hodges, who on the Bulls' visit to the White House after winning the championship gave President George Bush a letter expressing his concern at the administration's lack of involvement in the inner city, also criticized Michael Jordan and other star players for not doing enough for the ghetto poor.[2]

Equally important as the issues surrounding the NBA's approach to Islam is the league's complicity in containing the meanings of race and continually folding them into other categories, such as class (Grant Hill versus Allen Iverson), masculinity (Dennis Rodman), and nation (Dikembe Mutombo, Michael Olowokandi) such that the NBA has sought to undermine the power that race—as an independent, autonomous entity—has to construct identity and empower subjectivity. By configuring race within narrow confines and limiting the potential meanings of blackness, the league was able to condemn the actions of Abdul-Rauf, stripping them of any of the historical and racial specificity that has been so prominent in the oppositional cultural politics of Muslims in the United States.

The relative prominence of Muslims—both from the Nation of Islam and orthodox Islam—in professional sports began to reflect the broader politicized U.S. climate in the 1960s and 1970s, due in part to Malcolm X, Muhammad Ali, and emergent decolonizing countries in the Islamic world. In addition to Muhammad Ali, Dwight Muhammad Qawi, and Mustapha Hamsho in boxing and Ahmad Rashad (Bobby Moore) in football, the largest presence of Muslims was in professional basketball, in which numerous players changed their names in order to assert their newfound Muslim identities: Kareem Abdul-Jabbar (Lew Alcindor), Mahdi Abdul-Rahman (Walt Hazzard), Wali Jones (Wally Jones), Zaid Abdul-Aziz (Don Smith), Warren Jabali (Warren Armstrong), and Jamaal Wilkes (Keith Wilkes).[3] The presence of these Muslims in professional sports in general and in the league in particular was indicative of the manner in which race and the resistances to it have at times intersected with the cultural politics of Islam so as to open new spaces that articulate emerging oppositional subjectivities.

These subjectivities are present today as well, as Muslims continue to enact a space within popular culture. Sports continues to be a site in which these Muslim identities can be found, as basketball (Hakeem Olajuwon, Mahmud Abdul-Rauf, Shareef Abdur-Rahim, Tariq Abdul-Wahad, Larry Johnson), football (Karim Abdul-Jabbar, Rashaan Salaam), and boxing (Mike Tyson, Prince Naseem Hamed) indicate. But hip-hop music has also been a space where race and Islam have intersected prominently. Artists such as Public Enemy, Brand Nubian, Rakim, Gangstarr, Ice Cube, A Tribe Called Quest, Wu Tang Clan, The Roots, Nas, and Black Star, to name a few, have articulated identities that expressed the cultural politics of some branch of Islam. The assertions of these identities in sports and hip-hop music have provided alternative representations of Islam that confound the homogenizing tendencies that Orientalist clichés continue to animate regarding Islam. These Orientalist tropes, which characterize current political and cultural discourse, result from the burgeoning Islamic presence throughout the world since the late 1960s and continuing until today.

Beginning with the OPEC crisis in the early 1970s, and continuing through the Iran hostage crisis, the Persian Gulf War, the World Trade Center bombing, and other confrontations with "terrorists" (Qaddafi, Saddam Hussein, Osama bin Laden), anti-Islamic rhetoric in the United States has been steadily on the rise. Additionally, the increasing presence of Muslims in the United States— either through conversion or immigration—coupled with the

strategic role that the Middle East has played in United States foreign policy on the one hand and the rise of the Christian Right during the Reagan-Bush years on the other proved to be a volatile
combination, as Islam became a new ideological Other.

Cultural production began to reflect this increased hostility in
the 1980s and 1990s, as Hollywood weighed in on the topic. Films
such as *Not without My Daughter* (1991), *True Lies* (1994), *Executive Decision* (1996), HBO's *Path to Paradise* (1997), and *The
Siege* (1998), to name a few, presented Muslims in overtly reduc-
tive ways. But in addition to these overt, stereotypical views of
Muslims were subtler yet equally problematic representations of
the Islamic world. Films such as *Raiders of the Lost Ark* (1981), *The
Sheltering Sky* (1990), and *The English Patient* (1996) enacted
what Renato Rosaldo has called "imperialist nostalgia"–presenting
the relations of domination and subordination as elegant and genteel in order to counter the present-day resurgence of the Islamic
world and its supposed threat by invoking a period in colonial history in which a voiceless Islamic world was controlled, tamed, and
exoticized.

These films were not only reflective of the current mood but,
like the mainstream press, contributed to the general (mis)under-
standing of Muslims. In the print media, articles such as "The
Red Menace Is Gone, But Here's Islam," "Still Fighting the Crusades," and "Rising Islam May Overwhelm the West,"[4] just to
name a few, continually appeared in national newspapers and
journals. The circulation of this rhetoric throughout the cultural
and political apparatuses has had real material effects not only in
terms of America's aggression and domination in the Islamic
world, but also within the United States as Muslims or those who
may look the part have increasingly been the targets of brutality
and violence.[5] But, whereas Islam has been vilified as an extrem-
ist religion, no such characterizations have been made against
Christianity as a result of the Branch Davidian disaster in Waco,
Texas; the bombings of abortion clinics and the murdering of
doctors by the zealotry of The Army of God; or the white supremacist rampages by Buford Furrow and Benjamin Smith, both
of whom belong to white supremacist organizations that are un-
derpinned with elements of Christian doctrine.

New Orientalisms: Race, Resistance, and the Cultural Politics of Difference

In what ways did the social, political, and cultural discourses surrounding Islam inform the representation of Mahmud Abdul-Rauf? To what extent did this representation serve to reify the dominant discursive construction of Muslims as a homogeneous group? The Abdul-Rauf incident provides a lens with which to view how the overlapping and seemingly disparate fields of race, the national body, and cultural politics intersect so as to create an alternative form of subjectivity that destabilizes the monolithic construction of Islamic identity. Viewed in this manner, the insertion of race by way of African American conversion to Islam ruptures the Orientalist narratives of the American national project, which produce an essentialized Muslim identity. As an extension and embodiment of the national project, the NBA—with its own cultural and racial logics—served to articulate a narrative that pitted "America" against "Islam" while also undermining a raced subjectivity, ironically in a primarily black league. That the NBA, and the United States for that matter, has had a difficult time grappling with race becomes even more problematic when one examines the Abdul-Rauf incident in this light.

Mahmud Abdul-Rauf's refusal to stand for the national anthem and his assertion that the U.S. flag stands for "tyranny and oppression" is not ordained from the Qur'an. He stated that the Qur'an teaches him not to stand for "oppression"—and which religion doesn't? But what Abdul-Rauf did was to interpret the American flag as representative of that tyranny, and as such, he refused to stand for it. He was protesting what United States policy has been, both at home and abroad, with regard to human rights, and as such, his refusal to stand was a *political* act, not a religious one.

But as is the case with many incidents involving Islam throughout the world, instances of rebellion and resistance by those who happen to be Muslims are seen as religious in nature rather than as issues of human rights or civil and political equality. The label "Islam" is bandied about as if to highlight its seeming association to senseless violence and anti-Americanism, at the same time undermining the complex issues that such resistance is based on. For example, the struggle for a Palestinian homeland is couched in religious terms, not as a struggle for human dignity and equality. But the policies and the implementation of those policies in thwarting that struggle are seen as executed by a "democratic" Israel—which itself is a *Jewish* state. Rarely, if ever, are the policies of the Israeli government viewed as "divinely ordained." But with Abdul-Rauf, as with so many other Muslims operating out of a political context, his religion was foregrounded as a way of contrasting "America" (as represented by the flag) with "Islam." In this context, the recent historical meanings associated with Islam (irrational, savage, violent, and anti-American) are used to contrast with everything American (rational, civilized, and democratic).

The reaction against Mahmud Abdul-Rauf was swift. Because he was a Muslim, the media sought the opinions of other visible Muslims around the country. Leaders of mosques; heads of Islamic organizations (such as the Islamic Society of North America, the Muslim Public Affairs Council, and the International Institute on Islamic Thought); and other prominent Muslims were asked their opinions about the matter. Salam Al-Marayati of the Muslim Public Affairs Council said that "for American citizens, standing for the national anthem and the pledge of allegiance are required under Islam"[6] and pointed out that Muslims serve in the American military. The International Institute for Islamic Thought said that "for most Muslims the stance being taken by Abdul-Rauf is pure folly."[7] Yet it was the opinions of Hakeem Olajuwon, a prominent NBA player, that seemed to carry the most weight.

In a *New York Times* article titled "A Puzzled Olajuwon Speaks Out on Citizenship," Olajuwon, one of the top players in the NBA at the time and a Muslim, stated that being a good Muslim means to "be a good citizen . . . to obey and respect"[8] the customs and traditions in whichever country one lives in. Olajuwon's comments on the flag issue, the fact that he was a Muslim, and his position as one of the "gentlemen" and "role models" in the league served not only to alienate Abdul-Rauf within the Islamic community but also to legitimate the backlash directed at Abdul-Rauf by the NBA and the media.

The positions held by Hakeem Olajuwon and other Islamic organizations were attempts to undo America's marginalization of

Islam in contemporary discourse. But while their rhetoric was an attempt to include within America's social fabric Muslims and their contributions to America's so-called melting pot, they failed to engage and grapple with the issues of race that emanated from Abdul-Rauf's position. By examining more closely the context within which these comments were made, we can understand why, and in what sense, the discourse surrounding Islam in the America has been so problematic.

Black Steel in the Hour of Chaos: The Cultural Logic of Postindustrial Capitalism and the Politics of Identity

The construction of Islamic identity in the United States is complex and varied. Muslims in America must negotiate an identity that is constructed and reconstructed, being comprised of various overlapping fields that include race, ethnicity, and nationality. While differentiation does occur among immigrant Muslims along nationalistic and ethnic lines, one of the key tensions that exists in Islam in the United States has been between immigrant populations from the Muslim world and indigenous Muslims who have converted to Islam. The vast majority of Muslims who convert to Islam in the United States are African Americans, and their respective articulations of the religion are deeply embedded within the historically racialized climate of contemporary American society. It is this tension between the immigrant Muslim experience—and the associated cultural politics that this experience can engender—and the indigenous convert to Islam that frames and contextualizes the dynamic between Hakeem Olajuwon and Mahmud Abdul-Rauf.

The contemporary signification of African Americans as Muslims dates back to the presence of Islam among African slaves at the outset of the Atlantic slave trade. In refusing conversion to Christianity and in their resistances against the institutions of slavery, these African Muslims were precursors to future social movements in the United States that would rearticulate Islam to the social and political exigencies of the time. Whether in the pan-Africanist teachings of Marcus Garvey or in the urban philosophies of Noble Drew Ali, Elijah Muhammad, Malcolm X, and Louis Farrakhan, Islam has played a central role for African Americans in creating the impetus for political mobilization, social movements, and activism. While there are distinct ideological differences between these various figures and their significations of Islam,[9] it is important to understand the role that Islam has played in the historical narrative of slavery and its aftermath, since it has been instrumental as a strategy for African Americans to reassert some form of cultural and social independence from the oppressive regimes of power embedded in America's racial order.

America's racial hierarchy found its expression during slavery when slave names were used to identify Africans, instead of their original names—an attempt to replace black ethnic identity with a racial identity that would serve to configure blacks within a broader racial hierarchy. The creation of spaces of resistance through the adoption of a Muslim name and identity—as when Chris Jackson became Mahmud Abdul-Rauf—has signified "subtle and complex political positions in American racial discourse, and in the production of black cultural identities, that are based on the ethos and worldview of global Islam."[10] Discussions of Islam in the United States in general and in the African American community specifically cannot take place without examining an Islam refracted through the prism of race.

In contrast to Abdul-Rauf, Olajuwon highlights the cultural politics of assimilation and integration into the national political and economic terrain. Olajuwon came to America from Nigeria to play basketball for the University of Houston and, he hoped, for the NBA. Once in the league, he established himself as a dominant force. In addition to winning back-to-back championships and the league MVP award and being named as one of the fifty all-time greatest players in the NBA, he has been called the NBA's "most widely respected player among his peers, for his dignity and sportsmanship."[11] Olajuwon's talent and his status as the genteel role model of the league have given rise to portrayals of him as an anomaly among the supposedly overpaid, arrogant, and ungrateful players in the NBA. His success as a professional and his place within the game is the American Dream realized at its highest possible level.

Olajuwon's signification of Islam and his critique of Abdul-Rauf underpin an attempt to normalize Islam within mainstream American sociocultural discourse. With Olajuwon, as his game and his status in the league have improved, much has been made of his renewed commitment to Islam. Central to his representation, then, has been an emphasis on how Islam has played a major role in his life and career. By constructing and upholding a Muslim identity, Olajuwon has become one of the most identifiable Muslims in professional sports. And considering the negative image of Islam in the West, as well as the rhetoric surrounding it in the mainstream media, Olajuwon's "acceptance" in America signals an attempt to incorporate an Islam that is in concert with the cultural politics of dominant American society. As a member of the 1996 Dream Team (which has become for the NBA a major marketing vehicle), Olajuwon entered the realm of mass-market advertising and commodity culture. In exchange for visibility and acceptance, however, has come a lack of critical engagement of Islam and its dimensions, as well as a lack of understanding of the historical and continual misrepresentation and denigration of Islam in Western discourse. Achievement and middle-class acceptance, for Olajuwon, have masked an underlying problematic in which difference (the Otherness of Islam) has been reduced to cultural commodity, wherein Olajuwon, is Muslim enough to accept as such but not Muslim enough to offend anyone.[12]

Given his relative position in mainstream cultural discourse, Olajuwon has achieved a certain level of visibility as a commodity because his articulation of Islam is congruent with dominant American sensibilities. Had Olajuwon refused to stand for the national anthem at some point in his career, he would not have been a member of the 1996 Olympic Dream Team, nor the league's Most Valuable Player for that matter. His criticism of Abdul-Rauf—and the politics involved in that criticism—must then be viewed in light of Olajuwon's well-publicized naturalization as an American citizen (in order to play on the 1996 Olympic Dream Team) and his circulation within commodity culture. Olajuwon's embrace of the political sphere of national life (becoming a citizen) and his being embraced by the economic sphere (by way of becoming cultural commodity) have served to reinscribe onto the terrain of dominant

American culture a normalized articulation of Islam that lacks any cultural and political specificity.

This lack of a contextualized Islam became particularly problematic when Abdul-Rauf refused to stand for the national anthem. Olajuwon's critique of Abdul-Rauf serves to highlight the tension between a contextualized Islam and one that has been normalized, as it obscured the articulation of race in Abdul-Rauf's signification of Islam. America has historically had difficulty coming to terms with its colorful racial history. In attempting to uphold and normalize an Islamic identity in America, Olajuwon did not engage in the racial politics implicit in Abdul-Rauf's position. Instead, Olajuwon appealed to a Muslim identity that was congruent with the dominant American conceptions of patriotism and citizenship that the national project attempts to impart. Olajuwon's assertion that being a good Muslim means to "be a good citizen . . . to obey and respect" the customs and traditions of the country in which one lives is extremely problematic, as it assumes not only that there is *one* definition of a good Muslim but also that *that* definition be equated with good citizenship.

In addition, in an interview in the *Christian Science Monitor*, Olajuwon stated that "the call of Islam is not based on race or color" and went on to state that Abdul-Rauf "took things to an extreme, whereas Islam is a flexible faith, giving you a lot of choices."[13] There is no doubt that Islam is a multiracial religion, with followers in Africa, Asia, Europe, and North America. But at the same time, Islam has historically been a vehicle through which African Americans have resisted and deconstructed the racial discourse of American society. Olajuwon's position, and his critique of Abdul-Rauf, undermines the role that Islam has played in the African American community. The cultural identity assumed by African American converts has served to undercut an identity imposed on them through the structures of oppression and dehumanization. That Islam for Abdul-Rauf and other African American converts not only serves as a deconstruction of the racial project in the United States but is also a more empowered subject position is lost on Olajuwon, the NBA, and others who continue to subscribe to a view of Islam that is devoid of a racial subtext.

Additionally, Olajuwon's comment regarding the flexible nature of Islam and the possibilities inherent in the religion would seem to contradict his earlier critique of Abdul-Rauf. If, in fact, Islam is "flexible," then there should exist the space for personal interpretations that allow for a diversity of opinions on a range of issues. By critiquing Abdul-Rauf, Olajuwon, like Islamic organizations throughout the country, upheld and reinscribed a monolithic view of the nature of Islam. The position taken by most Islamic organizations throughout the United States, including the Muslim Public Affairs Council, the International Institute for Islamic Thought, and the Council on American-Islamic Relations, was that standing for the national anthem is in no way antithetical to Islam. Yet when, during the Abdul-Rauf incident, these organizations were questioned by the major media regarding the "official" position of Islam—as if one existed—they replied that patriotism and loyalty to the flag are a part of being a good Muslim. The assumption that there is a "true" Islam—an *acontextual* Islam—is problematic. To believe in such a notion is congruent with the construction of a monolithic Islam that the West has fostered with regard to Muslims throughout the world.

What must also be considered is that the leaders of these various Islamic organizations are reacting to the dominant perception in America that Islam is a religion of fanatics that wants to destroy America and all that it stands for. Clearly, then, the role they assume is one in which Islam must be viewed as compatible with the core notions of America: capitalism, individualism, democracy, and a self-serving patriotism. There is no doubt that an Islam exists that is congruent with some, if not all, of these characteristics. But by implying that there is but *one* interpretation, these organizations— and Olajuwon as well—undermine the histories and cultures of most of the Islamic world in the same way that the West has historically done.

NOTES

1. I am indebted to my conversations with Todd Boyd. For more incisive critique of basketball as cultural form, see Boyd's *Am I Black Enough*

for You? Popular Culture from the 'Hood and Beyond (Bloomington: Indiana University Press, 1997).

2. Ira Berkow, "The Case of Hodges vs. the N.B.A.," *New York Times,* December 25, 1996, p. B11.

3. Nelson George, *Elevating the Game: Black Men and Basketball* (New York: HarperCollins, 1992), p. 163.

4. Elaine Sciolino, "The Red Menace Is Gone, but Here's Islam," *New York Times,* January 21, 1996, sec. 4, p. 1; William Piaf, "Still Fighting the Crusades," *Foster's Daily Democrat* (Los Angeles Times Syndicate), November 27, 1990, p. B3; Patrick J. Buchanan, "Rising Islam May Overwhelm the West," *New Hampshire Sunday News,* August 20, 1989, p. A1. For an excellent analysis of the (mis)representation of Islam in the mainstream media and its perceived threat, see Edward Said's *Covering Islam* (New York: Vintage, 1997); and John L. Esposito's *The Islamic Threat: Myth or Reality?* (Oxford: Oxford University Press, 1995).

5. According to the Council on American-Islamic Relations (CAIR), 209 incidents of violence, one resulting in death, were *reported* against Muslims and Arab Americans immediately after the Oklahoma City bombing and before the arrest of Timothy McVeigh. In addition, the Arab-American Anti-Discrimination Committee reported that immediately after the U.S. attack on Iraq in August 1990, twenty incidents of violence were *reported,* whereas in June and July 1990, prior to the invasion, zero and one incident were reported, respectively.

6. Ken Denlinger, "Disorder on the Court: NBA Player's Refusal to Stand for Anthem Ignites Controversy," *Washington Post,* March 14, 1996, p. A1.

7. Ibid.

8. "A Puzzled Olajuwon Speaks Out on Citizenship," *New York Times,* March 14, 1996, p. B19.

9. Beginning in the early twentieth century, there have been two dominant strands within African American Islam: a multiracial Islam and a racially separatist Islam (the Nation of Islam). These two different discourses have provided a framework within which to understand the complex signification of African American conversion to Islam. The rhetoric of the Nation of Islam, as espoused by Elijah Muhammad and, later, by Louis Farrakhan, is one that emphasizes racial separatism as a response to the African American experience in America. Specifically, the Nation of Islam attempts to overturn the primary racial discourse in America: that of white supremacy. By espousing the richness of African history and attempting to restore cultural pride, the Nation has attempted to deconstruct the racial

myth of white superiority in order to empower blacks in America toward political mobilization.

African American conversion to Orthodox Islam, too, is informed by the racial politics of the United States, but it also suggests an embrace of a multiracial Islam—an attempt to create a broader racial identity that incorporates a global Islamic sentiment that unites disparate peoples of color throughout the world. Malcolm X, once a member of the Nation of Islam, traveled throughout the Islamic world and, as a result of his exposure to a multiracial Islam, became an Orthodox Muslim and subsequently left the Nation. His transition from the Nation of Islam to the multiracial Orthodox Islam in the early 1960s was similar to the path eventually taken by many African Americans in the early 1970s, as the Nation of Islam splintered after the death of Elijah Muhammad. Whereas the Nation of Islam viewed its struggle as specific to America (it has since, under Farrakhan, tried to build coalitions with the Islamic world), Orthodox Islam has been a vehicle that African Americans have utilized not only to deconstruct the political-racial history of the United States but also to construct an identity around the multiracial demographic of a global Islamic world. To try to configure African American signification of Islam as monolithic by conflating the Nation of Islam with Orthodox Islam is extremely problematic, as it obscures much of the difference between both groups' political, social, and ideological force.

10. Richard Brent Turner, "What Shall We Call Him? Islam and African-American Identity," *Journal of Religious Thought* 51 (1):25. Turner provides an excellent historical text in which to examine the role that Islam has played for African Americans in the United States.

11. Robert Marquand, "Hakeem Olajuwon: An Athlete and a Gentleman," *Christian Science Monitor*, February 5, 1997, p. 12.

12. We can trace the same trajectory when examining the recent acceptance by mainstream America of Muhammad Ali. Over the past two or three years, Ali has resurfaced as a presence in contemporary popular culture. He lit the flame at the opening ceremonies of the 1996 Olympic Games in Atlanta, and numerous television documentaries on his life have appeared, including the Academy Award–winning *When We Were Kings* (1996). In addition, he has made public appearances at numerous events, and his face has graced the April 1998 cover of *GQ (Gentlemen's Quarterly)*, proclaiming him "Athlete of the Century." What is curious about this recent trend is that Ali is now accepted and revered where he was once marginalized and reviled by mainstream America. Is the recent acceptance and adoration of him a result of his inability to express himself the way that only Ali knew how, thereby making him less intimidating now than

the figure he was in the 1960s and 1970s? Or is it that Ali and the rebellion that he represented have been reduced to a cultural commodity that masks any serious engagement with or understanding of Ali's historical resonance? The answer is probably a bit of both, but it leads one to wonder: If there was a critical examination of Ali and his indictment of America, would he still be the cultural icon that he has become? The answer to that is surely no. The point, then, is that, as Ali has become another sign of radical chic due to his access and acceptance as a cultural commodity in late-capitalist America, his identity as a Muslim and the politics associated with that identity have been diffused so that he is no longer viewed as a threat to America's racial order.

13. Marquand, "Hakeem Olajuwon," p. 12.

15

hoop dreams in black and white

race and basketball movies

AARON BAKER

*I can play basketball, that's the
bottom line. I can play East
Coast, West Coast, Space Jam
on Mars. I can play it.*
—Brent Barry

*Who knows but that, on the
lower frequencies, I speak
for you?*
—Ralph Ellison

SINCE THE EARLY 1980s, THE NBA HAS
become an important part of an increasingly spectacular, globalized, and racialized American popular culture. Broadcast revenues for the league rose
1,000 percent between 1986 and 1998 (the NFL
and Major League Baseball saw much smaller percentage increases during that time), as the NBA's
bursts of action, highlighted by dunks and three-
point shots, fit smoothly into the fast-paced flow
of spectacle that has come to dominate television
and, increasingly, the movies. During this period,
Michael Jordan replaced Muhammad Ali as the
best-known American athlete worldwide. A big
part of the NBA's greater appeal both at home and
abroad has come from its spectacle of Black style,

headlined for most of this period by Jordan; because more than 80 percent of the players are African American, the league exemplifies "the status of 'difference' as *the* commodity in postmodernity."[1]

In this chapter, I analyze how feature-film representations of a Black style of basketball drawn or modeled on the NBA offer an alternative narrative about the experiences of African Americans in this country but also how these representations reinforce the racial status quo. In the latter sense, such films reaffirm the values of Whiteness that still dominate American culture, despite the commodification of Blackness, and present what Stuart Hall calls "a difference that doesn't make a difference of any kind."[2] While African Americans have clearly been the primary victims of the justification of racial discrimination that I analyze, this biased thinking can affect Whites as well, so it is in their interest to recognize how it functions in media texts like these films. The overemphasis on individual exceptionalism in the representation of African American star athletes contributes to what bell hooks calls a "spirit of defeat and hopelessness" among poor and working-class Blacks, so that they "have no belief that they can attain wealth and power on any playing field other than [as elite athletes in professional] sports."[3] Yet absorption with such Black athletic excellence can also lead to belief in the inherent physical limitations of Whites. Another point I examine in analyzing these films is how they, at different points, both ignore and respond to economic inequality that crosses racial lines.

Although I attempt to link the films to the larger intertexual media framework that is contemporary American popular culture, my analysis here chiefly concerns several movies about basketball made during the period of the NBA's ascendancy. Because they incorporate the new difference yet are still strongly bound by formal and thematic conventions that have been used for decades to privilege the values of Whiteness, Hollywood films provide a good locus for analyzing competing discourses of racial difference. Many of these films are not specifically about the NBA; they instead feature "amateur" players or the playground game. Yet, even if they are not explicitly about the league, these movies often have in their utopian imaginations the NBA as the promised land or make reference to the constructions of Blackness featured there. They therefore share with other media representations of the NBA a similar dialogue about racial identity.

In his description of an ad for *Sports Illustrated* that offered a free Michael Jordan video to new subscribers to the magazine, John Edgar Wideman refers to the NBA's interest in a White audience:

> In this ad, which saturates the prime time on the national sports network [ESPN], a gallery of young people, male and female, express their wonder, admiration, awe and identification with Michael Jordan's supernatural basketball prowess. He can truly fly. The chorus is all white, good looking, clean cut, casually but hiply dressed. An audience of consumers the ad both targets and embodies. A very calculated kind of wish fulfillment at work. A premeditated attempt to bond MJ with these middle-class white kids with highly disposable incomes.[4]

This ad exemplifies how, with Jordan leading the way, what has sold the NBA to White consumers in recent years is what Nelson George calls a "Black athletic aesthetic." This aesthetic features constructions of Black masculinity that correspond roughly to traditional positions about identity in the African American community. On the one side is Jordan's creative improvisation, grounded in Black cultural tradition yet also an example of the "changing same," distinctive in the degree of its crossover appeal and its use as proof that (some) Blacks have full access to the American dream. Almost as widely commodified, but with a less sanguine view of race in America, is the flip side, the hypermasculine menace and intimidation represented in professional basketball by Charles Barkley and others, their "gangsta" personas overlapping to some degree with what certain rap performers have been offering (in part to young Whites) for most of the same period.

Much of the time, these different versions of Blackness are presented to a White audience in a solipsistic, apolitical manner at least as old as the rock-and-roll craze of the 1950s. Writing in the *New York Times* in 1993, Peter DeJonge described this White interest in a packaged, unchallenging version of Black identity:

In the last decade, the N.B.A., long considered too black to attract
a mainstream audience, has prospered by giving middle-class
whites, desperate for some semblance of a connection to black
America, a series of unthreatening yet bigger than life cartoon
superheroes called Magic, Michael, Charles and Shaquille.[5]

The civil rights movement awakened in some Whites an interest in
identity grounded in greater cultural specificity (often ethnicity),
rather than a racial subjectivity based primarily on their assumption of superiority over a non-White Other. Werner Sollors says
that this has gone so far that "casting oneself as an outsider may in
fact be a dominant cultural trait. . . . Every American is now considered a potential ethnic."[6] But since assimilation has made the
connection to ethnic heritage difficult for many, especially younger
European Americans, Blackness in popular culture offers a ready
substitute; its emphasis on the body presents a welcome alternative
to the deferred gratification of middle-class life and a physical dis-
traction for some White Christians from the hint of disembodi-
ment and death evoked by the spiritual quality that they regard as
making them superior.[7] A nostalgic basketball film such as *Hoosiers*
(1987) resists this use of Black culture as a response to White anxiety over identity. Instead, it celebrates small-town Indiana basketball and the values of homogeneity and community cohesion it represents. An all-Black team from the city becomes the threatening
Other that must be defeated in the climactic contest in order to
reaffirm the traditional White values that matter in this film. Con-
versely, more contemporary films such as *Grand Canyon* (1991)
and *White Men Can't Jump* (1992) demonstrate the widespread
White interest in Black culture. Both films contain scenes in which
African American men use basketball to help White men figure out
who they are.

   In addition to these movies that overtly link basketball to race,
many recent films about the sport try to erase any emphasis on social identity with stories that endorse utopian belief in color-blindness, equal opportunity, and the viability of simplistic moral judgments about individual responsibility as the final solution. To understand how this kind of utopian sports story works, let me briefly
describe how Black athletes have historically been shown in the

Hollywood cinema. The conventions that I refer to are still used by contemporary movies about basketball both to reinforce and to question White privilege.

With the exception of a few race films, African Americans appear only as minor characters (if at all) in feature-length movies about sports that date from the coming of sound in the late 1920s through the beginning of the civil rights movement. A cycle of Hollywood films in the early 1950s featured Black athletes, following closely on the opening of previously all-White professional sports to African Americans just after World War II, but in stories of self-reliance and White paternalism that attempted to de-emphasize social determinants of racial identity, much like the marginalization of African Americans themselves in previous sports movies. Black participation in Hollywood movies has increased slowly and unevenly in the almost half century since and, like their involvement in professional sports, has been restricted to a limited range of performative and behind-the-scenes roles.[8]

During the classic Hollywood period of the 1930s and 1940s, the majority of the infrequent appearances by Black athletic characters were in films about prizefighting, probably because it was the least exclusionary professional sport.[9] Similar to the representation of women in classic Hollywood films, Blacks functioned in these narratives of White male self-definition through athletic competition as either supportive—but self negating—helpers or, occasionally (along with Mexican or Chicano characters), opponents: obstacles that the protagonists overcome in order to realize their heroic identity. The primary focus on individual White protagonists in most classic sports films fits with what Robert Ray calls Hollywood's tendency to affirm "American beliefs in individualism, ad hoc solutions, and the impermanence of all political problems."[10]

In the 1940s and 1950s, this individualist emphasis manifested itself in the large number of biography films about athletes or coaches; almost thirty sports biopics were released in those two decades. George Custen points out that the inclination of biopics toward the stories of a few, mostly White men is an important part of a Hollywood version of history "limited in historical setting"—through its overvaluation of the actions of individuals—and therefore "ideologically self-serving" for those who run the movie business.[11] Biopics not only fit the promotion of self-reliance in classic Hollywood narrative structured around the desires and actions of one or a few main characters; they also demonstrate the symbiosis between professional sports and movies. Regardless of any gestures they might make to teamwork, fair play, and fan communities, throughout their history in the United States commercial sports have given the greatest recognition to individual star performances. Like Hollywood movies, professional sports fit squarely in the traditional American mythology that champions the promise of unified identity through individual achievement. The extensive discourse on star athletes in various media (including the Hollywood biopic) has been the principal voice of this mythology in American professional sports. Such belief in agency supports the utopian promise of sports: that once the contest begins, success depends primarily on one's preparation, determination, and effort. Even when teamwork figures prominently in narratives about athletics, it does not reduce the value placed on individual performance. Rather, like the nuclear family, the team operates as a social structure to foster the development of self-reliant individuals. Self-effacing play therefore subordinates itself to the more recognized actions of the star.

Borrowing from Richard Dyer's analysis of entertainment and utopia, I claim that the idealized identity of professional athletes responds to real needs that fans have: for greater economic means, for a sense of personal accomplishment, and for recognition from others.[12] What films about sports stars lack are specific strategies for how success in these areas can be achieved. Instead, they offer us spectacular celebrations of the achievements of stars, offset by a realist aesthetic of reportage which disavows that the whole performance is staged for our consumption and reassurance. This realist style figures most prominently in action scenes involving footage of actual contests or set in arenas or stadiums filled with crowds of extras, employing authentic uniforms, equipment, and often real athletes. These cinematic contests are frequently narrated by announcers in the style of television or radio coverage and shown with a continuity editing style that makes the sequence of shots seem motivated by the logic of the events, rather than being choices made by the filmmakers. Heightened realism in scenes in which the star competes is especially important in validating an ideology of agency which assumes that individual performance in these situations counts most in making the athlete what he (or she) is.

As Dyer points out, the conservatism of utopian entertainment comes from how it offers representations of a better life, if we just follow the rules and try harder. In other words, not only does such utopian entertainment avoid suggesting specific ways to change the current social reality, but it promises us happiness if we adhere to the status quo. Yet, Dyer adds, this utopian response works only if one ignores—as entertainment almost always does—how social identities such as race, class, gender, and sexuality complicate self-definition. On the contrary, the acknowledgment of social forces in the constitution of identity makes evident that the opportunity, abundance, and happiness in utopian narratives are not there for everyone to the same degree. Even when sports movies acknowledge the disadvantage of racism, sexism, or class difference (homophobia is still widely ignored), individual performance is generally held up as the best way to deny their influence.

The more one regards sports movies as historical—as relating the multiple determinants of the past as well as of the time when they were made and seen—and not just utopian stories about individuals, the more they reveal what Mikhail Bakhtin called "dialogism," or the combination of different discursive positions within one text. In applying Bakhtin's ideas about literature to ethnic and racial representation in film, Robert Stam has described his goal as to "call attention to the voices at play in a text, not only those heard in aural 'close-up,' but also those voices distorted or drowned out by the text."[13] Using this idea of textuality to approach sports films, one can see how their protagonists overcome external obstacles to succeed but are also formed in part by social forces—whether these work to define race or other types of identity—and the choices they offer.

> What drove me back . . . was I truly loved the game. I missed the
> enjoyment that it gave to me.
> —Michael Jordan about his return to the NBA

Basketball films of the 1980s and 1990s demonstrate this dialogism, not only between self-reliant gradualism and improvisational

pleasure but also through the more direct critique of American society presented by the gangsta identity. Michael Jordan figures in
several of these films, starring in *Space Jam* (1996), appearing in *He
Got Game* (1998), and invoked by *White Men Can't Jump, Hoop
Dreams* (1994), and *The Air up There* (1994). His importance to
these films does not come just from his being widely regarded as
the best basketball player ever; Jordan has a social significance that
goes beyond the basketball court. Writing in the *New Yorker* in
1998, Henry Louis Gates Jr. described him as representing one of
the two "forces that contend for the soul of contemporary America." For Gates, Jordan is not only the best on the court but also the
"greatest corporate pitchman of all time" and therefore the
supreme representative of the trend toward "'winner-take-all'
markets, visible in every economic and cultural realm but epitomized by the star system of the NBA." Gates also describes the
rival trend, "the fragmentation of culture into ever narrower
niches, from the proliferation of cable channels to the supposed
balkanization of the canon"—such that, within the context of basketball and juxtaposed to Jordan, it could refer to the outsider alienation of his NBA alter ego, the gangsta player.[14]

Gates therefore starts off his essay by placing Jordan very high
on the ladder of fame, fortune, and social significance. He subsequently goes back to chronicle Jordan's "modest origins"—the
"working class childhood in Wilmington, North Carolina (father a
foreman at a General Electric Plant; mother in customer relations
for the United Carolina Bank)"—and his down-to-earth, accessible
demeanor ("the manner—direct and artless—is familiar") so as to
cast Jordan's success as proof that the American dream still exists.
To ignore his down-to-earth and generous manner would leave Jordan as Mr. Winner Take All, vulnerable to association with the
greed that has accompanied the rise to fame and fortune and has led
to great wealth disparity in the United States.[15] Star athletes are
frequently attacked in the media for their large salaries and ego as
a way of displacing that glaring disparity. However, Gates isn't
naive about this success; he doesn't claim that it is available to all or
even most African Americans, or that Jordan himself doesn't suffer
from a certain degree of alienation. Nonetheless, the combination
of Jordan's ordinariness with the extraordinary fame and wealth he

has achieved make a strong endorsement for the all-American claim that there is the possibility for anyone to succeed. NBA commissioner David Stern sings the same tune of social mobility, describing Jordan as "a down to earth guy who defies gravity on the court," and Gates, remembering that in a global marketplace the promise of opportunity is also for overseas consumption, calls Jordan "an international symbol of America."[16]

In an attempt to remove race from the story in which Jordan stars, his agent, David Falk, states that "people don't look at Michael as being black." "They accept that he's different because he's a celebrity," he explains.[17] Falk here wants to convey a naive belief in color-blindness that tries to wish away racism in America. Stating that "people" (Whites) do not regard Jordan as Black fits the utopian assumptions of much of Jordan's media representation, suggesting that he proves race is no longer an insurmountable barrier in American society. I doubt that Whites ever forget Jordan is Black, however. They may choose to regard his race as what makes the story all that much more uplifting and inspirational; his celebrity proves for them how personal initiative and achievement can overcome even the obstacle of racial discrimination. Moreover, acknowledging Jordan's race fits the individual emphasis of sports stardom by invoking the physical essentialism still associated with African Americans and therefore suggesting that what makes him unique resides inside him, is part of his being and not created or influenced by environmental factors.

Falk played a major role in developing the film *Space Jam* as a star vehicle for Jordan, and its representation of his rise to success coincides with the race-blind utopia the agent describes. The film opens with a scene of Michael as a boy, shooting baskets late at night outside his family's North Carolina home. His strong, patient father comes out to get him to go back to bed, and when Michael asks, "You think if I get good enough I can go to college?" he reassures the boy: "If you get good enough, you can do anything you want to." The opening-credits montage that follows shows Jordan's career up through 1996, as if to reinforce that statement. We see Jordan's unimpeded rise to success from boyhood, through high school and college basketball to the championships with the Chicago Bulls. This climb seems fueled by the hard work and determination evidenced in the late-night practice session; Jordan's elevation in his spectacular moves to the basket appears in the credits as a metaphor for his rise to success and therefore implies that such achievement can occur simply through acts of physical effort.

Another part of placing Jordan in the raceless utopia wished for by a White audience involves making him familiar to us. Repeated references to him simply as "Michael" (shortened further in the "Be like Mike" Gatorade ad) suggest that we somehow know him. This familiarity plays on the assumption in the media regarding race that Benjamin DeMott describes as the friendship imperative. In DeMott's view, interracial friendships are widely represented in American popular culture as effortless and common, offering personal relations as a way of overcoming racism without the need for social movements or government action.[18] Calling Jordan by just his first name suggests that even as we consume him in a mediated, commodified form, we somehow achieve that friendship and contribute to the social harmony it creates.

Three basketball films, *White Men Can't Jump*, *The Air Up There*, and *Above the Rim* (1994), emphasize interracial friendship as important to the success of individuals of both races, while also using it to reaffirm conventions of Black representation. As I mentioned earlier, *White Men* portrays basketball as a venue in which a Black character (Sidney Deane) helps a White character (Billy Hoyle) find himself. Hoyle arrives in Los Angeles with his girlfriend Gloria, on the run from gamblers to whom they owe money. He then uses his unassuming appearance (specifically, his lack of height and his Whiteness) to hustle Sidney Deane in a Venice Beach game. Sidney, in turn, decides to put the "White boy can't play" assumption to work for both of them, and together they hustle Black opponents on playgrounds around South Central.

Though his trash talk and temper in early scenes might seem to portray the angry "don't give a fuck" attitude of a gangsta-style player, Sidney turns out to be representative more of Jordan's improvisational creativity and confidence than Barkley's belligerence. Michael Eric Dyson has described Jordan's playing style as having relied on three skills that have long had special importance in African American culture. The first is improvisation, the ability to spontaneously develop an effective response to a situation, which

Dyson says is learned through the "the honing of skill by the application of discipline, time, talent and energy." The second skill that Jordan employed Dyson calls the stylization of the performed self: the ability to mark what he does with an individual flair. Earlier in his career Jordan defined his distinctive style through what Dyson calls his "repertoire of dazzling dunk shots." His game later became less athletic but was still punctuated by moves to the basket that no one else could do. The third skill that marked Jordan's game was his use of "edifying deception," achieved by convincing himself, and everyone else, that he was the best. As Dyson points out, the main way in which Jordan initially achieved this deception was by creating the myth that he could outjump anyone, that he could literally hang in midair—hence his nickname, Air Jordan.[19] With a less high-altitude game but the accomplishment of several NBA titles, Jordan's psychological advantage became his reputation of being able to outplay any opponent at a crucial moment.

The Sidney Deane character in *White Men* plays a Jordan-inspired brand of ball in his playground games, supremely confident as he improvises in drives to the basket to elude taller opponents and creates distinctly stylized moves. To accommodate his White partner, Sidney's con game with Billy employs deception predicated on gaining an advantage over opponents through convincing them not that the pair is unbeatable but rather that they aren't competitive. The underestimation of Jordan's disproportionately White "supporting cast" with the Bulls (especially when Scottie Pippen was hurt) functioned in a similar manner.

In contrast to Sidney, Billy starts off the film playing a textbook game. Todd Boyd has described this kind of White basketball as one "in which adherence to a specific set of rules determines one's ability to play successfully and 'correctly.'"[20] Since basketball functions as a metaphor for racial identities, the textbook style suggests a White ideology that accepts the rules of the game, broadly defined. On the court, playing by the book means that Billy avoids the traits that mark the style Sidney employs. Billy's game is not improvisational but rather about mastering conventional moves and executing them. He therefore stresses controlling the ball, getting position, and hitting the high percentage shot. At times Billy's passes show some flash, but they merely hint at the White player's potential for improvisation before he reverts to the textbook game.

Even though Billy and Sidney win and make money working their hustle, their differences in style and in ideas of racial identity cause friction between them. A conversation in Billy's car articulates this cultural barrier. When Billy plays Jimi Hendrix on the tape deck, Sidney tells him that, though Billy may "listen," he doesn't "hear" the music. Sidney's point here is that Billy doesn't appreciate the improvisation in how Hendrix played the guitar. In Sidney's view, Billy may listen to Hendrix, yet his lack of interest in an improvisational game on the basketball court—what Stuart Hall calls "the metaphorical use of musical vocabulary" that characterizes Black popular culture—implies that he doesn't appreciate this style's broader cultural significance.[21]

Billy responds by voicing to Sidney his belief in the superiority of his textbook, "do only what you need to to win" view of the game. He tells Sidney, "You're just like every other brother I've ever seen on the playground. You'd rather look good and lose than look bad and win." Billy's comment represents a view commonly expressed in media discourse about the supposed ineffectiveness of a Black, "playground" style of basketball. *White Men Can't Jump* proves this critique wrong, however, by repeatedly showing that the White character, with his textbook style, is incapable of adapting to new challenges as they arise.

For most of the film, Billy makes bad decisions in response to situations that he encounters, whereas Sidney improvises viable responses to his own and also to Billy's problems. When Gloria leaves Billy because he loses all their money, Sidney figures out a way to repair the couple's relationship by getting her a chance to fulfill her dream of appearing on the game show *Jeopardy.* Through such effective responses, the film suggests that Sidney's confidence and improvisation can be as useful off as on the basketball court.

Even though *White Men Can't Jump* makes clear that Billy—like Sidney—has been forced to learn about hustling because he comes from a working-class background, the White character's style of play on the court conveys that he has yet to critique the bourgeois assumptions of a textbook game. The textbook approach is one that believes in the rules, the system whereby one defers in-

dividual pleasure (such as that found in improvisation and stylization) in order to win. It isn't until a climactic big-money game
against a legendary playground team that Billy begins to employ
the Black aesthetic that Sidney has modeled for him. Billy realizes
that the competition in this instance is so formidable that he has to
adopt an improvisatory style to create something new. Taking an
alley-oop pass from Sidney, he defies the statement of the film's
title and gets up and dunks the ball.

While *White Men Can't Jump* reverses the racist stereotype
voiced by Billy and represents Sidney's style of playing basketball
as part of an effective identity, the film also harks back to Hollywood's pre–civil rights pattern of using Black characters to define
White masculinity. By setting up the kind of easy friendship De-
Mott describes, *White Men Can't Jump* asserts that through respect for and loyalty to an African American, an individual White
liberal can overcome racism. In addition to subordinating him to
the role of defining Billy, the film decontextualizes Sidney's strategies by defining Black achievement "in terms of individualism and
exceptionalism."[22] While *White Men* shows numerous Black characters playing an improvisational, stylized brand of basketball, and
while an a capella vocal trio in the film recalls the grounding of improvisation in music, no other African American character is as capable as Sidney. To the contrary, in the scene in which their con is
first shown, Sidney's virtuoso performance as hustler and player
contrasts with the violent behavior of a defeated Black opponent
who angrily goes to get his gun. The latter character also fits within
the limited range of identities that American cinema offers to
Blacks, in this case their common portrayal "either as victims or
soulless predators who, because of fatal moral and character flaws,
cannot possibly transcend the limits of their condition."[23] Such
Black "loser" characters appear in many films as foils against which
protagonists (both Black and White) define their exceptional abilities; yet rarely do these films offer any explanation for criminality
or disadvantage. By default, we are asked to assume that individual
shortcoming is the reason.

These formulaic characterizations of African Americans operate
also in *Above the Rim*. The movie's main character, Kyle, is an exceptional high school point guard who hopes to win a scholarship

to play at Georgetown. Though less prominent than in *White Men,* a White friend, his high school coach Rollins, is crucial to the success of the Black protagonist in *Above the Rim.* Not only has the coach patiently endured Kyle's showcasing his skills and not involving the rest of the team, but he also brings in an ex-star player, Shep, to help keep the young player from making the wrong choices. As the film portrays Kyle's situation, he must choose between realizing his potential for success or adopting the gangsta life of Birdie (Tupac Shakur), a local drug dealer. Once again, this narrative conflict plays on the exceptional/pathological, Michael Jordan/gangsta character duality that dominates media representation of Black basketball in particular and African Americans in general. What *Above the Rim* adds to this Manichaean dualism of Black identity is a third, equally well-worn character: the outsider hero, Shep, Birdie's estranged brother who returns to the neighborhood to overcome his tragic past and help Kyle follow the path of self-reliance to success.

Although it doesn't hide that he deals drugs, the film initially presents Birdie as charismatic and—because of his new clothes, expensive vehicles, nightclub, and the attractive women around him—"successful" in the material terms that Kyle dreams about achieving through an NBA career. Birdie skillfully cultivates Kyle to play on his team in a neighborhood tournament, motivated by how the success of an aggressive gangsta style on the court will validate his "business" activities. Whereas Kyle at first seems unaware of how to conduct himself in order to land the scholarship offer from Georgetown he covets, Birdie is strategic and in charge. As part of his sales pitch, Birdie introduces Kyle in his club to an agent eager to represent him and to an attractive young woman. When Kyle and the young woman kiss and embrace too passionately, however, Birdie intervenes: "Alright, alright," he tells them, "I'm gonna get my club closed down." Later, when Kyle quits the team after he sees how ruthless and violent Birdie can be, the gangsta springs a carefully laid trap, telling the young star that he will reveal his acceptance of gifts and ruin his amateur eligibility if he doesn't let Birdie's team win.

Because the first half of the film emphasizes the similarities between the gangsta's highly rationalized criminal activity and the "legitimate" business world, in its second half *Above the Rim* emphasizes Birdie's sadistic side to distinguish his actions from the ladder to success that it has Kyle climb. When Birdie betrays Kyle, however, we should remember that there are plenty of agents like the one shown earlier in the nightclub, who "represent" young stars on a "legitimate" but no less manipulative basis. To arrive at its utopian message, the film must discredit this similarity, along with Birdie's politicized critique of the dead end of "an honest day's work," summed up by his taunting of Shep about his job as a security guard at the high school. Birdie therefore becomes a sadistic killer, the scar on his cheek linking him to earlier movie gangsters as he slices up a homeless man who disrespected him. However inconsistent such vindictive violence is with Birdie's previous careful, highly rational behavior, it allows the film to discredit the gangsta's cynicism about the efficacy of an honest job and the possibility of success for working-class Blacks in American society.

The Shep character is an important part of the film's inspirational message. Whereas Kyle had selfishly showboated and had been willing to throw the tournament after Birdie's threat, Shep takes the court for the coach's team in the championship game and models for the younger player the hard yet "clean" game that will get him his Georgetown scholarship. Shep's game is clean because it supports the rules of the existing social structure: like the image of Michael Jordan celebrated by the media, Shep's character reinforces the idea that individual excellence can carry the interests of the group. He is respectful of White authority, as represented by Coach Rollins, and while he uses the physical force that Birdie's team gangsta-rizes, it is only on behalf of masculine self-assertion, rejecting the angry statement such aggression makes about racist disadvantage.

Above the Rim celebrates Shep and Kyle as exceptional, "better" than the other young Black men in the film because these two individuals follow the rules of determined self-interest and respect for authority necessary to gain access to the few opportunities available. Kyle gets his scholarship at Georgetown once he tones down the self-gratification of his game and stops resisting the control of his coach. Shep, as well, benefits from his seemingly altruistic behavior; the film ends with the suggestion that he will accept the coach's offer to succeed him at the high school, a valued position in a community where basketball is highly regarded and the drug trade flourishes from a shortage of good jobs.

Whether in rap music and cinema or in representations of Black basketball culture, the toughness and self-sufficiency of the gangsta character are more appealing for a crossover audience than the statement about the nihilism created by racism. *Above the Rim* therefore emphasizes these traditional masculine characteristics in Kyle and Shep, meanwhile rejecting the racial critique implicit in Birdie's drug business and his denial of the rules of the game in how his team plays. As with the murder of the homeless man, the film shows the gangsta life leading to irrational violence; after Birdie's team loses, for example, he sends his enforcer Moe to shoot Kyle. Birdie's angry and eloquent justification of his criminal life to Shep earlier in the film gets lost once the shooting starts. The film focuses our attention instead on the destructiveness of violence, but no attention is paid to the roots of this behavior in social disadvantage. For *Above the Rim* to acknowledge such a contributing factor to the violence shown would compromise the utopian logic it puts forward as the solution to what is lacking in the lives of these young Black characters. Movies like *Above the Rim* and most other media representations of basketball avoid careful engagement with the moral and social complexities that confront working-class African American men. They prefer instead simplified constructions of masculinity that affirm the dominant values of competitive toughness and self-sufficiency, channeled within a utopian optimism and not as part of a racialized social critique.

Space Jam, as well, depoliticizes the gangsta response to disadvantage, casting it as both comical and driven by the desire to enslave and exploit others, in contrast to the self-reliant and generous success represented by Michael Jordan. The story of the film involves five diminutive aliens, abused and intimidated by their tyrannical boss, who arrive on earth to enslave the Warner Brothers cartoon characters and take them back to perform at an outer-space amusement park. The cartoon characters offer to play a basketball game for their freedom, but when the aliens show up with gangsta identities stolen from NBA players, the Looney Tooners do some kidnapping of their own, abducting Michael Jordan to help them win. Although Sean Bradley, one of the NBA players robbed of his "talent," is White, his presence seems an obvious attempt by the film to distract from the racialized character assumed by the aliens "Monstars." The Monstars take the floor to the sounds of "Hit 'Em High," performed by rappers Busta Rhymes, Coolio, LL Cool J, and others, and dominate the first half, led by the aliens who have adopted the identities of Charles Barkley and Larry Johnson—two NBA players strongly associated with the working-class cynicism and aggressive physicality of the gangsta identity. The subsequent victory of Jordan and the Toons in the face of the intimidation of the aliens reiterates a utopian view of basketball and criminalizes and ignores the racial critique of the gangsta style.

Jordan and the Critique of Style

In his *New Yorker* feature, Henry Louis Gates anoints Jordan as the ultimate representative of corporate success; yet he also reports instances of what can only be called the superstar's alienation, his disaffection from the economic system in which he has been such a hot commodity. For instance, Gates tells us that for eight years, as he led Chicago to NBA titles and his popularity grew to its unprecedented level, Jordan was undercompensated by the Bulls, stuck in a contract that paid him a salary below what other, lesser players were making in the NBA marketplace. Adding insult to injury, Bulls owner Jerry Reinsdorf refused to acknowledge this past unfairness, grumbling that he was sure he would regret the $30 million contract he signed with Jordan for the 1997–98 season. Gates quotes Jordan's response to Reinsdorf:

> All these years where you knew I was underpaid and you been making money and your organization's moved from a fifteen-million-dollar business when you bought it to a two-hundred-million-dollar business—all those years have gone down the drain because you have for once paid me my value. And you regretted that! That hit me so deep inside—the sense of greed, of disrespect for me.[24]

Because Jordan has earned so many millions as a player and for his endorsements and has achieved such praise for his achievements, to regard him as alienated initially seems absurd in comparison to millions of working people who have so much less. Yet, if even Michael Jordan has experienced denial of fair return for services rendered, that is evidence of just how typical such inequities are in an economic system for which he is offered as a testimonial figure. In this context, his expressive, improvisational style on the court becomes not just an example of competitive, entrepreneurial achievement—*creativity,* as the word is used in corporate market-speak for IBM computers ("Solutions for a Small Planet")—but a critique of alienation within a capitalist economy. His style, which emphasizes pleasurable creativity while competing, asserts the importance of finding for himself a return of expressive gratification without regard for whether the owners of the various venues in which he has performed (the Bulls, TV, advertising, the movies) will compensate him fairly for the profits he generates for them. Clearly, from his comments about Reinsdorf and the importance of his pleasure from playing, Jordan understands this return he must create for himself.

Jordan has commented that he doesn't know why his popularity continues to grow and has not dropped off, as it does for so many stars who enjoy only a brief time at the center stage of media attention.[25] One explanation may be that he symbolizes a utopian promise about the continued viability of the American dream, and about its greater access to African Americans. Jordan's popularity, however, may instead be grounded in the satisfaction he derives from work, which appeals to millions of people who do not find their jobs as meaningful. This dissatisfaction comes from an increasing lack of employment security and from inadequate salary increases and benefits but also as a result of the growing shortage of time that workers have for their personal and family lives. Writing in 1991, Juliet Schor reported that Americans were working more than in 1970, which was contributing to increased stress on their families, marriages, and health.[26] Jordan's apparent ability to deal with the tremendous pressures of his career and even to make that work experience expressive and enjoyable is a significant element of his appeal.

It is important to point out, however, that while the immense pressure and lack of management respect he has had to deal with may function to alienate him from his work, Jordan's situation is still, in a sense, utopian. His creativity and style may be attractive, but not everyone has a job that allows for such pleasures. In *Hoop Dreams*, we see Arthur Agee and his friend Shannon listening to music and dancing while working at Pizza Hut, but that scene seems an overly favorable presentation of the otherwise monotonous jobs that millions of people perform in the service economy. It is, in addition to the film's choice of blue-chip athletes as its subjects, another instance of how *Hoop Dreams* tries to understate the disadvantages facing Black youth in places like Cabrini Green and West Garfield Park.

Thus, while Jordan's agent David Falk may claim that audiences don't see Jordan as Black, in terms of both meanings I've just described, his career speaks directly to the situation of African Americans. As a model of mainstream success, he represents the gains of the post–civil rights talented tenth; in academics, Henry Louis Gates is an example of such improved possibilities for a limited group of African Americans. Yet, because Jordan also offers a strategy of resistance to alienation, he speaks to the plight of the Black working class, whose decline in wealth in recent years makes evident the continued importance of style and an improvisational aesthetic that provide a return for performance, even if not always in material terms.[27] Having said that, however, I would again underscore that the simple material limitations (the low wages and lack of benefits and paid time off) of so much of the work available in American society, especially to the working-class Blacks who make up a majority of the African American population, restricts one's ability (Jordan's inspiration notwithstanding) to make the work creative and meaningful.

In several recent films about basketball, an improvisational style of play functions to allow the characters employing it a return for efforts otherwise not rewarded. In *White Men Can't Jump*, Sidney's game may supplement his family's income during slow times in the building trade, but even more important to him is the expressive pleasure he gets from it. One reviewer of the film noted that, for both Sidney and his protegee, Billy, "the primary object of

their basketball hustling is the irresponsible delight it gives them.
The money they win buys them time, it keeps the heat off at home,
and enables them to live the playground life for a little longer."[28]
This description refers indirectly to the lack of adequate work for
both men but also to how the expressive, improvisational basketball
that Sidney plays and models for Billy creates meaning and pleasure, which they keep and do not exchange for a wage.

An awareness of such meaning and pleasure from basketball informs the following story that Sidney tells Billy when they first
meet on Venice Beach:

> Michael Jordan came down to the beach one time . . . took him to
> the hole, baby! You believe that? Took Michael Jordan to the
> hole! Michael said to me, he said, "Hey, you should play summer
> pro league." I said, "No! Shit might mess up my game."

This anecdote expresses Sidney's view of the pro game as about
playing basketball for money, where winning in the terms of the
larger White society matters so much that it becomes difficult to
hold onto the stylized game that counts for him as much as a pay-
day. In telling his story, Sidney shows he regards Jordan as a symbol of mainstream success, a Black man who has made it by the
White man's rules. Yet, rather than just mainstream success, what
makes Jordan special has been his ability to maintain a difficult balance of White approval and individual identity while in the media
limelight, by using what Todd Boyd calls a fusion of the "formal"
(textbook) and "vernacular" (Black) styles.

> When it's played the way it's spozed to be played, basketball hap-
> pens in the air, the pure air; flying, floating, elevated above the
> floor, levitating the way oppressed peoples of this earth imagine
> themselves in their dreams, as I do in my lifelong fantasies of es-
> cape and power, finally at last, once and for all, free.
> —John Edgar Wideman

The narrative conventions of racial representation that still dominate American popular culture strongly influence most films about
Black basketball, populating them, like athletic contests, with win-

ners and losers: exceptional individuals (Sidney in *White Men Can't Jump*, Jordan in *Space Jam*, Kyle and Shep in *Above the Rim*, Saleh in *The Air up There*, the Whoopi Goldberg character in *Eddie*, Jesus in *He Got Game*), and moral misfits (Birdie in *Above the Rim*; Raymond the sore loser with the gun in *White Men*; Denzel Washington's character in *He Got Game*; the gangsterized aliens in *Space Jam*; Arthur Agee's father and William Gates's brother in *Hoop Dreams*). Despite such stereotypes, which reduce Black identity to either self-reliance and moral strength or the lack thereof, the action sequences of these basketball films show the skills that make such exceptionalism possible; yet they often foreground as well styles that question such an easy prescription for success.

Above the Rim and *Rebound: The Legend of Earl "The Goat" Manigault* (1996) both present action scenes set on the playground in Harlem where Holcomb Rucker for decades ran a summer league so famous that top pro and college stars would come to meet the local talent. According to Nelson George, "At Rucker you played fly, flashy style (or at least tried to); otherwise you were just taking up space."[29] In *Rebound*, set during Rucker's era, and in *Above the Rim*, about a contemporary tournament reviving his memory, we see scenes in which a spectacular, improvisational game and the aggressiveness of the gangsta style question the conventional moral simplifications of their narratives.

In the early games of the tournament near the conclusion of *Above the Rim*, a lengthy montage presents numerous players, almost all of them Black, playing a fast-paced game of quick crossovers, no-look passes, and spectacular jams. The narrative function of this montage is to follow Kyle's and Birdie's teams as they win their way to an eventual showdown. Yet, inadvertently, the film qualifies its moralizing message about Birdie being the bad guy for breaking the rules and Shep and Kyle being heroes for following them. This montage shows so many players with outstanding skills that one can't help but wonder what makes Kyle, and later Shep, the best player on the court. The plethora of talent in this neighborhood tournament suggests that this story is not just about the importance of following the rules and succeeding but also about how few of these young men get a chance to move up. Except for a White point guard on an opposing high school team, no mention is made of any player from the neighborhood, besides Kyle, winning a scholarship to big-time college ball and possibly a pro career.

In *Rebound* we see several scenes in which the title character in this biopic, Earl "The Goat" Manigault, demonstrates the high-flying game that made him a playground legend in the early 1960s. The most spectacular of these scenes shows Manigault "double dunking," jamming with his right hand catching the ball with his left and redunking it. If the bane of many young Black players today is the power of the NBA dream despite the long odds, for Manigault in *Rebound,* the creative pleasure of playing means everything, because he never entertains such fantasies. When playground supervisor Rucker attempts to encourage Manigault to continue in school, assuring him that he has the ability to play college ball and then go to the NBA, Manigault dismisses such advice. He responds, "The NBA? Come on man! They ain't going to take me. You know they only take two brothers to a team if that." Despite Earl's talent (Rucker calls him the best player to ever grace his court), the film shows how an insecure Black college coach obsessed with playing textbook basketball later ruins Earl's chances to showcase his skills and make it to the NBA. The ending of the film retains the tension between Rucker's message of self-reliance as a ticket to success and Earl's stylistic critique. After breaking a heroin addiction, Earl gets the scornful approval of the dealer who controls the neighborhood to clean up Rucker's playground and restart the league in which, presumably, style will continue to count—even while dreams of the NBA are also born.

Through this emphasis on improvisational and gangsta styles, *White Men Can't Jump, Above the Rim,* and *Rebound* acknowledge the structural barriers that limit the opportunity that Michael Jordan is often used to symbolize. Although they dismiss gangsta cynicism and violence as destructive, an exaggeration of what Cornel West calls the selfish "market values" that have contributed to the lack of opportunities for young African Americans in the first place, the stylistic critique of utopian success in these films recognizes the gap between promise and reality that is a major factor in such nihilism.

While he notes how an essentialized notion of Black identity has been useful to avoid the domination of a discriminatory (White) mainstream popular culture, Stuart Hall also points out the problems that result from a dehistoricized and uncritical understanding of African American culture. Hall says that Black popular culture can be better understood as overdetermined, constituted from "two directions at once," not as either Black or American but as both Black and American.[30] The identities presented in the film representations of basketball I've analyzed here communicate such a hybrid notion of Blackness, as they offer both the expressivity of a Michael Jordan, which has given the star player his access to mainstream success, and the denial of opportunity that fuels the anger of the gangsta. However, to the degree that Michael Jordan is offered to us as simply a utopian figure, as someone whose success proves that social mobility is available to everyone, he doesn't meet Hall's criteria for insight into African American identity. Such utopian interpretations of Jordan ignore the disadvantaged experience of many African Americans, as well as Jordan's own expressive critique of the alienation that White culture continues to insist on as a prerequisite of equality.

NOTES

1. Jay Coakley reports the revenue increases in his book *Sport in Society: Issues and Controversies* (St. Louis: Times Mirror, 1998), 378. Todd Boyd has made the point that basketball is "a game perfectly suited to the fast paced visual culture [of] television"; see *Am I Black Enough for You? Popular Culture from the 'Hood and Beyond* (Bloomington: Indiana University Press, 1997), 117. About the commodification of difference, see Gitanjali Mararaj, "Talking Trash: Late Capitalism, Black (Re)Productivity, and Professional Basketball," *Social Text* 50 (Spring 1997): 101.

2. Stuart Hall, "What Is This 'Black' in Black Popular Culture?" in *Black Popular Culture*, ed. Gina Dent (Seattle: Bay Press, 1992), 23.

3. bell hooks, "Neo-Colonial Fantasies of Conquest: *Hoop Dreams*," in *Reel to Reel: Race, Sex, and Class at the Movies* (New York: Routledge, 1996), 79.

4. John Edgar Wideman, "Michael Jordan Leaps the Great Divide," *Esquire*, November, 1990, 210.

5. "Talking Trash," *New York Times Magazine*, June 6, 1993, 34, 38.

6. My analysis here was influenced by Frank P. Tomasulo's writing

about his experience as an Italian American in "Italian Americans in the
Hollywood Cinema: Filmmakers, Characters, Audiences," *Voices in Italian
Americana*, vol. 7, no. 1 (1996): 69. Quotation from Werner Sollors, *Be-
yond Ethnicity: Consent and Descent in American Culture* (New York:
Oxford University Press, 1986), 31, 33.

7. Richard Dyer, *White* (New York: Routledge, 1997), 207.

8. Kenneth Shropshire has written about the lack of Black access to administrative, front-office, and ownership positions in sports in his book *In
Black and White: Race and Sports in America* (New York: New York University Press, 1996).

9. Sports historian Steven Riess reports that there were eighteen hundred Black professional fighters in the 1930s, and by 1948, nearly half of
all contenders were Black; see his *City Games: The Evolution of American
Urban Society and the Rise of Sport* (Urbana: University of Illinois Press,
1989), 116.

10. Robert Ray, *A Certain Tendency in the Hollywood Cinema
1930–1990* (Princeton: Princeton University Press, 1985), 31.

11. George Custen, *Bio/Pics: How Hollywood Constructed Public History* (New Brunswick: Rutgers University Press, 1992), 8.

12. Richard Dyer, "Entertainment and Utopia," in *The Cultural Studies Reader*, ed. Simon During (London: Blackwell, 1993), 271–83.

13. Robert Stam, "Bakhtin, Polyphony, and Ethnic/Racial Representation," in *Unspeakable Images: Ethnicity and the American Cinema*, ed.
Lester D. Friedman (Urbana: University of Illinois Press, 1991), 286.

14. Henry Louis Gates Jr., "New Worth: How the Greatest Player in
the History of Basketball Became the Greatest Brand in the History of
Sports," *New Yorker*, June 1, 1998, 48.

15. Relying on the work of New York University economist Edward
Wolff, Ralph Nader has recently written a letter to Bill Gates, asking
Gates's assistance in responding to the wealth disparity in the United
States, which is such that the top 1 percent in this country own more than
the bottom 90 percent. See "Nader Urges Gates to Tackle Wealth Dispari-
ties," Associated Press wire story, July 28, 1998.

16. Gates, "New Worth," 51, 61.

17. Quoted in ibid., 54.

18. Benjamin DeMott, *The Trouble with Friendship: Why Americans
Can't Think Straight about Race* (New York: Atlantic Monthly Press,
1995), 1–6.

19. Michael Eric Dyson, "Be Like Mike? Michael Jordan and the Pedagogy of Desire," in *Reflecting Black: African-American Cultural Criticism*
(Minneapolis: University of Minnesota Press, 1993), 67–69.

20. Boyd, *Am I Black Enough for You?* 115.

21. Hall, "What Is This 'Black' in Black Popular Culture?" 27.

22. Herman Grey, *Watching Race: Television and the Struggle for "Blackness"* (Minneapolis: University of Minnesota Press, 1995), 156.

23. Ibid., 156–57.

24. Gates, "New Worth," 51.

25. Ibid., 58.

26. Juliet B. Schor, *The Overworked American: The Unexpected Decline of Leisure* (New York: Basic Books, 1991), 1–15.

27. Edward N. Wolff states that:

The racial distribution of wealth deteriorated in the 1980s from an already unacceptable level. Relative income of African American households held steady at about 60 percent of white income in the 1980s, but the relative wealth position of most black families deteriorated. Historically, black wealth always has been much lower than that of whites, the legacy of slavery, discrimination, and low incomes. Between 1983 and 1989, a bad situation grew worse. In 1983, the median white family had eleven times the wealth of the median nonwhite family. By 1989 this ratio had grown to twenty. Middle class black households did succeed in narrowing the wealth gap with whites, but most nonwhite families moved even further behind.

Edward N. Wolff, *Top Heavy: The Increasing Inequality of Wealth in America and What Can Be Done about It* (New York: New Press, 1995), 2.

28. T. Rafferty, "Boys' Games," *New Yorker*, June 6, 1992, 80–82.

29. Nelson George, *Elevating the Game: Black Men and Basketball* (New York, HarperCollins, 1992), 74.

30. Hall, "What Is This 'Black' in Black Popular Culture?" 29.

contributors

ALPHA ALEXANDER, as director of Health and Sports Advocacy for the YWCA, oversees the health, sports, and education program development for 354 community and student member associations in fifty states. Alexander is a member of the United States Olympic Committee (USOC) board of directors, a position she has maintained since 1988.

AARON BAKER is an assistant professor in the interdisciplinary Humanities Program at Arizona State University. He is co-editor of *Out of Bounds: Sports, Media, and the Politics of Identity.*

MARK CONRAD is associate professor of Legal and Ethical Studies at Fordham University. He writes and comments frequently on sports law issues. Conrad is the editor of the internet publication, "Mark's Sports Law News."

SOHAIL DAULATZAI is a doctoral candidate at the University of Southern California. He has recently published "(Re)Birth of a Nation: Islam, Cultural Politics and the Rhetoric of Empire" in the Fall/Winter 1998 issue of *Spectator.* His research interests include postcolonial criticism, race, and the cultural politics of globalization—particularly in film, sports, and hip-hop culture.

GERALD EARLY is the Merle S. Kling Professor of Modern Letters in Arts and Sciences at Washington University in St. Louis. He is the author of numerous works, including *The Culture of Bruising: Essays on Prize Fighting, Literature, and Modern American Culture* and *The Muhammad Ali Reader* and *Body Language: Writers on Sport.*

TINA SLOAN GREEN is a professor in the College of Education at Temple University. She is also president and co-founder of the Black Women in Sport Foundation. Before retiring, she coached three national championship teams and was the first African

American woman inducted into the National Lacrosse Hall of Fame.

DAVIS W. HOUCK is an assistant professor in the communications department at Florida State University. He has recently completed work on his third book, *Rhetoric as Currency: Hoover, Roosevelt and the Great Depression*. His most recent work on sports involves the gender and sexual politics of "selling" the WNBA.

JULIANNE MALVEAUX, Ph.D., is an economist, author, and syndicated columnist. She writes about politics, economics, gender, race, and popular culture. Malveaux's most recent book, *Wall Street, Main Street and the Side Street: A Mad Economist Takes a Stroll* (Pines One Publications, 1999) is a collection of her best columns from 1994 to 1998. Malveaux's work appears in *Essence* magazine, the *San Francisco Examiner*, and other newspapers, magazines, and academic journals.

TARA McPHERSON is an assistant professor of Critical Studies and Gender Studies at the University of Southern California, where she teaches and writes about popular culture, feminism, and new technologies. She is co-editor of *Hop on Pop: The Politics and Pleasures of Popular Culture* and is currently completing *Reconstructing Dixie: Race, Place and Femininity in the Deep South*, both forthcoming from Duke University Press.

CHARLES J. OGLETREE, JR., is the Jesse Climenko Professor of Law at Harvard Law School. He has published numerous articles on criminal and civil rights legal issues. He often serves as a moderator on PBS forums.

JAMES PETERSON is a doctoral candidate in English at the University of Pennsylvania, contributor to *XXL* and *Philly Word*, editor of *Hip Hop Scholarly*, and CEO of Critical Mass Consulting Corporation. He was born and raised in the underground of Newark.

LARRY PLATT is a writer and commentator whose work has appeared in *GQ, Details, Philadelphia Magazine*, and *Salon*. His most recent book is *Keepin' It Real: A Turbulent Season at the Crossroads with the NBA.*

SUSAN J. RAYL is an assistant professor at Bridgewater State College in Massachusetts and author of a forthcoming book on Bob Douglas and the New York Renaissance basketball team.

EARL SMITH is the Dr. Ernest Rubin Distinguished Professor of American Ethnic Studies and chairman of the Department of Sociology at Wake Forest University. He is the author of numerous sports sociology articles and is at work on the book *The Sporting World of African American Athletes: From Jackie Roosevelt Robinson to Eldrick "Tiger" Woods.*

about the editors

TODD BOYD is a professor of Critical Studies in the University of Southern California School of Cinema-Television. He is the author of *Am I Black Enough for You? Popular Culture from the 'Hood and Beyond* and editor of *Out of Bounds: Sport, Media, and the Politics of Identity.* A prominent media commentator, Boyd has written extensively for both the *Los Angeles Times* and the *Chicago Tribune.* He is also writer and producer of the Paramount Pictures film *The Wood* (1999).

KENNETH L. SHROPSHIRE is a professor of Legal Studies and former director of Afro-American Studies at the Wharton School at the University of Pennsylvania. He is the author of several books, including *In Black and White: Race and Sports in America,* the winner of a 1996 Outstanding Academic Book Award from *Choice* magazine and a 1997 Gustavus Myers Center for the Study of Human Rights in North America Outstanding Book Award. He may be contacted via his website at http://www.kennethshropshire.com.

Nutshell Series

of

WEST PUBLISHING COMPANY

P.O. Box 3526

St. Paul, Minnesota 55165

May, 1983

Administrative Law and Process, 2nd Ed., 1981, 445 pages, by Ernest Gellhorn, Dean and Professor of Law, Case Western Reserve University and Barry B. Boyer, Professor of Law, SUNY, Buffalo.

Admiralty, 1983, approximately 325 pages, by Frank L. Maraist, Professor of Law, Louisiana State University.

Agency-Partnership, 1977, 364 pages, by Roscoe T. Steffen, Late Professor of Law, University of Chicago.

American Indian Law, 1981, 288 pages, by William C. Canby, Jr., former Professor of Law, Arizona State University.

Antitrust Law and Economics, 2nd Ed., 1981, 425 pages, by Ernest Gellhorn, Dean and Professor of Law, Case Western Reserve University.

Church-State Relations—Law of, 1981, 305 pages, by Leonard F. Manning, Late Professor of Law, Fordham University.

Civil Procedure, 1979, 271 pages, by Mary Kay Kane, Professor of Law, University of California, Hastings College of the Law.

Civil Rights, 1978, 279 pages, by Norman Vieira, Professor of Law, Southern Illinois University.

Commercial Paper, 3rd Ed., 1982, 404 pages, by Charles M. Weber, Professor of Business Law, University of

I

d Richard E. Speidel, Professor of Law, Northwestern University.

Community Property, 1982, 423 pages, by Robert L. Mennell, Professor of Law, Hamline University.

Comparative Legal Traditions, 1982, 402 pages, by Mary Ann Glendon, Professor of Law, Boston College, Michael Wallace Gordon, Professor of Law, University of Florida and Christopher Osakwe, Professor of Law, Tulane University.

Conflicts, 1982, 469 pages, by David D. Siegel, Professor of Law, Albany Law School, Union University.

Constitutional Analysis, 1979, 388 pages, by Jerre S. Williams, Professor of Law Emeritus, University of Texas.

Constitutional Power—Federal and State, 1974, 411 pages, by David E. Engdahl, Professor of Law, University of Puget Sound.

Consumer Law, 2nd Ed., 1981, 418 pages, by David G. Epstein, Professor of Law, University of Texas and Steve H. Nickles, Professor of Law, University of Minnesota.

Contracts, 1975, 307 pages, by Gordon D. Schaber, Dean and Professor of Law, McGeorge School of Law and Claude D. Rohwer, Professor of Law, McGeorge School of Law.

Contract Remedies, 1981, 323 pages, by Jane M. Friedman, Professor of Law, Wayne State University.

Corporations—Law of, 1980, 379 pages, by Robert W. Hamilton, Professor of Law, University of Texas.

Corrections and Prisoners' Rights—Law of, 2nd Ed., 1983, approximately 365 pages, by Sheldon Krantz, Dean and Professor of Law, University of San Diego.

Criminal Law, 1975, 302 pages, by Arnold H. Loewy, Professor of Law, University of North Carolina.

Criminal Procedure—Constitutional Limitations, 3rd Ed., 1980, 438 pages, by Jerold H. Israel, Professor of Law, University of Michigan and Wayne R. LaFave, Professor of Law, University of Illinois.